Constructing Educational Inequality

1 7 MAY 2021

D1141994

York St. John College

3 8025 00427054 5

We dedicate this book to
all the researchers whose
work we have discussed —
it is offered in the
spirit of critical
friendship.

Constructing Educational Inequality:
An Assessment of Research on School Processes

Peter Foster
Roger Gomm
Martyn Hammersley

YORK ST. JOHN
COLLEGE LIBRARY

 Falmer Press

(A member of the Taylor & Francis Group)
London • Washington, D.C.

UK The Falmer Press, 4 John Street, London WC1N 2ET
USA The Falmer Press, Taylor & Francis Inc., 1900 Frost Road, Suite 101, Bristol, PA 19007

© P. Foster, R. Gomm and M. Hammersley, 1996

All rights reserved. No part of this publication may be reproduced, stored in a retrieval system, or transmitted in any form or by any means, electronic, mechanical, photocopying, recording or otherwise, without permission in writing from the Publisher.

First published in 1996

A catalogue record for this book is available from the British Library

Library of Congress Cataloging-in-Publication Data are available on request

ISBN 0 7507 0388 1 cased
ISBN 0 7507 0389 x paper

Jacket design by Caroline Archer

Typeset in 10/12pt Garamond by
Graphicraft Typesetters Ltd., Hong Kong

Printed in Great Britain by Biddles Ltd., Guildford and King's Lynn on paper which has a specified pH value on final paper manufacture of not less than 7.5 and is therefore 'acid free'.

Contents

Acknowledgments

The authors are grateful to the School of Education, Open University and the School of Education, Manchester Metropolitan University for grants towards the completion of the work on which this book is based. We would also like to thank Barry Cooper, Donald Mackinnon, and John Scarth for contributing to the discussions out of which this book arose, and for providing comments on various drafts. Needless to say, responsibility for any errors remains with us.

Chapter 1

Educational Inequality as a Social Problem

Educational inequalities between children from different social classes have been a central political concern in Britain since before the Second World War. Various government-sponsored reports addressed this issue (such as those of the Hadow and Norwood Committees), leading up to the 1944 Education Act. This Act was a milestone in the development of policy to bring about educational equality between the social classes, but concern about educational inequalities continued to grow in the post-war period, reaching a peak in the 1960s and 1970s. And at that time other kinds of inequality, notably between the sexes and between majority and minority 'racial'/ethnic groups, also became the focus of political attention, at both national and local levels. More recently, under the influence of Thatcherism, the salience of educational inequality as an issue in government policy has been reduced, in favour of a preoccupation with declining academic standards and a heightened concern with the contribution of education to economic productivity, manifested in the 1988 Education Act and subsequent legislation. However, educational inequality has by no means disappeared from the agendas of political parties, interest groups, and local authorities.

Inequality has also been the central focus of most sociological research concerned with education. Early work in this field dealt with social-class inequalities in the workings of the free place system (Lindsay 1926; Gray and Moshinsky 1938). After 1944, the task became to investigate the extent to which the new tripartite system had reduced educational inequality. And, indeed, this research played an important role in shaping government policy. In the 1960s the work of Floud, Halsey, Douglas and others, whose relationship with government ministers and civil servants was often close (Kogan, 1971), paved the way for the establishment of comprehensivization as national policy.[1] The diminishing salience of the problem of educational inequality in government policymaking in the past two decades has been accompanied

---

[1]   Key examples of this research are: Halsey and Gardner, 1953; Glass, 1956; Floud and Halsey, 1956; Floud, Halsey and Martin, 1956 and Douglas, 1964. It is worth remembering that moves toward comprehensive schooling at local level long pre-dated Circular 10/65; and that the latter only 'invited' local authorities to draw up comprehensive schemes, comprehensive reorganization never being carried out in some areas, and in some senses never being fully achieved anywhere.

by a decline in the influence of sociological and other research. Nevertheless, educational inequality still remains a central concern for many educational researchers. And their work has succeeded in highlighting gender and ethnic inequalities, and has provided resources for those campaigning against these.

In this book we shall look at a significant portion of the large body of research on educational inequality which has been produced in Britain since the Second World War. Our particular focus will be on studies which have been concerned with inequalities in the internal organization and functioning of schools.[2] The aim is to determine what conclusions can be reached on the basis of this work. This means that our orientation is necessarily methodological. We shall look at the variety of claims which have been made about educational inequalities, and ask whether the evidence offered in support of them is convincing. This is by no means a straightforward matter, however, as we shall see.

One way of conceptualizing our project is as an exercise in reflexivity. In recent years there has been much argument to the effect that social and educational research is and/or should be reflexive (Gouldner, 1970; Young, 1973; Jenks, 1977; Hammersley and Atkinson, 1983; Woolgar, 1988; Ball, 1990; Troyna, 1994). Of course, the word 'reflexivity' has been used in many different ways. Most fundamentally, though, it signals the fact that social researchers are necessarily part of the world they study. This has several aspects.

In epistemological terms, it means that in formulating their problems, devising their methods, and interpreting their data and findings, researchers cannot but rely on the particular cultural resources available to them. Thus, to some extent at least, their conclusions will reflect the limitations of those resources. What is being rejected here is any sort of epistemological foundationalism which claims to build research on a bedrock of data whose validity is universal and absolutely certain. Furthermore, reflexivity implies that the *orientations* of researchers will also be shaped by their socio-historical locations, and in particular by the values and interests that these locations induce in them. So, it is not just that the resources available to researchers are socio-historically determined but that the use made of those resources is itself socially structured.

The concept of reflexivity also points to the fact that knowledge production requires participation in the social world to collect data; participation which can have effects, desirable and undesirable, on the people studied, and on the researcher. Likewise, the transmission of knowledge has consequences. The publication of research findings can (and, many believe, should) shape the climate in which political and practical decisions are made, and even stimulate particular sorts of action. In this way, and others, research may change the phenomena it studies.

Reflexivity, in these senses, is not something which is an optional feature

---

[2] One result of this choice of focus is that almost all of the work we discuss will be concerned with schools in England, rather than Wales, Scotland, or Northern Ireland. This needs to be borne in mind throughout our discussion.

of research: it is unavoidable. But there is an additional component of the meaning of 'reflexivity', referring to the researcher's level of awareness of the inter-relationship between research and the world it studies. It is often argued that researchers have not always been as aware as they should be of the ways in which their work is party to the social world, and of the implications of this. It is this kind of awareness which calls for research to be more reflexive are intended to encourage. This is often seen as forming the basis for researchers and/or others to exercise greater control over the process and consequences of research. What is frequently demanded is that research be made self-conscious and self-directing in its interaction with its environment; though what this implies in terms of the theory and practice of research is a matter of considerable disagreement.

One recommendation which is sometimes made is that the analytic resources of sociology be applied to sociological work itself (Gouldner, 1970). And it certainly seems to us that the reflexive implications of sociological arguments for sociological research should be explored, and taken into account in their assessment. So, we will begin our consideration of research on educational inequalities in schools by locating it in its social context, and examining some of the ways in which it has been pursued; doing this from the point of view of what has been one of the most influential sociological perspectives within the field, social constructionism.

Social Constructionism and Social Problems

A feature of sociological research on education, remarked upon recurrently, is its tendency to become detached from developments elsewhere in the discipline (Floud and Halsey, 1958, p. 165; Young, 1971, p. 1). Of course, those who have made this complaint have often gone some way towards rectifying the situation. Thus, Floud, Halsey and others sought to distinguish the *sociology of education* from *educational sociology* by stressing its social scientific orientation and its substantive links with other fields of sociology. And, central to the 'new sociology of education' (Gorbutt, 1972) was an insistence on 'making' research problems, rather than simply 'taking' them from the agendas of policymakers and practitioners. Moreover, this 'new sociology' adopted a radical stance, drawing on theoretical ideas in the sociology of knowledge, symbolic interactionism and social phenomenology, to argue that the knowledge purveyed, the learning promoted, and the abilities rewarded in schools are social constructions, and must be investigated rather than taken as given.[3]

Since that time social constructionism has continued to be influential within the sociology of education, as it has been elsewhere. However, the development of this approach has taken somewhat divergent forms in different areas. This is revealed if we compare its application within the sociology of education

[3] A key source was the phenomenological sociology of knowledge developed by Berger and Luckmann (1967) on the basis of the work of Schutz, Mead and others.

with social constructionist approaches to the study of social problems.[4] This is an especially appropriate comparison because, as we noted earlier, the sociology of education has been preoccupied (indeed, almost obsessed) with educational inequality, treated as a social problem (Flude, 1974, p. 42). What is surprising, however, is that in terms of social-problems theory the new sociologists of education and their successors, like the 'old sociologists' against whose work they reacted, must be seen as adopting a social causation rather than a social constructionist approach. This is because they have been primarily concerned with identifying the nature and scope of a problem (the incidence and extent of educational inequality in relation to various categories of people), diagnosing its causes (often with a view to recommending policies), and assessing the success of policies designed to alleviate it. By contrast, a social constructionist approach to social problems involves a shift in focus away from the conditions identified as problematic towards a concern with the political activity by which these came to be recognized and treated as a problem. In this way, social problems are seen as produced by a definitional process embodied in political struggles, in which social groups first identify some feature of their environment as a problem and as requiring treatment (or redefine an old problem in a new way), and then engage in political activity to get their definition recognized and acted on.

This kind of social constructionism provides a quite different perspective on educational inequality from those which have predominated in the sociology of education. Moreover, one of its implications is that the work of sociologists adopting a social causation approach comes into the focus of analysis as, at the very least, a source of argumentative resources available for use in the micro-politics of social problem formation. In fact, their work has been rendered even more central by recent developments within social constructionism. Ibarra and Kitsuse's (1993) formulation of what has come to be called 'strict constructionism' narrows the focus of analysis entirely to the rhetorical formulation of social problems. Here social constructionism turns into a kind of discourse analysis; and sociological writing itself constitutes a substantial proportion of the data available for such analysis.

As developed in social-problems theory, then, social constructionism provides a distinctive perspective on the study of educational inequality; and one which offers to facilitate reflexive analysis of research in this field. It highlights the fact that most of this work treats educational inequality as an objective feature of the world, albeit one that can and should be eradicated. Of course, sociological work on education has emphasized that inequality is a *social* product, not the result of psychological or biological factors; but it has treated it as existing independently of the researcher, and indeed of beliefs about it

---

[4]   On social constructionist approaches to social problems see, for example, Spector and Kitsuse, 1977 and Holstein and Miller, 1993. Social constructionism has also been influential in other fields, for example in the sociology of health (Wright and Treacher, 1982) and, especially, in the sociology of science (for a discussion, see Sismondo, 1993). There is also a constructionist movement in psychology, see Gergen, 1985.

on the part of individual members of society, both those who benefit and those who suffer from it. By contrast, a thoroughgoing social constructionist perspective would emphasize that educational inequality is only constituted as a social problem in particular societies at particular times; and that this occurs in, and through, the work of powerful groups and individuals who operate in the context of particular, historically generated forms of social organization, and deploy particular rhetorical strategies. From this perspective, to argue that educational inequality exists as a social problem in societies irrespective of whether it is recognized as such by members of them would be to impose a construction which reflects presentist and ethnocentric presuppositions. Similarly, it is implied that to treat the existence of educational inequality in Britain today as a social problem is to accept taken-for-granted assumptions which should be opened up to sociological scrutiny. For constructionists, educational inequality constitutes a social problem now only because of the activities of those in the past who construed it as such and engaged in political mobilization to get it recognized as a problem; and as a result of the work of those in the present who keep it on the political agenda, including many educational researchers. In the next section we provide a sketch of a social constructionist analysis of the emergence and development of the problem of educational inequality.

The Socio-historical Construction of Educational Inequality as a Social Problem

There was a time in Western societies when neither educational nor any other form of inequality was widely regarded as a social problem amenable to change, not just by those in power but even by most of 'the lower orders' themselves. In the Middle Ages, for example, differences in social status, wealth and power, and the inheritance of these, were generally treated as facts of life and/or as part of a natural and divinely ordained social order. As Coleman (1968) has pointed out, this was not just a matter of ideology, material factors were important too; notably the all-encompassing role played by the family. It was only from the seventeenth century onwards that this started to change to any extent, partly as a result of the gradual spread of the idea that all human beings are born equal and that they should enjoy opportunities to rise (and fall) in the social order, according to talent.[5] This change was particularly associated with the rise of the commercial, urban middle classes, and was accelerated by the industrial and political revolutions they subsequently sponsored (Hobsbawm, 1962).

[5] The idea of the equality of human beings was of course enshrined in Christianity, but the revolutionary potential of that idea was defused by other worldliness. And, as Christianity became institutionalized, it legitimated social hierarchies, not least those of the Church itself. See Chadwick, 1967 and Southern, 1970. On the idea of equality and its development generally, see Abernethy, 1959; Lakoff, 1964 and Benn, 1967.

Educational inequality seems to have emerged as a social problem only relatively recently. Even in nineteenth-century Britain, the class structure was still widely regarded as static, and as properly so. What social mobility occurred was viewed as individuals 'bettering themselves'; it was not generally treated as something which ought to be the goal of public policy. In this context, different social classes were believed to require different sorts of education. Indeed, at the beginning of the nineteenth century it was still widely assumed that the working classes did not need any formal schooling at all, and that providing them with it could be dangerous. It was quite late in that century before the State took direct responsibility for supplying universal elementary education. And even by the beginning of the twentieth century, access to secondary education was very restricted for the working class, and this came to be the central issue for campaigns against educational inequality.[6]

The roots of the problem of educational inequality stretch much further back than the nineteenth century, however. There seem to have been at least two conditions associated with its emergence. One was the widening influence of the idea that to be truly human is to be educated. The influence of the Renaissance was of particular importance here, with its expansion of the scope of secular learning and knowledge; while the Reformation had the effect of promoting literacy in vernacular languages and thereby further weakening priestly control of knowledge. On top of this, the scientific revolution of the seventeenth century presented knowledge as something which could be acquired by anyone who was prepared to learn by means of scientific method: it did not require a level of classical erudition which was only available to those with the money and leisure to access the literature of the ancient world, nor did it require religious virtue or perhaps even intellectual genius. These various ideas were combined by the Enlightenment thinkers of the eighteenth century, many of whom placed scientific investigation and education at the centre of social reform. And, in the nineteenth and early twentieth centuries, we find education treated as essential to human life both by those who stressed science as the spearhead of modernity, and therefore campaigned for scientific and technical education, and by those who saw the humanities as the true source of human knowledge, emphasizing personal and cultural development. Moreover, once education had come to be regarded as constitutive of true humanity, calls for equal access to it followed almost automatically, given the growing influence of egalitarian arguments of various kinds.

The second condition that set the stage for the emergence of educational inequality as a social problem was the increasing role of literacy and numeracy in a variety of social spheres over the course of the eighteenth, nineteenth, and twentieth centuries: in the growing activities of the State, in the running of economic organizations that were getting larger and more complex,

---

[6] Within each social class, of course, educational opportunity was much more restricted for females than for males; and, where education *was* provided for girls and young women, it was generally designed to prepare them for marriage and the domestic sphere, see Purvis, 1991.

and in the widening realm of political and cultural activities. Schools became important as providers of literacy and numeracy skills, these being essential in many new and expanding occupations. And later, with the increasing role of standard qualifications in occupational selection, schools began to prepare candidates for examinations of various types and at various levels. In this way, schooling came to take on an increasing role in the process of occupational recruitment. As a result, educational inequalities were linked with social inequalities; and remedying the former came to be seen as a means of remedying the latter.

This is the general historical background against which campaigns against educational inequalities have taken place in the twentieth century, campaigns in which psychologists, sociologists and other researchers have played an important role. In the next section, we shall examine the work of social scientists in the formulation of educational inequality as a social problem.

Research and the Conceptualization of Educational Inequality

In the first half of the twentieth century psychologists, and particularly those involved in the development of intelligence tests, had a considerable influence on how the problem of educational inequality was conceived. Dominant figures here were Godfrey Thomson (Sharp, 1980) and Cyril Burt (Hearnshaw, 1979). Central to this work was the idea that intelligence is genetically determined, in large part; with different social classes varying in average intelligence, and members of the lower classes being generally less intelligent than those of the middle and upper classes. The existence of mismatches between intelligence and social-class background in many individual cases was recognized, however. Indeed, the regression to the mean characteristic of a genetically inherited characteristic made such mismatches inevitable. Thus, intelligence testing was required to identify the kinds of education appropriate to each child; though the amount of educational inequality which existed was generally assumed to be relatively small.

Partly as a result of this work more attention came to be given to identifying individual working-class children who showed exceptional ability, and to providing them with the opportunity to develop their talents. This was achieved through increasing the provision of free places, creating a ladder of opportunity from elementary into secondary schools.[7] In this way, it was believed, not only could the system be made fairer but the nation could also capitalize upon more of its talent.

The numbers of free places available for secondary education increased dramatically in the early twentieth century. They were filled on the basis of competitive examinations (oral and/or written), teachers' reports, and/or

[7] While originally intended as free places for which candidates merely had to qualify, they quickly became competitive scholarships (Gordon, 1980, Ch. 8).

intelligence test results, the methods varying from local authority to local authority and over time. However, while these developments increased the number of working-class students in secondary schools, there was growing criticism of the free system as inadequate, both because many places were taken by middle-class children and because the number of academically able working-class children came to be seen as greater than had previously been recognized (see Floud, Halsey and Martin, 1956, pp. 139–49). The work of sociologists, notably that of Lindsay (1926) and Gray and Moshinsky (1938), played an important part in this. Political pressure to recognize social-class inequalities in access to secondary education as a social problem came initially from the labour movement, but later gained broader support, particularly as a result of the change in political climate produced by the Second World War.[8] The 1944 Education Act, which was the product of this pressure, was an attempt to open up educational opportunity to all working-class children, though it was still based on the idea that an academic secondary education should be available only to those with a high level of inherent ability.

In the 1950s and 1960s there was widespread questioning of some of the basic assumptions of this first stage in the development of the problem of educational inequality. In particular, the claim that intelligence was largely inherited came to be challenged, and greater emphasis was placed on the effects of social environment (Simon, 1953; Vernon, 1969; see also Vernon, 1979). Psychologists had not denied the role of the environment; indeed, the provision of increased access to secondary education had been motivated in part to facilitate realization of the intellectual potential of able working-class children by countering the effects of their home backgrounds. But built into this point of view was the idea that there is a definite limit to the number of academically able working-class children. This idea was enshrined in the Norwood report, where three types of child were identified: what might be referred to as the academic, the technical, and the practical (Committee of the Secondary School Examinations Council, 1943, Ch. 1). This influenced the implementation of the 1944 Act, resulting in the prevalence of the tripartite system (though in most places it became a bipartite system, technical schools being rare). However, with growing doubts about the heritability of intelligence, differences in home background came to be seen by many commentators as the major factor behind variation in school achievement. The focus of much research became 'the social determinants of educability' (Floud and Halsey, 1958, pp. 181–5); and in the wake of this, the concept of cultural deprivation was imported from the United States and became influential in explanations for the differential school achievement of the social classes (see, for example, Schools Council, 1970). Thus, the relative failure of working-class children in schools, compared to middle-class children, began to be explained by many

[8] On the politics of reform in the interwar period, see Simon, 1974. Silver, 1973 provides a brief overview, along with extracts from some of the key documents. Banks, 1955 traces the development of different types of secondary education, of varying prestige and function, up to, and including, the establishment of the tripartite system.

in terms of the effects of culturally deficient home backgrounds which failed to provide the cognitive and attitudinal socialization believed to be a prerequisite for academic success.[9] This explanation stimulated proposals that there should be direct action by schools in the form of compensatory education (Halsey, 1972), and calls for stronger links between home and school (Craft *et al.*, 1972).

These changes in view about the nature and origin of academic ability, along with doubts about the capacity of intelligence tests to measure it in a culture-fair way, also led to pressure for comprehensive secondary schooling. It was argued that to select at 11+ was too early, denying a large number of intelligent working-class children access to a grammar-school education who could have benefitted from one. In 1956 Floud, Halsey and Martin pointed out that 'the likelihood that a working class boy will reach a grammar school is not notably greater today, despite all the changes, than it was before 1945' (Floud, Halsey and Martin, 1956, p. 33). Furthermore, Douglas's (1964) work suggested that even where measured ability was equal, social-class differences in obtaining grammar-school places persisted. Also of considerable political significance at this time was that, as a result of the post-war baby boom, a substantial proportion of children from middle-class backgrounds found themselves in non-selective education. One consequence of this was that a growing number of secondary-modern schools started to offer an academic education to top-stream students, leading to their entry for GCE examinations. This had the effect of revealing the extent to which the 11+ had consigned academically capable students to non-selective schools. Another result was the expansion of local experiments with comprehensive schooling and pressure at national level for comprehensivization, culminating in Circular 10/65 (Rubinstein and Simon, 1969).

Where the shift from the first to the second stage in the development of educational inequality as a social problem coincided with a change in the relative influence of different disciplines, from psychology to sociology, subsequent reconceptualizations of the problem occurred primarily through internal transformations of the sociology of education itself; transformations which involved challenges to the domains of other disciplines.[10] These later changes provided the basis for much of the research we shall examine in this book.

One early development was a focus on the effects of streaming in schools. A major criticism of the 11+ had been that it had a backwash effect, encouraging streaming in the later years of primary schooling and thereby effectively

---

[9] It was argued that whereas in the past the material circumstances of their homes disadvantaged working-class children, by the middle of the century these were no longer a key factor, hence the emphasis on cultural features. See Banks, 1971, Ch. 4 for a review of research in this area. See also Craft, 1970.

[10] The economics of education also played an important role, particularly through promoting the idea that education must be seen as investment not just consumption, see Blaug, 1987. For useful histories of the sociology of education in the period we are examining, from different perspectives, see Flude, 1974 and Banks, 1982.

pushing the point of selection even earlier (Douglas 1964; Jackson 1964; Barker Lunn 1970). Equally, though, attention came to be given to streaming in secondary schools. The argument here was not just that such internal selection reinforced the effects of differences in home background, but also that these processes themselves had consequences which increased social class disparities in academic achievement. It was claimed that streaming, and the differentiation of students on academic-behavioural grounds generally, served to depress the academic performance of those ranked lowest, through generating negative attitudes towards school. Moreover, since a higher proportion of working-class children found themselves in low streams, this exacerbated social class differences in educational achievement (Hargreaves 1967; Lacey 1970). Here, the emphasis in the explanation of educational inequalities started to move away from the personal characteristics and social backgrounds of students back once again to processes of selection within the education system. This fed into the promotion of comprehensive schooling, suggesting that the new schools should be organized on the basis of mixed ability teaching groups. At the same time, these arguments about the effects of streaming and other forms of academic differentiation provided a bridge to the more radical arguments about educational inequality, and about the role of schooling in society, which were to follow.

Crucial to these subsequent developments was the emergence of the 'new sociology of education'. This shifted the focus of debate among sociologists dramatically. As we have seen, most previous discussion of educational inequality had been concerned with working-class children's access to secondary education, or with what needed to be done to facilitate their capacity to benefit from it. Now, however, attention started to be given to the nature of the education that was on offer, to the sort of academic ability on which school achievement depends, and to the kind of learning schools fostered.

In some respects these preoccupations were a development of earlier themes (see, for example, Halsey, 1961; Williamson, 1974; Bernbaum, 1977). Within the campaign for comprehensive education, the grammar-school curriculum had often been dismissed as too narrow, and intelligence and achievement tests had been criticized for being subject to middle-class bias. However, the new sociologists pursued a much more radical line in relation to these issues; drawing not just on the theoretical resources we mentioned earlier, but also on the arguments of radical educators and de-schoolers which were influential in the late 1960s and early 1970s.[11] They began to challenge the whole nature of the education provided in schools. This was itself now seen as a barrier to the achievement of educational (and social) equality. One aspect of this was the argument that the knowledge and skills purveyed, or at least those accorded high status, stem from the culture of dominant social groups. In other words, the very knowledge schools offer reflects the unequal social structure of the wider society. This involved a challenge to the idea that

---

[11] See the discussion and references in Hargreaves, 1974.

what counts as knowledge transcends society. And associated with this was the claim that the study of school knowledge lies within the domain of sociology, rather than in that of the philosophy of education. As a result, sociological attention started to be given to how and why particular forms of knowledge had come to be included in the curriculum, this being explained in terms of the influence of powerful groups and their struggles with those who opposed them (see Young, 1971; White and Young, 1975; Whitty, 1985).

In this way, schooling came to be seen as involving the imposition of a dominant culture on subordinate groups. Previously, a distinction had been drawn between educational and social selection, between selection on the basis of relevant abilities and attitudes, on the one hand, and selection by social-class characteristics spuriously associated with ability, on the other. Now, by means of a theoretical 'stepping back', the whole notion of academic ability came to be bracketed and treated as a socio-historical construction, rather than as something which could be taken for granted (Hudson, 1970; Squibb, 1973). Here the new sociology also challenged the domain of the psychology of education, and in a much more direct manner than the old sociology had done.[12]

The new sociology of education completed the shift begun by Hargreaves, Lacey and others from explanations of educational inequalities in terms of the individual and social characteristics of students to explanations which emphasized the role of the education system. From now on, any attempt to explain differences in educational achievement in terms of students' differential abilities, or of the effects of their home background on their motivation and capacity to learn, was ruled out on the grounds that it took for granted the education system's definition of what counted as knowledge, learning, ability, and motivation; definitions which reflected the dominant culture and were discrepant with working-class culture. As a result, the focus of research within the sociology of education, and in educational research generally, shifted away from being primarily concerned with the effects of home background towards analysis of the education system itself. The central issue for the new sociologists became the inequality of power between the social classes in their capacity to define what counts as education. And the remedy recommended, or at least implied, was a transformation of society as a whole. What emerges here is a conception of the problem of educational inequality as in large part the product of an education system which constructs a conception of knowledge and ability that discriminates against working-class children.

Closely associated with this was a methodological shift towards the use of qualitative methods. Here too the new sociology of education extended a development started by Hargreaves and Lacey. Largely under the influence of

[12] In these ways, academic politics were closely intertwined with wider political struggles: the 'new sociology' emerged as part of a conflict amongst the disciplines making up the curriculum in teacher education. See Bernbaum, 1977 for an account of the historical background to this. For a discussion of sociological imperialism in another area, see Strong, 1979.

social anthropology, these researchers had adopted an ethnographic approach, focusing on patterns of social relations in particular schools, these being treated as case studies of general types. Lacey had studied a boys' grammar school (Lacey, 1966, 1970 and 1975), Audrey Lambart (the third member of the team) had investigated a girls' grammar school (Lambart, 1976 and 1982), and Hargreaves had studied a boys' secondary modern school (Hargreaves, 1967). While they employed some quantitative techniques, notably sociometry and questionnaire data, these researchers placed considerable reliance on participant observation and informal interviews with teachers and students. The new sociology of education rendered this trend toward qualitative method virtually complete. And subsequently, under the influence of phenomenological and symbolic interactionist ideas, a considerable amount of research on schools and classrooms was carried out, most of it relying primarily on qualitative study of a small number of cases. Indeed, usually the research took place in a single school, and very often it focused on a small subset of the teachers and small groups of students.[13]

Like many social movements, once it had achieved dominance the new sociology of education tended to fragment into competing factions. Some researchers concentrated on documenting the school and classroom processes which had previously been so neglected. Others reverted to a focus on the operation of the education system as a whole, albeit in a very different manner from earlier work. Under the growing influence of Marxism, they came to see the cultural domination taking place in schools as generated by wider social structural forces, especially capitalism. Marxist accounts became influential which portrayed the whole structure and content of education systems in modern societies as functionally tuned to reproduce social inequality: in providing recruits of appropriate kinds for different levels of the social structure, by legitimating this inequality through transmitting ideological accounts of why society must be like it is, and through ensuring that for the most part children ended up in social-class positions that were much the same as those of their parents (Althusser, 1971; Bowles and Gintis, 1976). From this point of view, 'ability' became little more than an ideological cipher for the characteristics or interests of the dominant classes, and/or for the capacities needed to function in capitalist society. Schooling was widely regarded as implicated in a process of direct social reproduction.

This view was clearly at odds with the phenomenological and interactionist emphasis on teachers and students playing an active role in constructing the social reality of schooling. And, over time, it came to be rejected even within the Marxist camp, on the grounds that it failed to allow any scope for resistance on the part of students and teachers, and thereby ruled out any prospect of change (see Arnot and Whitty, 1982; Whitty, 1985). However, the Marxist framework was still retained by these critics, with capitalism as the determin-

[13]   For an account of the diverse qualitative approaches which emerged at this time, see Atkinson *et al.*, 1993. For some examples of this work, see Willis 1977; Woods 1979; Hammersley and Woods 1984; Hargreaves and Woods 1984.

ant in the last instance; even though emphasis was now placed on the relative autonomy of both the education system and the State from the economy (see Hargreaves, 1982; Harris, 1992).

The 'new sociology' differed from earlier work, then, both in its definition of the problem of educational inequality, and in how inequality was to be explained. Where previously the failure of working-class children to achieve at the same level as middle-class children had been accounted for, to a large extent, in terms of features of their cultural backgrounds, now this failure was reinterpreted as a product of the school system. It was just one part of the process by which capitalist society reproduced itself. The criteria of assessment and the whole manner in which schooling was organized were seen as functioning to bring about that failure. And, along with this, there was a shift in the conceptualization of working-class children, away from portraying them as victims of their cultural backgounds, or even of specific organizational features of the education system, towards treating them as suffering and resisting oppression, that oppression having its source in the very structure of British society. In short, the education system was now regarded as an agency of the capitalist state; and as directly, albeit subtly, implicated in the reproduction of educational and social inequality.

We can illustrate some of the more recent of these shifts in the construction of the problem of educational inequality by looking closely at two classic studies in the sociology of education from different periods.

From Working-class Victims to Potential Revolutionaries

David Hargreaves' book *Social Relations in a Secondary School* (Hargreaves, 1967) was written at a time when the problem of educational inequality was still seen primarily in terms of the differential capacities for academic success provided by working-class and middle-class homes. As we noted, Hargreaves' work, along with that of Lacey, was distinctive in placing emphasis on features of secondary-school organization which disadvantaged working-class children, though neither of them denied the influence of social-class differences in home background.

Hargreaves argues that in the English tripartite education system of the early 1960s students in the lower streams of secondary-modern schools, who were predominantly working-class, bore a double stigma: they had failed to get a selective school place, and they had failed to get a top-stream place in their secondary-modern school. In terms of the values on which the education system was based their status was undeniably low, and he argues that as a result they experienced status frustration: they had desired high status but had been denied this by the school system. Drawing on theories of delinquency and analysing data collected at 'Lumley', a secondary-modern school located in a northern English conurbation, Hargreaves claims that the response of lower-stream students to this was to form a subculture which inverted school values. In this way, they produced an alternative status hierarchy to that of the school, and one in terms of which they could be successful. Anti-school attitudes, 'delinquent' behaviour, and a reduction in motivation for school work, followed from this.[14]

The implication of Hargreaves' account is to present the attitudes and behaviour of working-class boys placed in the lower streams of secondary-modern schools as caused not by low intelligence, or even primarily by the shortcomings of their cultural backgrounds, but to some considerable extent by the social organization of schooling: by selection at 11+, streaming in schools, and differentiation on the basis of academic ability and 'behaviour' by teachers in the classroom. He argues that, since their self-esteem is threatened through being placed in low streams, the boys 'are thus *forced* to seek a substitute system which can confer prestige in proportion to the degree of rejection of the school's values' (p. 172; our emphasis). Here, then, the students are portrayed as victims of the way in which the education system is organized. This involves a moral re-evaluation of the problem of educational inequality, one which contrasts with earlier accounts as well as conflicting with the prevailing views of many secondary-school teachers at the time.

Hargreaves' account can usefully be compared with a later book, which has probably been even more influential within sociology: Paul Willis's *Learning to Labour* (Willis, 1977). While carrying out his research some ten years later, Willis focuses on a group of students who are very similar to those studied by Hargreaves. Again, the site of investigation is a secondary-modern school; and, even more than in the case of Hargreaves, it is working-class boys in the lower streams who are centre stage. Furthermore, the attitudes and behaviour of 'the lads' Willis describes are very similar to those reported in Hargreaves' account of 'delinquent youth'.

Nevertheless, the two authors differ significantly in how they account for the attitudes and behaviour of the boys they studied, and in their evaluations of these. One important difference is that Willis brings the students' home background back in as a central variable. Where Hargreaves had tended to portray the nature of the anti-school subculture he found in the lower streams as the result of an inversion of school values, Willis presents it much more strongly as an expression or development of working-class culture. Even more important, that culture is no longer treated as a source of deprivation or even of disadvantage. Rather, it is celebrated as containing important insights into the nature of the wider society, and of the role of schooling within that. Furthermore, where Hargreaves sees the anti-school subculture of the lower-stream boys as a response to failure, for Willis it is a response to the attempt of the school to control 'the lads' and to impose middle-class culture and incorporate them into capitalist society.

---

[14] Hargreaves saw this process of polarization as occurring across all four streams (he excluded from his focus 5E, a class which contained 'boys who were considered back-ward or retarded', Hargreaves, 1967, p. 2), but with the anti-school subculture being dominant in the bottom streams.

What we have in Willis's work, then, is a further re-evaluation of the attitudes and behaviour of recalcitrant, low-stream, working-class boys. Where these were negatively evaluated by Hargreaves, albeit without this constituting grounds for blaming the students, for Willis this evaluation is reversed. For him, the counter-culture is superior to school culture because it contains 'penetrations', true understandings of the nature of society; whereas, by contrast, school culture is primarily ideological in character, functioning to preserve an unequal society. Similarly, whereas Hargreaves tends to portray the attitudes and behaviour of students as a causal product of the organizational features of the secondary school, Willis presents 'the lads' as playing a much more active role in making sense of their environment and determining their actions. Indeed, it is the 'ear 'oles', the conformist students, whose behaviour is treated as causally determined: 'the lads' resist the efforts of the school to control them, making use of working-class culture as a resource in this resistance.[15]

After the New Sociology of Education

In the late 1970s and 1980s, the sociology of education developed against the background of what has come to be referred to as the collapse of the social democratic settlement (CCCS, 1981). As we noted earlier, there was a shift to the Right at the level of national government, and in the political agenda towards a concern with educational standards and what was seen as the failure of education to contribute to economic growth. Moreover, the sociology of education was itself in the firing line, as one of the main sources of the progressivism and educational radicalism which had allegedly deformed teacher education and resulted in the decline of standards and the transmission of anti-capitalist ideology in schools.

At the same time, internally, the subdiscipline began to be influenced by the spreading influence of feminism in the academic world and by the emergence of multi-culturalism and anti-racism as key strands of Leftist politics. Attention shifted from the fate of white, working-class boys to the educational experiences and fortunes of girls and of ethnic minority (particularly Afro-Caribbean and Asian) students. Educational inequalities between the sexes and among ethnic/'racial' groups now became the focus for much research. Those involved in this drew on many of the same theoretical resources employed in the identification of educational inequalities between the social classes. Thus, it was claimed that the capabilities of girls had been systematically underestimated by schools and teachers, especially in science and mathematics. It was also argued that their access to some courses had been restricted by the assumption that they would not go on to higher education, or take up

15   There is, of course, an ironic twist in Willis's account, in that it is the lads' resistance which dooms them to working-class jobs. However, Willis does not present this in tragic terms, but rather as an outcome which could be changed if the revolutionary potential of the school counter-culture could be realized.

employment requiring high-level academic knowledge, but choose marriage and a family instead. In addition, though, it was claimed that the nature of school knowledge reflects patriarchal assumptions, with the result that it either demotivates girls or socializes them into forms of knowledge and learning which are alien to them. In addition, schools came to be seen by many feminists as institutions which inculcate traditional conceptions of masculinity and femininity, directly and indirectly, thereby reproducing patriarchy (Deem, 1978 and 1980; Stanworth, 1983; Arnot and Weiner, 1987; Weiner and Arnot, 1987; Measor and Sikes, 1992).

In a similar way, it was argued that ethnic minority students suffer sub-stantial discrimination in schools: that teachers tend to see Asian children as suffering from language problems and as having cultural backgrounds which disadvantage them, while Afro-Caribbean students (particularly boys) are re-garded as highly disruptive. These stereotypes were regarded as informing both the treatment of students in classrooms and their allocation to bands and sets in secondary schools. Furthermore, it has been suggested that much the same consequences follow from this for ethnic-minority students as for white working-class ones: in the case of Afro-Caribbean students, in particular, it leads to the development of anti-school subcultures, which increase their antagonism to teachers and depress their academic performance. And, equally important discrimination against black students in schools has been seen as arising not merely from prejudice on the part of teachers, but as reflecting the fundamentally racist character of the whole society. It is suggested that much of what is valued in schools, both in terms of curricular and behavioural norms, is based on 'white culture'. Alongside this, there has been a concern not just to avoid 'blaming the victim' but also to portray black students as perceptively and actively resisting the discrimination they face (Wright, 1986, 1992a and 1992b; Mac an Ghaill, 1988; Gillborn, 1990a; Mirza, 1992).

As with earlier work on social class, this research has constructed educa-tional inequality as a problem requiring political intervention. Some formula-tions of sexual and racial inequalities took a less radical position than the new sociologists had done, focusing on unequal access to, and unequal opportun-ity to benefit from, what was offered by schools. To a large extent this con-stituted an internal critique of the education system for not achieving its own ideal of equality of opportunity, albeit now interpreted in terms of equality of outcome.[16] However, there was also a more radical response present from the beginning, influenced by developments within feminism and by the black power movement in the United States, as well as by the new sociology; and this became more prominent as work in these fields developed.[17]

[16] See, for example, Byrne, 1978, whose arguments parallel those of the old sociolo-gists in many ways.
[17] For discussions of the diversity of orientations to be found amongst educational researchers working in the fields of gender and 'race' see Weiner, 1985 and Troyna, 1987, respectively.

As a brief illustration of these later developments, we will look at some influential work by Mary Fuller (Fuller, 1980, 1982 and 1983). In one of her articles, Fuller presents her work against the background of findings from the mid-1970s that many Afro-Caribbean girls were performing better in school than white working-class girls and than Afro-Caribbean boys. This ran counter to what might have been predicted from assumed patterns of discrimination and oppression. It seemed that Afro-Caribbean girls, as blacks, should have been performing worse than whites; and, as an oppressed gender, worse than males. In short, they should have been at the very bottom of the performance league. The fact that this was not the case constituted a potential challenge to the prevailing paradigm. The conclusion seemed to be drawn by some that black girls suffered less from gender discrimination than white girls. Fuller comments that 'using some conceptual sleights of hand', commentators had contributed to 'the myth that black women are not subordinated on the basis of their sex, and, indeed, may even be privileged in relation to other women' (Fuller, 1982, pp. 87–8).

Fuller's work challenges this interpretation. She claims to show that the effects of the double subordination of black girls can be detected even in the case of the group of academically successful students she studied, who were located in the top fifth year band of a large London comprehensive school. These girls did well at school, eventually obtaining 'a mean of 7.6 passes at O level or CSE and generally with creditable grades' (1983, p. 178). However, there is an interesting contrast between Fuller's portrayal of the 'subculture' formed by these girls and Hargreaves' account of top stream boys' attitudes and motives. Fuller sees the subculture formed by the girls she studied as a product of their experience of sexism and racism, rather than of streaming or even of home background. She reports that they were aware of the significance of being black and of being women in a society which discriminates against members of both these categories. Thus, they complain about the double standards parents maintain towards boys and girls, both in terms of the performance of domestic chores and of personal freedom; they note the sexism of black peers; and they recognize that there is discrimination in the labour market. Indeed, according to Fuller, it is precisely this knowledge about discrimination which motivates their commitment to succeed academically. They also differ from Hargreaves' pro-school boys in that they are not conformist in orientation. Fuller reports their critical attitudes towards the school and towards most teachers, and their non-conformist behaviour in the classroom. In this respect, she brings them closer to Willis's 'lads', even though they differ from the lads dramatically in their academic aspirations and success. Like the lads, the girls are taken to have an accurate understanding of the world and of their own place within it. And they too resist the pressures operating on them. In a novel rhetorical reversal, their pro-educational attitudes and the behaviour following from it are portrayed as a form of resistance, albeit of a distinctive kind.

Reviewing the Sociological Construction of Educational Inequality

If we look back across the three studies we have examined, we find some interesting shifts in the textual strategies used to formulate the problem of educational inequality. To a large extent these involve the differential assignment of positive or negative moral evaluation to various features of the scenes described; and, along with this, ascription of freedom, knowledge, and responsibility (or lack of these) to the agents involved.[18]

In the case of Hargreaves' work, moral worth is assigned to the education system and to what it offers, but the academic failure of working-class children is negatively evaluated as unjust. This is because it does not accurately reflect their real intelligence and moral character. And, while negatively evaluated, their low academic achievement and anti-social behaviour are portrayed as determined to a large extent by the selection procedures of the education system. Furthermore, for the most part, the students are not aware of the causes of their own attitudes and behaviour, nor are they presented as able to do much about these. Responsibility lies with teachers and schools; and, once the source of the problem has been drawn to their attention, the remedy is in their hands (see Hargreaves, 1967, Ch. 9).

The situation is very different with Willis. Here, moral worth is assigned to 'the lads'; while the school, along with the society of which it forms part, is negatively evaluated. Moreover, the lads are portrayed as having knowledge that others (including teachers) do not have, and as playing an active role in resisting the system; though they do not have the power to succeed in transforming it. The problem lies in the very structure of society. What is required, it is implied, is that radical intellectuals and teachers help the working class to overthrow capitalism.

Fuller's scenario is different again, and is more complex and ambivalent in character. Discrimination against blacks and women is negatively evaluated. However, its source is not clearly indicated, and (for the most part) it does not seem that Fuller's account is based on the same sort of thorough-going rejection of the larger society as that of Willis. Nevertheless, the girls are portrayed as having already taken responsibility for their own lives, and she ascribes to them both knowledge about discrimination and an active role in resisting it; though what results from this is a commitment to work for individual success within the existing educational and occupational systems.[19]

Of course, these three studies do not provide a comprehensive picture of the rhetorical formulations of the problem of educational inequality to be

[18] It is possible, of course, that these shifts reflect changes in the character of students over time, or differences between the groups of students which these researchers studied. From a social constructionist point of view, however, such considerations are not relevant.

[19] Fuller's three articles differ somewhat in the extent to which they are located within a macro-critique of British society: compare Fuller, 1980 with 1982. She also denies that

found in the research literature, even in its most recent phases. But they do give some sense of the range of formulations employed, and of the changes that have taken place in these over time. In summary form, we can recapitulate the main stages in the construction of educational inequality as a social problem as follows, though there is considerable overlap in time between them:

Initially, it was customary and financial barriers against working-class access to schooling which were seen as constituting educational inequality; and, subsequently, inadequate provision of free places and the failure to provide a secondary education for all. These factors were criticized for preventing intelligent working-class children from rising in the occupational structure.

Later, attention came to focus on *cultural* barriers to working-class participation and success in the education system. Now it was the effects of their home backgrounds on early cognitive and attitudinal development which were believed to lead to the underachievement of working-class children.

At around the same time, emphasis was also laid on organizational barriers to working-class achievement *within* the education system. Selection for different kinds of secondary school at too early a point, along with the demotivating effects of streaming, were regarded as preventing working-class children from achieving their full potential.

With the new sociology of education, the focus shifted sharply. Schooling was no longer portrayed as a modernizing and enlightening force in the world but came to be regarded as itself part of the problem. It was seen as involving the imposition of the dominant culture, and as functioning to reproduce the social-class structure. Effectively, it was now treated as constituting cultural and social discrimination against working-class children, though it also generated resistance on their part. The whole nature of the education offered by schools came to be questioned, this sometimes being seen as inherently ideological and oppressive.

Finally, the focus was extended to educational inequality between the sexes and between ethnically and 'racially' defined groups. Work in this phase drew on the rhetorical resources developed in earlier phases: it was argued both that girls and ethnic-minority students are denied their fair share of educational success; and that the very nature of school knowledge and learning, as currently constituted, discriminate against them.

the girls' behaviour amounts to 'individualistic self-improvement', suggesting that it is rather 'a necessary strategy of survival' (Fuller, 1982, p. 98). However, her arguments are not convincing on this point since the 'subculture' seems to amount simply to shared orientations rather than to active collaboration, and the girls' goal is clearly their own individual educational success. There is an interesting comparison to be drawn here with Hargreaves' account of the solidaristic character of the anti-school subculture at Lumley (Hargreaves, 1967, p. 172).

Conclusion

In this chapter, we have used a social constructionist approach to the study of social problems as a way of providing a reflexive perspective on the sociology of education. This highlights the fact that much work in this area has been closely associated with political pressure to eradicate educational inequalities. Moreover, the conceptualization of inequality, the explanations presented for it, and the policies recommended to deal with it, have changed radically over time, reflecting changes in the wider political climate. What this reveals is that the phenomenon with which this research has been concerned does not exist independently of it. Rather, researchers have themselves been involved in constructing the problem of educational inequality, defining and redefining it. This is true most obviously at a discursive level, but also to some extent at the level of the shaping of public policy.

This social constructionist account of the sociology of education shows something even more important from our perspective. As we noted early on, social constructionism was a major factor in the development of the new sociology of education. What is striking from the point of view of the study of social problems, however, is that it was applied selectively.[20] The new sociologists dismissed the existence of differences in ability or intelligence, the alleged cultural deprivation of working-class homes, and the assumed superiority of the forms of knowledge promoted by schools, by arguing that what counts as intelligence, culture, or knowledge is a matter of social definition; and that it is the definitions of powerful groups which prevail within the education system. Thus, the concept of academic ability on the basis of which schools operate was reinterpreted as a social construction which functions to serve the purposes of schools, of the State, and of dominant social classes; the implication being that it does not reflect any actual or relevant differences amongst children. In this way, a social constructionist approach was used to throw doubt on the claims of researchers, policymakers, teachers and others who had sought to explain differences in the academic performances of students in terms of their differential ability or the cultural features of their home backgrounds. These views were treated as ideological, in both content and function, because they failed to recognize the socially constructed character of social phenomena. At the same time, however, the real existence of dominant groups, of their power, of the process of social reproduction, and indeed of educational and social inequalities themselves, was never regarded as in the least doubtful by the new sociologists. The socially constructed character of *these* phenomena was ignored.

Much the same tendency can be seen operating in more recent work on educational inequality in relation to gender and ethnicity. Arguments to the effect that there may be actual differences in ability or orientation between girls and boys, or between members of different ethnic groups, and that these

[20] This was pointed out by a number of early critics, but to no avail. See Shipman, 1973 and Bernbaum, 1977.

generate differential educational achievement, have been ruled out on the grounds that such alleged differences are social constructions produced by sexism or racism; not least by the sexism and racism of those who claim that such differences exist. However, patriarchy and racism are not treated as social constructions, but as social forces actually operating in the world. Here too we have a selective scepticism: some features of the world are treated as social constructions, and therefore as less than fully real, while others are not.

Such a selective application of social constructionism is by no means unusual. Indeed, it is to be found elsewhere in the study of social problems. Woolgar and Pawluch (1985) have referred to it as 'ontological gerrymandering'. These authors point out that while constructionists have often portrayed social problems as mere constructions, they have not done this in all cases. For instance, sometimes they have focused not so much on the processes by which a social problem has become defined as such but on the social factors which caused its previous neglect. By implication at least, some social problems have been treated as spurious, others as genuine. Which approach was adopted depended on the researcher's values.

As Woolgar and Pawluch point out, however, no justification can be provided by social constructionists for this selective scepticism. Logically, constructionist arguments apply to all social phenomena. From this point of view, our account in this chapter might be seen as remedying the one-sided application of social constructionism which has previously prevailed in the sociology of education. By treating the problem of educational inequality as itself a social construction, we have highlighted what is typically, but unjustifiably, left outside the framework of analysis in this field.

However, even our account in this chapter does not escape the charge of ontological gerrymandering. After all, social constructionist analyses of social problems still present as real the socio-political or discursive processes involved in the construction of those problems. Thus, most social constructionist accounts do not give attention to the work of the sociologist in 'constructing' what is described. To be fully consistent, social constructionism has to include within its focus the work of the constructionist herself or himself. The result of this is best exemplified in Ashmore's social constructionist account of the sociology of scientific knowledge (Ashmore, 1989). This not only assumes that natural scientific knowledge constructs the objects to which it refers, but also that the sociology of scientific knowledge fabricates the natural science it studies. Moreover, aware that the argument applies even to a sociology of sociology, Ashmore continually subverts his own account in order to remind the reader that he is in fact constructing the very sociology of scientific knowledge which he is studying.

The upshot of Ashmore's work seems to be a form of sociological analysis which cannot provide knowledge of any kind, even on its own terms. Instead, it is ensnared in an endless process of self-subversion. Of course, it might be concluded that, even if not a desirable state of affairs, this consistent constructionism is the only legitimate option. But, for a constructionist, any such appeal to legitimacy can itself only be an occasion for further deconstruction. In this way, like all forms of scepticism and relativism, social constructionism implodes.[21]

However, if ontological gerrymandering is unacceptable, and the consistent application of the sceptical implications of social constructionism is futile, what conclusion should be drawn? What this dilemma shows, we believe, is that there is a fallacy at the core of constructionist reflexivity. As Button and Sharrock (1993) have made clear, to focus on the social constitution of knowledge is not necessarily to imply that the objects it refers to do not exist. Nor does it mean that those phenomena are illegitimate, or that they can be easily changed. In large part, the problem here stems from the term 'social construction' itself: it seems to carry the implication that social phenomena are the product of conscious and deliberate processes, that they could have been constructed differently, and that the process of construction can be reversed. Yet this is by no means implied by the fact that they are the products of human activity. In this way, social constructionism takes over the distinction between what is caused and what is constructed from the social causation approach it reacted against; and, along with this, it inherits the idea that only the former is real, in the sense of existing independently of human beings. Yet, phenomena produced by the activities of human beings *can* exist independently of the intentions and desires of the people involved in producing them. Indeed, in some senses they necessarily do so.

Despite its failings, however, social constructionism does usefully direct our attention to the fact that researchers construct (or at least construe) the phenomena they investigate, as well as to the way in which their work is shaped by the social contexts in which they operate. It also shows that in an important sense research on educational inequality has been largely unreflexive. Researchers in this field have looked at the education system with a view to detecting and explaining educational inequalities, without giving much attention to the way in which their own concern with this form of inequality, and how they conceptualize and explain it, are themselves social products; and the implications of this. So, while the fact that educational inequality is a social construction does not imply that it does not exist, or that it is not a legitimate target for sociological investigation, it remains true that research in this area needs to be much more self-consciously reflexive than it has been. The question arises, though, of the form which this reflexivity should take. This is the issue we will address in the next chapter.

[21] Using a different metaphor, Craib, 1993 has described social constructionism as a form of social psychosis.

Chapter 2

Methodological Preliminaries

In Chapter 1 we introduced our work as reflexive in character, as being concerned with making a methodological assessment of research on educational inequality. And, in that chapter, we used a social constructionist perspective as a way of gaining sufficient distance to obtain a reflexive stance. However, we came to the conclusion that, while social constructionism can be a valuable analytic device, and while it provides some insights into this body of research, it does not constitute a sound approach. Applied consistently, it undermines the very possibility of sociological knowledge; and, ultimately, it destroys itself as well. We shall not, therefore, be adopting a constructionist perspective in the remainder of this study.

So, what position will we be taking? We can begin to answer that question most usefully, perhaps, by locating ourselves within the field of inquiry mapped out in the previous chapter. And, as we hinted there, one of the most important benchmarks in that field is the distinction between the old and the new sociologies of education.

The Old and the New

As we saw, the work of both the old and the new sociologists can be seen as having formed part of a political campaign for educational (and social) equality. However, they differed in their conceptualizations of their own relationship to that campaign, as well as in their interpretations of what equality means. The old sociology of education was explicitly political in some senses. Adoption of the label 'political arithmetic' by some of its leading exponents is significant here, since the term signalled not just that the 'arithmetic' engaged in was to do with public policy but also that it was motivated by a particular ethical vision. Thus, in their review of the history and character of the political arithmetic tradition, Halsey *et al.*, emphasize that those belonging to this tradition:

> [. . .] were concerned to describe accurately and in detail the social conditions of their society, particularly of the more disadvantaged sections, but their interest in these matters was never a disinterested

academic one. Description of social conditions was a preliminary to political reform. They exposed the inequalities of society in order to change them. The tradition thus has a double intent: on the one hand it engages in the primary sociological task of describing and documenting the 'state of society'; on the other hand it addresses itself to central social and political issues. It has never, therefore, been a 'value free' academic discipline, if such were in any event possible. Instead, it has been an attempt to marry a value-laden choice of issue with objective methods of data collection. (Halsey, *et al.*, 1980, p. 1).

And the underlying commitment of the political arithmetic of the old sociologists was to social democracy, to the kind of ethical socialism exemplified in the writings of Hobhouse, Orwell, Marshall and Tawney (Dennis and Halsey, 1988; see also Halsey, 1982 and 1994).

The new sociologists of education also regarded the old sociology as political in character; but in a different way. They saw the work of their predecessors as reinforcing the political status quo. It did this, they claimed, because its promotion of explanations for educational failure in terms of the cultural characteristics of working-class homes and communities confirmed the stereotypes of working-class children which were already prevalent within the education system. It was also argued that, even when the old sociology criticized the institutional arrangements of the education system, it took for granted as legitimate the fundamental character of the education offered, as well as the legitimacy of the wider society which this system served (see Flude, 1974).[1]

In this way, the new sociology of education represented a break with social democratic ideals in favour of more radical views, combining Marxism (especially the young Marx) with libertarianism.[2] Here the new sociologists reflected the political spirit of the 1960s. Gone was the previous sense of slow evolution in a Leftwards direction. There was, if anything, an even greater optimism about the prospects for change; but this was to be *fundamental* change. It would not be a mere continuation of what had gone before, managed by those already in power, but rather a change to a new form of society forced by rebellion from below; and one which involved a transformation of the balance of power towards some sort of participatory democracy. It was these political views which led to a shift in the conceptualization of educational inequality. As we saw, whereas the political arithmeticians had been concerned with the unequal distribution of education, the new sociologists subjected to scrutiny what counted as education in contemporary society

[1] What we are presenting here is, of course, no more than a sketch of the two positions. An obvious omission is the work of Bernstein, which took up a distanced relationship to both the old and the new sociologies; see, for example, Bernstein, 1970. See Atkinson, 1985.
[2] In this it was paralleled by developments in other fields, notably the sociology of deviance: see Downes, 1979.

and rejected much of it as cultural domination and/or as socialization into capitalism. Thus, a great deal of what the previous generation of English sociologists of education had believed should and would be inherited by a socialist society, for example a central role for science and for professional expertise, began to be jettisoned. Many now regarded these as merely devices by which dominant groups maintain their power.

There was, however, another important difference between the old and the new sociologies of education, and this lay in their divergent understandings of what it meant for sociological research to be political. Despite their explicit rejection of the doctrine of value freedom, the political arithmeticians' view of the relationship between research and politics was, in fact, quite close to that of Weber. They retained the idea that, while choosing topics for investigation was a political matter, establishing the facts about those topics was not. They differed from Weber only in that they saw a close empirical relationship between their own political position and their sociology: the two were aspects of the same progressive social trend.[3] Where Weber had emphasized the considerable scope for irreconcilable value conflict in the modern world, and the resulting absence of any basis for claims about progress, they believed that the world was moving (however haltingly) towards the realization of at least some of their intellectual and ethical ideals. Thus, while they shared with Weber the distinction between facts and values, they saw rather less scope for conflict between the two than he did. This reflected the fact that they also drew on the rather different views of Marx and Durkheim about this issue; for both of whom how society ought to be was an objective matter which could be discovered through socio-historical analysis (Bryant, 1976).

Thus, the old sociologists of education viewed scientific and political progress as built into the process of historical change, albeit as potentialities rather than inevitabilities, and as closely related to one another. Implied here was a substantial optimism about the ability of researchers to produce the knowledge that is required by policymakers and practitioners, and about the capacity of that knowledge to generate desirable change (see, for example, Halsey, 1961, p. 42). As Bryant (1976, p. 20) notes, in Europe generally in the 1950s there was a somewhat inchoate belief in a sociological contribution to the renewal of European societies. Sociology was widely heralded by sociologists and others as a subject fit for the times.

It is much more difficult to characterize the views of the new sociologists about the relationship between research and politics; partly because the movement was so diverse. Useful here, though, is Whitty's distinction between its 'analytic' and 'possibilitarian' strands. Whereas the latter was concerned with 'the possibility of transcending the experienced realities of everyday life' (Whitty, 1977, p. 31), the former aimed solely at documenting the constitutive features

---

[3] Weber's sense of the relationship between his political and academic work was complex and underwent some change over time, as did his degree of pessimism, see Beetham, 1985. He was, however, a staunch opponent of any sort of progressivism or historicism.

of lived reality, effectively 'leaving everything as it is' in practical terms. At first, these were little more than competing accents within the writings of the new sociologists. But, over time, there was a tendency towards fragmentation which resulted in a variety of approaches, ranged between analytic and possibilitarian poles.[4]

The 'analytic' stance retained the distinction between facts and values from the old sociology, and emphasized rigorous but qualitative description of the social world. Of particular importance was portrayal of the diverse perspectives to be found among people in that world, and description of the realization of these in patterns of social interaction. However, the knowledge produced was not necessarily seen as having any direct bearing on the achievement of particular political goals. Indeed, the task was to document the plurality of values, with no single prespective being privileged over others. Great emphasis was placed on the 'appreciation' of deviant or marginal points of view and on identification of the taken-for-granted assumptions through which mundane reality is constituted. And while this sometimes reflected a political commitment that privileged marginal perspectives, some of the key sources from which such work drew emphasized the need to avoid romanticism (Blumer, 1969 and Matza, 1969) and insisted on the 'indifference' of analysis towards practical concerns (Garfinkel, 1967). On this basis, the old sociology of education was criticized as taking for granted much that needed to be investigated, as failing to adopt the radical suspension of commonsense knowledge and of practical commitments which is necessary for rigorous analysis. What we have here, then, is a theoretical rather than a political radicalism. This is exemplified by ethnomethodological work, though much interactionist research was also towards this analytic end of the spectrum.[5]

By contrast with this, possibilitarians saw all research as a thoroughly political matter. For them, unlike the old sociologists of education, the politics did not stop with the selection of topics for investigation and then restart with the interpretation of the findings: political considerations permeated every aspect of the research process, whether researchers were aware of this or not. However, there was an important tension within the possibilitarian stance between Marxist and what we might call decisionist alternatives; even though, in practice, these were not usually distinguished.[6]

---

[4] In many ways this division corresponds to the contrast between Husserlian and existential phenomenology, on which see Hammond *et al.*, 1991. Whitty criticizes what he refers to as 'the sort of possibilitarianism which verges on a romantic individualism' (p. 33), but his remains a possibilitarian position, broadly defined. The papers in Jenks, 1977 provide examples of the sort of blending of analytic and possibilitarian orientations which occurred, and which still occurs to some degree.

[5] For examples of predominantly analytic work, though not without possibilitarian tendencies, see Hammersley and Woods, 1976 and 1984; Hargreaves and Woods, 1984. Some ethnomethodological work later turned in more practical, but largely nonpossibilitarian, directions: see Payne and Cuff, 1982.

[6] Examples of possibilitarian research can be found in Whitty and Young, 1976. The term 'decisionism' is borrowed from Habermas, 1971, pp. 263–8.

Marx inherited from Hegel a position that is similar in some respects to the views of the political arithmeticians. Both involve a belief in the potential for comprehensively progressive social change; though, of course, they differ in their conceptions of the sort of society which is at the terminus of social development. Both also treated scientific knowledge as carrying direct implications for how society could and should be. In the case of Hegel and Marx this took a particularly strong form. They believed that the distinction between fact and value is open to historical transcendance. For the later Hegel this had already occurred, and all that was needed was for the way in which human ideals had been realized in the Prussian State of the early nineteenth century to be rationally demonstrated; this, indeed, was the task he set himself in his *Philosophy of Right*. For Marx, of course, the historical realization of human ideals lay in the future (though in the not too distant future, since the material conditions for this had already been established). He believed that the scientific analysis of capitalism could demonstrate not just the nature of modern Western societies and how they would develop, but also how they could *and ought to be* transformed to realize human species-being. And, in one way or another, most forms of Marxism have inherited this conception of transformative knowledge.

By contrast, decisionists reject such claims as a form of rationalist historicism: they dismiss attempts to derive human values from the process of historical development, for much the same reasons that earlier attempts to derive them from nature had been rejected. They regard both these positions as forms of false consciousness which perpetuate human alienation. For decisionists, people's value-positions are a matter of commitment: one must choose one's values, and this requires a 'leap of faith' or an act of will, since their validity can never be rationally demonstrated.[7] This inevitably means that within any society there will be conflicting values; and that, often, one group will be in a dominant position and will impose its values on others. Two moral commitments typically drive this perspective. One is the value of authenticity, of explicit recognition of one's own values and of the nature of one's commitment to them. The other is the ideal of a society in which power is equally shared, so that there is no imposition of values by one group or person on others.[8]

[7] This is what Sharp (1980, p. 82), in criticizing Young, describes as 'the existentialist wager'; see Young, 1973. And, indeed, existentialism was an important early source of decisionism in the social sciences. This philosophy denounced the idea that history has a rational essence which is being progressively realized. It drew on nineteenth-century criticism of Hegel as affirming bourgeois society's domestification of the non-rational (of what in more recent times has been referred to as 'the Other'). There is an important link here with some forms of post-structuralism, notably the work of Foucault.

[8] Here we are characterizing decisionism as it is to be found within recent sociology. It does not have both of these characteristics elsewhere. Thus, Weber, one of the chief targets in Habermas's critique of decisionism, was not committed to equality in any sense beyond freedom before the law and perhaps also equality of *access* in educational, economic, and political realms.

Developments in the 1980s and 1990s have generally favoured possibilitarianism, in a blending of Marxist and decisionist forms. However, there has been a broadening of the subordinate groups whose cause is to be supported, so as to include not just the working class but also women and ethnic minorities. Feminism and anti-racism have emerged to play something of the same role as Marxism did previously, but these movements (themselves internally divided) have been forced to negotiate with one another, and attempt to conceptualize the relationships among the various sorts of inequality they emphasize (see La Rue, 1970; Barrett, 1980; Kuhn and Wolpe, 1978; Carby, 1982; Lugones and Spelman, 1983; McDowell and Pringle, 1992). Equally important has been the growing influence of post-structuralism and postmodernism. In the French context, these were to a large extent directed against Marxism, and in some respects they have worked to reinforce decisionism. At the same time, they have injected a radical scepticism about claims to knowledge, exacerbating the influence of the social constructionism already built into the new sociology of education; though, in general, this scepticism has been deployed selectively, as we saw in the previous chapter.

A Different View

While we share the old sociology's commitment to scientific research (and our political views are not far from theirs in many respects), we do not inherit their optimism about the prospects for desirable social change or about the role of research in generating such change. They appeal to a concept of progress which is assumed to be built into the development of modern Western society. We find this implausible, whether in its positivist or its Marxist form. The arguments against teleological views of history hardly need rehearsing: such views assume the validity of inference from factual to value conclusions, and presuppose that modern society constitutes an integrated system which is subject to developmental laws (Hammersley, 1992, Ch. 6). Once those premises are abandoned, as surely they must be, a teleological view of history cannot be sustained. The commitment of the old sociologists to such a view was never whole-hearted, and weakened over time in the face of events; but something very like it seems to have underpinned much of their work.

As we noted, the old sociology also presupposed a strong relationship between research findings and policymaking. It is our view, however, that research can never provide the *basis* for policy or practice. It can inform these, but its contribution is distinctly limited, and can be negative as well as positive. Not only do policy and practice involve value considerations that are outside the scope of research, they also necessarily depend on a broad spectrum of practical knowledge based on experience, including local knowledge of the contexts of action. In addition, they rely on judgments, both about the relevant characteristics of situations and about the most appropriate ways of dealing with them. Marxist and positivist claims to have integrated scientific theory with political practice are fantasies, and the effects of attempts to realize them have not been encouraging.

In these respects, our views are close to those of Weber. However, even he tended to exaggerate the role of scientific inquiry in relation to practice: he assumes that inquiry can assess the logical derivation of value judgments from ultimate values and the appropriateness of means for achieving given ends (see Bruun, 1972). We doubt that there are ultimate values whose character is such that they can form the basis for deductive inferences about what is to be done in particular circumstances. There seem to us to be no better reasons for believing that there is a foundation of absolute certainties in the value sphere than for assuming that there is one in the sphere of factual knowledge.

We have rather less in common with possibilitarianism than with the old sociology of education. To us, both the conception of politics which it assumes and the relationship between politics and research which it proposes are unconvincing. As was noted earlier, the new sociology differed from the old in terms of the frame within which the problem of educational inequality was viewed. In the case of possibilitarianism, this involved a move away from seeing inequality as a contingent problem within society which can be remedied if not eradicated by piecemeal changes, towards treating it as a problem whose existence derives from the very nature of that society, and which can only be rectified by changing the latter fundamentally; in fact, by transcending it. There is reliance here on a utopianism whereby much of what we currently take to be human nature, or to be general features of all societies, is treated as merely a feature of pre-history, of the imperfect forms of society that have been possible hitherto. Such a view is characteristic of Marxism, as well as of those forms of decisionism which see a radically different *natural* humanity beneath the conventions of modern society (in the terms of Paris 1968, a beach beneath the paving stones of city streets).[9]

We regard such utopianism as misconceived and dangerous. For one thing, it rests on a conception of society as a theoretical entity whose true essence can be discerned and realized. Hindess has pointed out that Marxism and economic neo-liberalism are mirror images of one another in this respect. One treats market relations as 'a sign of exploitation and [of] the anarchy of capitalist production', the other regards it as 'an index of freedom' (Hindess, 1987, pp. 8–9). Both neglect the contingency of social processes, and the resulting need for evaluative and prescriptive judgments to take account of the particularity of circumstances; not least about what sorts of intervention will and will not be effective in particular cases. Equally important, utopianism's denial of the implications of what we know of human behaviour and of social arrangements up to the present point in history has the effect of unhooking

---

[9] Of course, Marx rejected utopianism. For him, as for Hegel, this was a term to be applied to those who sought to impose 'external' ideals on reality. He believed that his own position was not utopian because he could demonstrate that the ideals to which he was committed were built into the process of historical development. However, if one finds this demonstration unconvincing, one cannot but see Marxism as utopian.

ideals from all experience. While the empirical record displays a very great deal of diversity, it also reveals some relatively fixed features which seem unlikely to be open to much change. In particular, there have not been societies, certainly not on any scale, where the universal human lot consisted of a person hunting in the morning, fishing in the afternoon, raising cattle in the evening, criticizing after dinner 'just as I have a mind, without ever becoming hunter, fisherman, shepherd or critic' (Marx and Engels, 1845–6, p. 53). And, of course, Marx does not deny this. To the contrary: it is a central feature of his position that such a possibility can only be realized in the future, by a transformation of capitalism which moves human society on to an entirely new plane. Yet, while it is important not to be misled into thinking that everything which is characteristic of one's own society is a feature of human nature and thus fixed for all time, it is equally important not to mistake everything that is common to human societies as merely historical. Both universalism and historicism have their dangers.

When urged to embrace the radical possibility of a totally different kind of society as a leap of faith, one must wonder, as with the claims of supernatural religions, why a leap in one direction is preferable to that in any other. More than this, discarding the empirical record in favour of such a leap would only be worth considering if its failure merely risked leaving us back in the status quo. Yet, if the history of the twentieth century can teach us anything, it is that there is a strong chance of landing somewhere worse.[10]

Possibilitarian utopianism, whether Marxist or decisionist, also proposes a direct relationship between intellectual work and political action. Like political arithmetic, it assumes that the production of knowledge (or at least of knowledge of the right sort) feeds the process of progressive social change; though this time the target is change of a revolutionary rather than an evolutionary kind. Indeed, the rhetorical structure of possibilitarianism is such as to construct two opposed political sides: there are those who support the status quo, wittingly or unwittingly; and there are those who are working to overthrow it, so as to bring about human emancipation. Once we apply this framework to sociological research itself, there arises the question 'Whose side are we on?'[11] But this involves an over-simplification of political realities. There are, of course, occasions when political situations are reduced to a battle between two sides, but it is false to see the general run of politics as only two-sided. This is patently obvious even on the Left where, as we saw earlier, there are now competing claims from socialists, feminists and anti-racists, each of these groups themselves being internally divided. More important still, in our view, possibilitarianism involves a deflection of research away from its primary task, which is the production of knowledge. Possibilitarianism involves sub-

[10] For a complementary critique of utopianism in the field of the sociology of deviance, see Downes, 1979.

[11] This is the title of Becker's influential article (Becker, 1967). His argument was not possibilitarian, yet that is how it has been interpreted by many subsequent writers; including, for example, Troyna and Carrington, 1989.

ordinating research to practical and political goals. And, in the absence of some benign force working to harmonize such goals with the pursuit of social inquiry — of the kind assumed by positivism, Hegelianism and Marxism — this can only result in the distortion of research findings.

Despite their differences, both the old sociologists of education and the possibilitarian new sociologists treated their central task as the documentation of educational inequalities, and the explanation of these; and both assumed that value conclusions could be drawn directly from their analyses. This was because, for both, value issues were believed to be already largely settled: as a result of social democratic assumptions, Marxism's scientific overcoming of the fact–value distinction, and/or sheer (and necessarily irrational) commitment. By contrast, for us value issues are rarely settled; and sociological research can do only a little to resolve them. In this respect, our position is closest to the 'analytic' strand of the new sociology of education. We regard the existence of conflicting evaluations as an inevitable feature of human society. These do not necessarily reflect irrational commitments, so that reasoned discussion may sometimes overcome disagreements; but very often it will not do so. Above all, scientific research offers no prospect of providing a value consensus, and it should not pretend that it can. For us, then, the task of sociology is restricted to the production of descriptions, explanations and theories. It cannot validate evaluations and prescriptions. Thus, we draw a sharp distinction between the orientation of the researcher and that of the policymaker and practitioner. We believe that this is a distinction which cannot be eliminated or transcended, and that attempts to do this distort both realms.[12]

We also adopt the 'analytic' commitment to suspend any evaluation of the perspectives of the people studied, for the purposes of describing and explaining their behaviour.[13] This involves a rejection of those forms of analysis which treat the cognitive validity of perspectives as closely related to, if not entirely determined by, their social origins, functions, or consequences (see Geuss, 1981). One resource employed by this kind of analysis is the concept of ideology, and this has been central to much of the work of possibilitarian new sociologists and their successors (see, for example, Sharp, 1980). In our view, this approach reduces the chances of effective understanding by taking for granted the evaluative preconceptions of the researcher. This is exemplified in Willis's division of the perspectives of 'the lads' into 'penetrative' and 'ideological' components (Hammersley, 1981; Walker, 1986).

Another important inheritance from the analytic tradition is a recognition of the role of contingency in social life. This originally stemmed from rejection of functionalist and Marxist theories for their oversimplified and

---

[12] For a more extended account of the arguments presented here, see Hammersley, 1995a. The classic statements of the difference between research and politics are, of course, Weber's speeches on the vocation of science and the vocation of politics. See Weber, 1948 and Lassman and Velody, 1989.

[13] See Matza's, 1969 recommendation of 'appreciation'; also, Polsky, 1971 and Rock, 1979b.

overdeterministic conception of social processes. It built on the concept of unintended consequences which was already present in some forms of functionalism (Merton, 1936), but it went beyond this to deny that society constitutes a system. Instead, the focus became situationally located complexes of action, macro and micro, and their contingent and changing interrelationships; echoing Weber's 'realism', and leading to an emphasis on the complexity of the social world (see Collins, 1977; Beetham, 1985; Rock 1979a and b).

Despite considerable agreement with the analytic orientation, however, we see the goal of research rather differently; at least to the more extreme versions of that perspective, such as ethnomethodology. For most ethnomethodologists, the rigorous study of the social world is only possible on the basis of a radical shift in attitude away from that characteristic of everyday life, suspending belief in the validity of all commonsense knowledge. This shift is modelled on the phenomenological *epoché* of Husserl, so that there is a switch in focus from the study of social phenomena as they appear in the world to a theoretical concern with how they are socially constituted as the phenomena they appear to be. Both the end-product of research and the means by which it is to be pursued are viewed as involving a break with the pragmatic orientation of everyday life. This approach is also exemplified in what has come to be called 'strict constructionism', whose focus is on how social problems are discursively constructed in public talk.[14] We outlined the problems with this position in the previous chapter: either it involves a selective scepticism in which, at the very least, its own activities are treated as standing apart from the construction of the social world, or it adopts a more consistent but self-destructive scepticism. Furthermore, the idea that the scientific or rigorous study of the social world can only be carried out on the basis of this kind of radical *epoché* is misconceived. It arises from the inheritance of foundationalist assumptions from phenomenology and positivism (Hammersley, 1995c).

In our view, it is necessary to distinguish among three types of inquiry which have quite different characters. First, there is what we might call practical inquiry, which can be a phase of, or an adjunct to, any kind of practice. In the course of practice, problems may arise for the resolution of which new information is required. Whether the practical inquiry needed to supply this information is carried out by practitioners themselves or by others who specialize in such inquiries, the process of investigation and its outcome will be framed by practical goals and by the perspectives that practitioners have developed for pursuing these.[15] Whether or not one refers to this as 'research' is partly a terminological matter; what it is important to recognize is that, despite some commonalities, it is a very different activity from academic research. The key characteristics of the latter, in our view, are that its goal is producing knowledge which is of general value, rather than being designed to

[14] Ibarra and Kitsuse, 1993 label their approach interactionist, but it is heavily informed by ethnomethodology and conversation analysis. At the same time, their work has been criticized by ethnomethodologists, see Holstein and Miller, 1993.

[15] Many, though not all, forms of action research would fall under this heading.

meet the needs of some particular set of practitioners, and that it is validated through a process of collegial assessment.

It is also necessary to distinguish between two forms of academic research. This distinction broadly conforms to one that Parsons makes in discussing Weber's methodological work: between the analytic and the historical sciences (Parsons, 1937, pp. 597–601).[16] Parsons' terms are not entirely happy ones, and we shall refer instead to the distinction between theoretical and substantive social research.

Theoretical research, as the name implies, is devoted to the development and testing of theories. While this involves investigation of particular empirical situations, the focus is not on these in their own right but only as instances of theoretical categories. The goal is to produce well-established accounts of causal relationships among specific categories of social phenomena: relationships which occur anywhere and at any time where the relevant conditions hold, other things being equal. The theories produced serve as resources which can be used for the development of explanations in both substantive academic and practical inquiries.[17]

Substantive research, on the other hand, is concerned with the description and explanation of particular situations or phenomena, micro and macro. These are selected for study because they are value-relevant; they either have importance in themselves, or they have importance because of their relationship to other things which are significant from some value perspective. However, the role of values goes beyond this. The descriptions and explanations produced by substantive research do not simply reproduce what actually exists or happens in the world. Indeed, they could not do this: endless numbers of accurate descriptions could be produced of any situation or event. All description is selective, then, and in substantive research selectivity is based on value-relevance. In much the same way, explaining a phenomenon does not involve merely finding what caused it. There is an infinite number of potential causes to which appeal could be made. There are immediate causes, but each of these is itself caused, as is every more remote cause. What is selected out of this expanse of causal potential as 'the cause' or 'the causes' involves considerations that are additional to judgments about causality. It depends on such matters as which potential causes offer hope of remedial action, which represent grounds for culpability, etc. In short, explanation as well as description is value-dependent.

The aim of substantive research, then, is to provide factual information which is relevant to at least some of the value arguments which surround the phenomena investigated. Such research may even be concerned directly with showing whether or not a situation matches some ideal, and why it does or does not do so. In other words, it may consist of what is often referred to as

[16]   This distinction derives from the neo-Kantian philosophy of Windelband and Rickert, see Oakes 1988. The discussion which follows draws on this background.
[17]   We are using the term 'theory' here in only one of its many senses, see Hammersley, 1995b.

'evaluation research'. Nevertheless, for us, this is distinct from practical evaluation, in two respects. First, it takes only one value ideal (or a small complex of them) as the basis for describing and/or explaining phenomena, whereas practical evaluation must take into consideration all the values relevant to the practical activity which it serves. Second, the products of evaluation research can and must be factual, not value, arguments. No commitment should be implied or assumed on the part of the researcher to the ideal on which reliance is placed: it is employed simply as a methodological device for constituting the phenomenon investigated. Above all, in our view, there should be no promotion or criticism of such ideals in the context of research, since research cannot validate or discredit ideals.[18]

For us, then, by contrast with the views of some 'analytic' sociologists of education, including 'strict constructionists' and ethnomethodologists, investigation of the nature and causes of social problems, including educational inequality, is a legitimate and important focus of academic research. It falls into the realm of what we have referred to as substantive inquiry. It is perhaps necessary to reiterate, however, that we believe that inquiry into educational inequalities must be governed by the principle of value neutrality: it cannot and should not pretend to validate practical evaluations and prescriptions. The aim of such research is to put information into the public domain which is relevant to professional and political debates. It is *not* to aid particular sides in those debates.[19]

Explicit commitment to the principle of value neutrality is rare today, largely as a result of the influence of possibilitarianism. It is rejected not just on the grounds that it is undesirable but also because it is believed to be unachievable. It is generally accepted that all interpretation of the social world is necessarily shaped by presuppositions deriving from the socio-historical location of the interpreter. And it is often concluded from this that the way in which claims and evidence about educational inequality are assessed necessarily depends on the political perspectives of those doing the assessment. This relates to what might be referred to as the problem of justification, the topic of the next section of this chapter.

The Problem of Justification

One can characterize much recent writing about sociological and educational research methodology as a response to the acknowledged failure of epistemological foundationalism. In the past, largely as a result of the influence

---

[18] The dichotomy presented here between research 'evaluations' and practical evaluations parallels Nagel's distinction between 'characterizing' and 'appraising' value judgments (Nagel, 1961, pp. 492–5).

[19] Needless to say, it may have this effect, in combination with other factors, but this should not be its goal; and without such a goal the direction of effect is unlikely to be consistent over time.

of positivism, there had been a tendency to see research as committed to reaching conclusions on the basis of empirical evidence, where that evidence was treated as independent of the researcher and of his or her theoretical framework, political beliefs, and even philosophical assumptions. Science was assumed to require the wholesale rejection of metaphysics, and the suspension of political and ethical commitments. While the arguments against foundationalism have a long history, their force has been rediscovered by philosophers and sociologists in the past forty years and deployed against positivist foundationalism (see Hammersley, 1995a, Ch. 1). This has been rejected on the basis of several arguments, but the most fundamental is that the very idea of a foundation of absolutely valid knowledge is unintelligible. All knowledge claims are, by definition, potentially open to challenge, so that reasons for believing them may always need to be provided. This is an essential feature of the very idea of a knowledge claim. To suggest that there are some such claims, notably sense data, which are not open to possible challenge because they are simply given as part of our experience is to misuse the concept of knowledge. It is to treat sense data simultaneously as things that happen to us and as beliefs we can rationally decide to accept, thereby confusing two quite different categories of phenomena.

While there is now widespread agreement that foundationalism is indefensible, there is little agreement about viable alternatives. Within social-research methodology three possibilities have been widely canvassed: standpoint epistemology, instrumentalism, and relativism. And, we can relate these back to our earlier discussion, since the first two are loosely associated with Marxism, the last with decisionism.[20]

While standpoint epistemology has its origins in Marxism, it is also employed by some feminists and anti-racists; indeed, the term itself derives from feminism (Hartsock, 1983). Central to this epistemological argument is the idea that members of an oppressed group (for example, the working class or women) have exclusive access to true knowledge of the social world, so that for its findings to be valid research must be founded on the experience of that group. This 'standpoint' argument is modelled on Marx's claim that, because of the dialectical character of societal development, under capitalism the working class have uniquely valid insight into the character of that social formation. This relies on a Hegelian epistemology whereby subject and object are reunited over the course of historical development (Lowith, 1949). Often, standpoint epistemology is adopted without any explicit philosophy of history; though there have been attempts by feminists to provide such support (see, for example, Flax, 1987 and Smith, 1987, pp. 78–81).

Instrumentalism is also to be found in Marxism (Prokopczyk, 1980), though it is most characteristic of pragmatist philosophy. Here the validity of

---

[20]   As with Marxism and decisionism, these three alternatives are often conflated or used simultaneously by the same author, even though they are mutually incompatible. For a more conventional Marxist approach in epistemological terms, see Sharp, 1980 and 1981.

knowledge is defined solely according to whether action on the basis of it has desirable effects. In other words, research must be pursued in close associa-tion with practical activities, including political struggle, and judged in terms of its contribution in that context. Mies quotes Mao's dictum that 'in order to understand a thing one has to change it' (Mies, 1983, p. 125). Thus:

> According to (the historical, dialectical and materialist theory of knowledge) the 'truth' of a theory is not dependent on the application of certain methodological principles and rules, but on its potential to orient the processes of praxis towards progressive emancipation and humanization. (Mies, 1983, p. 124).

On the basis of this instrumentalism Mies criticizes academic feminists, arguing that research must be subordinated to the political aim of the women's move-ment, which 'is not just the study but the overcoming of women's oppression and exploitation' (Mies, 1991, p. 61).

The other alternative to foundationalism represents an extension into the cognitive realm of the value relativism that is characteristic of decisionism. Thus, it is not uncommon to find it suggested that the conclusions of social and educational research are necessarily determined by the presuppositions of the researcher, and as such represent just one view of the world amongst others; the implication is explicitly or implicitly, that different views are valid in their own terms. The arguments relied on here are those long deployed by philosophical sceptics, notably the point that we can have no direct know-ledge of the world and that no ultimate criterion for judging the validity of accounts is available. The most common use of this scepticism or relativism is to challenge others' claims to knowledge. In other words, it is typically used in a negative and selective fashion, as we saw in our discussion of social constructionism in Chapter 1.

In our judgment none of these alternatives to foundationalism is convinc-ing. In particular, they are wrong about the epistemological implications of the failure of foundationalism: they are overreactions to that failure. Thus, contrary to the arguments of relativists, to accept that we cannot produce knowledge that is absolutely certain in its validity is not to deny that we can produce conclusions which are more likely to be valid than particular alternatives. To ignore this is to take over the foundationalist conception of knowledge as findings whose validity is known *beyond all possible doubt*. Accepting that judgments are involved in the assessment of validity does not imply that such assessments are simply determined by prior commitments and are therefore not subject to reason.[21]

Moreover, neither scepticism nor relativism provide a satisfactory alter-native to foundationalism. Like consistent constructionism, they are self-undermining, being subject to the liar paradox: if true they imply their own

---

[21] It does lead, however, to recognition that the hope of achieving a universal con-sensus which represents the whole truth about the world is a forlorn one.

invalidity. In the case of relativism, if the validity of all arguments is frame-work-relative then so too is the validity of the claim that the validity of all arguments is framework-relative. And this implies that even from the relativist point of view relativism is false for non-relativists. Thus, non-relativists are not only correct to reject relativism from their own point of view but from that of relativists too![22]

Instrumentalism is also unconvincing. While we recognize that the value of research should be judged partly in terms of its political and social rel-evance, the claim that its *validity* should be judged in this way is much more questionable. Like relativism it relies on a self-undermining argument. Insofar as the production of desirable consequences is taken as defining validity, this position proposes a replacement for the correspondence theory of truth, yet implicitly relies on that theory. This is because claims about the effects of act-ing on the beliefs being assessed cannot themselves be judged instrumentally (otherwise we are in an infinite regress).[23] And even where instrumentalism implies treating desirable consequences only as an indicator of validity, this assumes a much stronger relationship between the truth of a belief and the practical consequences of acting on it than is justifiable: the validity of assump-tions is neither a necessary nor a sufficient condition of practical success.

Standpoint epistemologies also suffer from severe problems. We must ask on what grounds we can decide that one category of person has superior insight into reality. This cannot be simply because they declare that they have this insight; otherwise everyone could make the same claim with the same legitimacy (we would be back to relativism). This means that some other form of ultimate justification is involved, but what could this be? In the Marxist version of this argument the working class are the group with privileged in-sight into the nature of social reality, yet it is Marx and Marxist theorists who confer this privilege on them by means of a particular philosophy of history. Something similar occurs in the case of feminist standpoint theory, where the feminist theorist ascribes privileged insight to women, or to feminists engaged in the struggle for women's emancipation (Hartsock, 1983; Harding, 1986). However, while we must recognize that people in different social locations may have divergent perspectives which give them distinctive insights, it is not clear why we should believe the implausible claim that some people have privileged access to knowledge while others are blinded by ideology, simply by virtue of their social positions (Merton, 1972).

In our view, then, none of the alternatives to positivist foundationalism adopted by the new sociologists and their successors constitutes a sound epistemological position. All of these reject not only foundationalism but also the idea that sociological inquiry can be distinct in its goals and guiding

[22] For a much more sophisticated critique of scepticism and relativism than we can present here, see Williams, 1991. Many of the key points were made by Pring in his early critique of the new sociology of education: Pring 1972.

[23] This is a criticism which Sharp, 1980, p. 83 directs against Young's instrumentalism; she also criticizes him for relativism.

principles from other forms of practice, notably politics. And therefore all of them reject the conventional model of research as involving the assessment of claims to knowledge on the basis solely of criteria of logical consistency and empirical adequacy. By contrast, in our view, even without a foundation of absolutely certain knowledge, it is possible to make reasonable judgments about the validity of factual arguments on the basis of these criteria.[24] Of course, those judgments will necessarily be more uncertain, and more open to disagreement, than if there were a foundation of absolute givens to which we could appeal. And the obvious problem which arises is how potentially endless requests for justification can be reasonably curtailed. In other words, we need to be able to answer the question of when evidence is sufficient to accept a claim as true.

This is a practical matter which we all routinely and recurrently resolve in everyday life. Among the means of resolving it are appeals to plausibility and credibility; and these are central to assessments of research findings. By 'plausibility' here we mean the relationship between a claim and existing knowledge, the validity of which is currently taken to be beyond reasonable doubt. By 'credibility' we mean the likelihood that the process which produced the claim is free of serious error. Relevant here, for example, is whether or not the claim relates to matters of a kind which could be determined with minimal risk of error by looking and seeing, whether the promoter of the claim has an interest in it being believed etc. Where a knowledge claim is neither sufficiently plausible nor credible to be accepted at face value, as is almost inevitably the case with any interesting research finding, evidence must be sought and provided. However, this evidence can be assessed only in terms of *its* plausibility and credibility; and so on until a judgment can be made, or until judgment has to be suspended for want of the necessary evidence (see Hammersley, 1990b and 1992, Ch. 4).

Plausibility and credibility are matters of degree, but there must be a cut-off point at which knowledge claims become *sufficiently* plausible and/or credible to be accepted as true. In practical affairs this seems to be decided, very often, on the basis of such considerations as the relative costs of different types of error, the possibility and price of obtaining further evidence, the likelihood that this would improve the decision etc. Such practical considerations are not appropriate in the context of academic research, given that its aim is the production of knowledge that is of general value. However, there is a mechanism built into the operation of academic research communities which provides a means of resolving this problem.

Individual researchers must, of course, make judgments about the plausibility and credibility of arguments and evidence for themselves; and these will necessarily reflect their own backgrounds and personal characteristics, to some extent at least. However, in the context of academic research they are

---

[24] A substantial body of work in the philosophy of science takes this position. For discussions of this in the context of educational research, see Phillips, 1990a and 1990b.

accountable to others for their judgments, so that they must take due note of what their colleagues would and would not accept as beyond reasonable doubt. Needless to say, in the absence of a foundation of absolutely valid knowledge to which ultimate appeal can be made, there is no guarantee that disagreement will be resolved. However, the chances that agreement can be reached in this way, and that the resulting consensus will capture the truth, is maximized to the extent that the behaviour of a research community is guided by the following norms.[25]

1   The overriding concern of researchers is the truth of claims, not their political or practical implications.
2   Arguments are not judged on the basis of the personal and/or social characteristics of the person advancing them, but in terms of their plausibility and credibility.
3   Researchers are willing to change their views if arguments from common ground suggest those views are false; and, equally important, they assume (and behave as if) fellow researchers have the same attitude.
4   The research community is open to participation by anyone able and willing to operate on the basis of the first three rules. In particular, there must be no restriction of participation on the grounds of political or religious beliefs and attitudes.
5   Where substantial agreement does not result, all parties must recognize that there remains some reasonable doubt about the validity of their own positions, so that whenever these are presented they must be accompanied by supporting argument or reference to where such argument can be found.

In our view, a research community committed to the above norms maximizes the chances of uncovering error in factual claims, and of thereby discovering the truth about particular matters. It encourages the cumulative development of a body of knowledge whose validity is more reliable than that of lay views about the same issues. This is not to say that in any particular instance current research-based knowledge will be correct, and commonsense wrong; simply that it is likely to be closer to the truth on the average. Furthermore, it should be noted that this advantage is bought at some considerable cost in terms of the time taken to complete inquiries in this way, and (correspondingly) the limited size of the body of research-based knowledge which can be produced.

This view of academic research places the process of critical assessment of claims and evidence at its centre. And, indeed, we see our work in this book

[25] These norms are similar to Merton's early account of the norms of science, see Merton, 1973. There is also a close parallel with Habermas's idealization of rational discourse, see McCarthy, 1978.

as an example of the sort of collegial assessment that is essential to the operation of an academic research community. This is especially important in a context where possibilitarianism has been and continues to be influential. That position has the effect of leading researchers to address their research to particular political constituencies: to those who already have, or who can be persuaded to adopt, the same political commitments. Meanwhile, the responses of those who do not share these commitments tend to be explained away as ideological.[26]

Conclusion

In this chapter we have outlined our methodological position in the context of the recent history of research on educational inequalities, in relation to the old and the new sociologies of education. For us, the social problem of educational inequality is a legitimate and important focus for sociological inquiry. However, the contribution of such inquiry is much more limited than either the old or many of the new sociologists supposed. Indeed, in our view, the purpose of research in this area should be to produce knowledge relevant to public debates, not to eradicate inequality. In other words, it should be guided by the principle of value neutrality, as well as by that of value relevance.

In response to arguments to the effect that such a project is impossible, given the failure of positivist foundationalism, we argued that the alternatives to foundationalism adopted by the possibilitarian new sociologists and their successors are defective. Furthermore, we suggested that the absence of a foundation of epistemic givens does not vitiate the assessment of factual claims in terms of logical consistency and empirical adequacy. It is possible to come to reasonable conclusions about the validity of such claims on the basis of judgments about their plausibility and credibility. We also emphasized the importance of the research community in providing accountability for these judgments, forcing conceptual clarification and the provision of evidence where disagreement occurs, in pursuit of a rational consensus. The assessment of claims to knowledge, one's own and those of others, in the context of such a community is what we mean by reflexivity.

[26] Our own previous work has been responded to in just this manner. See Connolly, 1992; Blair, 1993; Gillborn and Drew, 1993; Gillborn, 1995, Ch. 3.

Chapter 3

Assessing Research on Educational Inequalities

In the previous chapter we outlined the methodological position we adopt in this book. Our task in this chapter is to spell out its implications for the assessment of research on inequalities in schools. What is involved here is assessment of the *products* of research, not of the process of producing them; though, of course, information about the latter is also relevant. Thus, the procedure is almost the reverse of that involved in doing research: we start with research reports, and we examine the claims they make and how convincing these are on the basis of the evidence provided.

In order to do this, we need to identify the requirements which a study must meet if conclusions about educational inequalities are to be established convincingly. We will discuss four of these:

- clarity of argument;
- descriptive adequacy;
- explanatory power; and
- generalizability.

Clarity of Argument

It is a presupposition of our approach here that the main function of a research report is to present an argument; in other words, a conclusion about some matter (however tentative) plus the grounds for believing that it is true. This implies that research reports will have a hierarchical structure. At the top will be the main conclusions, and beneath these will be the substructure of the argument: claims about relevant features of the cases studied and evidence relating to them (Hammersley, 1990b). As an example, Figure 3.1 outlines the structure of a research report concerned with the consequences for educational equality of the allocation of students to sets by secondary schools (Abraham, 1989a).

The top line of this diagram presents the central argument of Abraham's article. Then, listed under each element of that argument, are the claims he makes about the school which he studied and, below these, a summary of the empirical evidence he provides for these.

Main Conclusion	Setting causes a polarization in attitude to school which			increases the difference in school achievement between working class and middle class students
Main claims (relating to the school studied)	Setting is a weaker form of academic/ behavioural differentiation than streaming or banding, but it still causes polarization	There is a polarity in attitude to school among fourth-year students, as follows: *Low sets* negative attitude towards school *Top sets* positive attitude towards school	This polarization has increased over time from the point at which setting occurred	
Evidence	There is considerable overlap in membership among top sets	There are significant differences in time spent on homework as reported in questionnaire responses	There have been increasing differences between top and bottom sets in missed assignments and bad behaviour reports from the end of the first year, when setting occurred	Middle-class students are overrepresented in top sets
	There is a correlation within and across sets in teachers' rankings of academic performance and 'behaviour'	There are significant differences in missed school work as reported in school records		
		There are significant differences in the number of bad behaviour reports, as reported in school records		
		There is a high correlation among the above three indicators		
		There is a polarization in friendship choice *re* attitude to school.		

Figure 3.1: The structure of Abraham's (1989a) argument

Research reports can involve a variety of kinds of argument and sub-argument, and these need to be clearly identified. A crucial distinction is between factual and value claims. By 'factual claims' we mean those which seek to document how things are in the world, rather than how they ought to be or how we would like them to be. There are various kinds of factual claim. Some, notably descriptions and explanations, are concerned with phenomena existing in particular, temporally and spatially defined, contexts. Both these types of claim are to be found in the substructure of Abraham's argument. Thus, he *describes* the attitudes to school and the friendship choices of students; but he also argues that these are, in part, the product of the school's differentiation of students along academic/behavioural lines, thereby integrating his descriptive claims into a larger *explanatory* framework. Descriptions and explanations are the main kinds of argument to be found in substantive academic research. However, explanations also depend on another type of factual argument: theories.

We are using the term 'theory' in a rather specific sense. For us, theoretical arguments differ from other sorts of factual claim in that, rather than dealing with particular phenomena located in particular places and times, they refer to categories or types of phenomena. And these categories are open-ended: they include all phenomena — past, present, future and possible — which meet the criteria defining membership of the category. A theory states a relationship between phenomena belonging to two or more categories; a relationship that it predicts will hold if certain conditions are met. The relationship is usually a causal one, though it may be probabilistic — occurring in most (or a certain proportion) of cases relevant to the theory. An example is the differentiation–polarization theory which was the focus of Abraham's research. This states that if students are differentiated by schools according to an academic-behavioural standard, for example by being streamed or banded, their attitudes to that standard will become polarized: in particular, those given the lowest rankings will tend to reject it and the values which it embodies (see Hammersley, 1985). Abraham's concern was to investigate whether setting also has this effect.

By contrast with factual claims, value arguments not only describe, explain, or theorize social phenomena but also express some view about them in terms of one or more values. Actions may be portrayed as desirable or undesirable, situations as better or worse, people as blameworthy or blamefree etc., on a wide variety of grounds. We argued in the previous chapter that academic research should not draw value conclusions. Thus, in the chapters which follow, we will concentrate primarily on factual claims about educational inequalities, leaving any value conclusions on one side. However, we cannot ignore values entirely. In the previous chapter we noted how all substantive academic inquiry is value-dependent, in the sense that it uses particular value ideals as a methodological device for identifying and describing significant phenomena, and for selecting relevant explanatory factors. We will therefore need to give some attention to the role that values play in this respect. In the case of research on educational inequalities in schools, this means providing clarification of the conceptions of equity, and the other values, which may be employed to identify inequalities and the discrimination which is often held to cause them.

Equity, Equality and Discrimination

It is rare for research on educational inequality to make any explicit reference to the concept of equity.[1] A consequence is that, in this area as in many others, the term 'equality' has acquired a complex logical grammar. Westen (1990) points out that it has the paradoxical feature of seeming to be one thing to all people but of actually meaning different things to different people. One of the problems is that it is used in both descriptive and prescriptive senses, without these being clearly distinguished.

Westen defines descriptive equality as referring to 'the relationship that obtains among two or more distinct things that have been jointly measured by a common standard of comparison and found to be indistinguishable by reference to that standard' (Westen, 1990, p. 33). This specification is important because it points to the comparative and relational character of judgments of equality and inequality. It simply makes no sense to refer to some person or category of person as being in an unequal position unless it is made clear with whom they are being compared and in terms of what standard. Moreover, in descriptive terms there are innumerably many ways in which any set of objects can be described as equal or unequal to some other set.

Prescriptive equality, or equity, presupposes descriptive equality, and so is also comparative and relational. But here the standard consists of some notion of justice, and there is also a clear indication that the implied descriptive equality should prevail. Equity is concerned, then, with what *ought* to be treated the same; though it also (necessarily) prescribes what ought to be treated differently. As Aristotle pointed out, it is just as wrong to treat people who are dissimilar the same as it is to treat those who are similar differently.[2]

Judgments of inequity can be based on several sorts of ground. In the context of educational inequalities the most important distinction is probably between equity relating to the distribution of some good, and that concerning the distribution of opportunities to obtain a good.

The first kind of inequity claim involves the argument that something of value has been unequally distributed between two or more categories of person when it should have been distributed equally; or, alternatively, that some good has been distributed equally in some respect when it should have been distributed in unequal portions. We can see notions of equity at play in this sense in judgments about the distribution of educational resources. Here are some examples:

[1] For exceptions, see Secada, 1989 and Gallagher *et al.*, 1994.
[2] The clearest presentation is in the *Nicomachean Ethics*, 1131[a]27, see Aristotle, 1925, p. 112.

- At any time, the education of each child or student should involve the same level of educational expenditure as that of every other.
- The education of each student should involve the same level of educational expenditure as that of every other over the course of their school careers.
- Educational expenditure should co-vary with student ability (such that the least able, or the most able, get the most resources).
- Educational expenditure should be distributed according to need. More should be spent on those with the greater need.
- Educational expenditure should co-vary with merit, in the sense that those students who work hard and behave well should receive more of the benefit of educational spending than those who do not.
- Students vary in the importance of the contribution they are likely to make to the public good later in life. Educational expenditure should be allocated in direct proportion to estimations of eventual public benefit.

What we have here is a variety of arguments about what would be an equitable distribution of educational expenditure between categories of student. And, of course, in any particular case these arguments are likely to be in conflict with one another: they recommend quite different educational policies.

Much the same sort of debate can arise about the distribution of other resources, such as the attention of the teacher in the classroom. Here the issue is even more complex, however. This is partly because in this case there is no standardized medium of exchange to provide the basis for measurement. As a result, there are problems about how we are to identify different amounts of teacher attention, especially since it can be given unequally to several students simultaneously, and can vary not just in duration but also in intensity and character. There is also the problem that the distribution of a teacher's attention is not completely under his or her control: students make differential demands for attention. Moreover, a teacher giving attention to one student might be in the interests of others (for example because it curtails the harassment they were previously experiencing from that student). And, following on from this, we must recognize that the effects of a teacher's attention may not always be benign for the student who receives it.

This concern with equity in the distribution of goods does perhaps sometimes underly research on educational inequality; but a rather different, and more complex, concept of equity of opportunity seems more usually to be involved. This is concerned with differences in the *opportunity* to acquire an education or to achieve high levels of educational achievement. Equity of opportunity relates to goods which it is not within anyone's power to distribute, or which it is believed must be distributed according to the possession of some quality on the part of recipients. Thus, the level of academic achievement which students reach is widely held to depend on their ability and on the effort they expend in its pursuit, not just on the activity of teachers; in other words, it is not a good which is within teachers' power to distribute. Furthermore, it is generally believed that educational credentials, such as GCSE certificates, should be distributed according to level of educational achievement. In these terms, equity of opportunity requires that individuals who are similar in their potential to achieve a given level of qualification experience an equal chance of getting it. However, as Williams (1962) has pointed out, this notion of equality (or equity) of opportunity assumes that some conditions are to be equalized in order to allow inequality of some other (justifiable) kind to be revealed and rewarded; and there is no logically determinable stopping place in arguments about what should be equalized (see also Mackinnon, 1986). As a result, there is great scope for disagreement about what does and does not constitute equity of opportunity; over and above the question of whether the sort of meritocratic regime it implies is justifiable.[3]

Here again, then, we are faced with a range of different interpretations of what equity implies. Indeed, Ennis (1978) argues that equity is a formal concept, the content of which must be supplied by one or other substantive conception of what would be desirable, just etc. We can get some sense of the sort of disagreement involved if we look again at the redefinition of the problem of educational inequality which has taken place over the course of the twentieth century, which we outlined in Chapter 1.[4] The starting position was the argument that the pre-1944 education system was inequitable because many children of working-class parents who had the same ability as middle-class grammar-school entrants could not and did not get a secondary education, because their parents could not afford the fees and because there were insufficient free places. However, following the 1944 Act, views about equity of opportunity were revised: it was now argued by many that working-class children still did not have equal access to an academic secondary-school education, because they did not have the same level of opportunity to develop academic ability as middle-class children. Where previously the distribution of ability had largely been taken as given, as lying outside the responsibility of the education system, now it was itself treated as something the opportunity to acquire which was subject to legitimate (indeed obligatory) state intervention. One result of this was proposals for compensatory education.

Here, then, we have variation in judgment about what does and does not constitute an educational opportunity. What this points to is that the mean-

---

[3] From this point of view, the frequently drawn contrast between equality of opportunity and equality of outcome is rather misleading. In general, those who argue for equality of outcome are simply proposing a particular interpretation of equity of opportunity and a means of measuring it. This is clear in Halsey's (1981, p. 111) argument that, 'unless there is proof to the contrary, inequality of outcome in the social distribution of knowledge is a measure of *de facto* inequality of access' (see also Coleman, 1968). Rarely do proponents of equality of outcome argue explicitly that education is a good which can and should be equally distributed, in the way that educational expenditure or teacher attention can be, at least in principle.

[4] For a parallel account, relating to both Britain and the United States, see Coleman, 1968.

ing of 'opportunity', like that of 'equality', is relational. Rubinstein (1993) has argued that the opportunities available to people cannot be defined independently of the goals and desires which they have; and that the latter are not simply a product of their circumstances. Because they have different orientations, people may respond quite differently to 'the same' situation. He criticizes what he refers to as 'the structural approach', in which opportunities are conceived of as external and objective: 'like doors that can be there or not, open or closed'. Instead, he argues that '[...] actors and their cultural values do not merely react to or reflect opportunities: they [...] *constitute* them' (Rubinstein, 1993, p. 277).

Rubinstein illustrates his argument with a discussion of MacLeod's ethnography of two groups of young men living in the same public housing project in a city in the United States (MacLeod, 1987). Despite the similarity of their circumstances, they live radically different lives. In particular, they have very different attitudes to schooling:

> The (white) Hallway Hangers incarnate all the vices ever attributed to the underclass. Fighting is their main source of status. They have numerous arrests for theft, violence, etc. and they consume and sell a pharmacopeia of intoxicants. They hate schools and teachers and disdain academic achievement. In contrast, the (black) Brothers, while facing essentially the same [objective circumstances], do well in school and are persuaded that this will ensure their futures. They eschew the violence, drugs, and thieving of the Hallway Hangers as pointless and self-destructive. (Rubinstein, 1993, pp. 275–6)

In addition to this, Rubinstein argues that opportunities are also constituted by capabilities. Here he draws on Gibson's (1979) notion of affordances, this term referring to features of an environment which facilitate possibilities of action, but which are necessarily relative to the capabilities of the actor. Thus, to take a trivial example, a mail box is an opportunity to mail something, but only for someone who understands the concept of 'mailing' (Rubinstein, 1993, p. 279).

As Rubinstein makes clear, then, opportunities must be defined in relation to both goals and capabilities. However, it seems to us that since attitudes may be changed and capabilities developed, it is legitimate to identify opportunities as open to people even though they would not recognize these or be able immediately to take advantage of them, given their current attitudes and capabilities. In other words, opportunities may be ascribed not just on the basis of the goals and capabilities *actually* possessed by the actors concerned but also in relation to ones which they *could* acquire or adopt. What this indicates is that, like the identification of equalities/inequalities the description of opportunities is value-dependent. While it is a factual matter, it depends on some conception of the goals and capabilities which people legitimately have or ought to have. And, of course, different value judgments, reasonable and less reasonable, might be made about this. What is important in the context of research on equality of educational opportunity is that the factual and value assumptions on which the identification of opportunities is based are made explicit.

The changes that have occurred in definitions of educational equality have arisen, then, not just because of changes in view about the empirical nature of academic ability but also as a result of changes in judgment about where the responsibility lies for ensuring that ability and aspiration are developed. As Coleman (1968, p. 22) comments, with early definitions of educational equality, 'the responsibility for profitable use of [the free public resources provided by the education system] lay with the child and his family. But the evolution of the concept has reversed these roles. The implication of the most recent concept [. . .] is that the responsibility to create achievement lies with the educational institution, not the child'. Of course, as we saw, this was not the end of the process of redefinition, in Britain at least. Even Coleman's 'most recent concept' assumes that the form of education offered in schools is a good to which all students should properly aspire. And this highlights another value assumption involved in the concept of equity of opportunity.

One of the distinguishing features of the new sociology of education was that it questioned this aspect of previous definitions. There were two alternative arguments here, though they were not always clearly distinguished. The first was the claim that all education is culturally relative, so that what form of education is a good, and a proper aspiration, for one category of student may not be for others. Equity here would be each person receiving the kind of education which is appropriate to him or her. Ironically, this is a form of argument which was used in the nineteenth and early twentieth centuries to deny the working class a secondary education, or to offer them an equitable but different one (Banks, 1955). However, in the new sociology of education it was given a different political inflection, being tied to the idea that society must be transformed so that power is equally distributed across a plurality of cultures. The other argument, very different in its implications, is that the education currently offered within schools is a deformation of what a true education would be, so that school success is not a proper aspiration for anyone. Equity here would be equal opportunity to benefit from a true education; though the question remains open as to the nature of that education.

From all of this it should be clear that the descriptive equalities and inequalities to be found within the education system at any time are manifold; and that focusing on one or other of these relies on value-based interpretations of the concepts of equity, opportunity, and education. Given that there are always competing interpretations of these concepts, there is no such thing as educational equality or inequality *per se*; there are only equalities and inequalities. And which of these are treated as significant, as equitable or inequitable, depends on the value perspective adopted. For the reasons which we explained in Chapter 2, we do not believe that it is legitimate for sociologists to argue in favour of, or against, the value of particular definitions of equity, though they can point to the implications of adopting particular definitions, in terms of what these highlight and neglect. Instead, the task of research is to provide factual information relevant to definitions which are current in public debate, or for which reasonable justificatory arguments can be offered.[5] But, given the diversity which exists in interpretations of educational equity, it is important that the value assumptions underlying researchers' identification of educational equalities and inequalities are made explicit.

As we noted in Chapter 1, in parallel with shifts in the definition of educational equality, there also occurred changes in the explanations provided for inequalities. In general, this involved a move towards emphasis on features of the structure and functioning of the education system itself, as opposed to the individual and social characteristics of students. The research we are concerned with in this book relates to the latest phase in that development, in which the primary focus has been on the role of discrimination by schools against particular categories of student.

The concept of discrimination is, of course, dependent on that of equality. Like the latter, it has both descriptive and evaluative senses. In its descriptive sense discrimination (or differentiation) is ubiquitous. We are all constantly distinguishing some things and some people from others, and acting differently towards them. In its evaluative sense, however, discrimination refers to the differential treatment of those who should have been treated the same.[6] Here again, though, in our view research ought to be restricted to value-relevant descriptive statements; it should not include claims about the injustice, unacceptability etc. of unequal treatment of particular kinds, since it cannot validate such claims. There is a significant distinction between the factual statement that in terms of some conception of equity teachers or others have discriminated against some category of student, and a negative evaluation of that action as discriminatory. There are two reasons for this. One is that, as we have emphasized, there are different conceptions of what is equitable. The other is that practical evaluations of discrimination are a matter of judgment, and depend on a wide range of considerations, including the scope for alternative action, its 'opportunity costs' etc.

A distinction is often drawn between direct and indirect discrimination. The former refers to policies and actions which have the effect of preserving or increasing inequality of opportunity (in a defined sense) and which are adopted *because they have that effect*. This may be done because it is believed that some category of student should not have the opportunity to obtain an education of a particular kind, that they cannot benefit from

[5] This seems to be the position which Coleman, 1968 adopts, though he also refers, confusingly, to the notion of 'complete equality of opportunity' (p. 21).
[6] There is another sense of 'discrimination' in which a positive rather than a negative evaluation is implied (see, for example, Thompson, 1973). However, this is rarely if ever used in the field with which we are concerned.

such an 'opportunity', and/or that they should be encouraged to acquire a very different kind of education. By contrast, indirect discrimination refers to policies or actions which have the effect of preserving or increasing inequality of opportunity, in some sense, but which are not adopted for that reason, and whose consequences in this respect may not be known to the relevant policymakers or practitioners. Indirect discrimination can result from conscious judgments about the characteristics of some category of person which are believed to be correct, from decisions on the basis of unconscious stereotypes of some group which would be abandoned if recognized, or from assumptions about other matters which when translated into policy have a differential effect on particular categories of person. For example, the decision to stream students in secondary schools could be designed to separate middle-class and working-class students, on the basis that each requires a different kind of education; and in this case it would constitute direct discrimination. However, streaming could also be motivated by the belief that children of different abilities require different sorts of education, or different forms of teaching. This would not constitute direct discrimination, in relation to social class; but it would represent a form of indirect discrimination if the allocation of students to streams was based on judgments of ability which were influenced by irrelevant social-class characteristics. However, on some definitions, indirect discrimination might also be said to occur even if the teachers allocated students to streams solely on the basis of judgments of academic ability, where ability of this kind is distributed unequally between the social classes; so that middle-class students predominate in the higher, and working-class students in the lower, streams.

Which form of discrimination is being claimed, and how it is held to occur, need to be made explicit; both because they involve different conceptions of equity and opportunity, and because they demand somewhat different kinds of evidence. For example, direct discrimination requires evidence to show that the intention was to treat the relevant categories of student differently, whereas indirect discrimination does not. However, both require that the equity assumptions on the basis of which they have been identified are spelled out. And it is also necessary to make explicit the *factual* assumptions which are involved in the identification of inequalities of opportunity, and of the forms of discrimination held to produce them. These assumptions concern the effects of various policies and actions on the learning or educational achievement of students. And in the case of *these* assumptions, unlike those relating to values, it is the responsibility of the researcher to provide evidence in support of them.

The conceptual issues surrounding the identification of inequalities and discrimination are not the only ones which may require clarification in research on educational inequalities. As we noted, a feature of the concept of equality is that it is comparative; and, in general, research on educational inequality has been focused on inequalities between social classes, genders, and ethnic groups. And these categories are also by no means unproblematic.

Categories of Student

The three sets of social categories most commonly used in research on educational inequalities vary somewhat in their degree of conceptual complexity. While there are some common problems, there are distinctive issues relating to each.

Gender

From one point of view, sex or gender is the least problematic of the three sets of categories. We can be reasonably sure that sex as operationalized in one study will be much the same as sex operationalized in another. In practical terms, the categorization of students by sex is a relatively straightforward matter: there are just two categories, and allocation to one or the other is rarely contentious; at least not by comparison with the considerable difficulties involved in operationalizing 'race'/ethnicity and social class.

However, there are some questions to be raised about exactly what is being categorized in this process. A distinction is often drawn between sex and gender; that is, between male/female and masculine/feminine.[7] Moreover, it has been pointed out that (on some definitions) both of these involve bipolar distributions rather than dichotomies; and that they do not always vary together, either for particular individuals within a given culture or across cultures. A further complication is that both sex and gender are interrelated with sexual orientation, and this too is not simply dichotomous. For these and other reasons, there has been considerable debate amongst feminists about the problems of adopting essentializing definitions of womanhood.[8] Similarly, there has recently emerged a small body of research concerned with the role of schools in reproducing sexualities (see Mac an Ghaill, 1995; Epstein, 1995). While for many research purposes the complexities surrounding sex/gender may not be a crucial issue, they should not be forgotten. And they may turn out to be more significant than is currently assumed.

'Race' and Ethnicity

The concept of 'race' shares similar conceptual problems with that of sex; but these are generally thought to be more fundamental, hence the common use of scare quotes around the term.[9] It is argued that here we have a concept which refers to a false perception: that the only legitimate use of the term 'race'

[7] One of the main sources of this is de Beauvoir's *The Second Sex*, and her arguments are by no means uncontroversial, see Butler, 1987.
[8] See Alcoff, 1988 and Spelman, 1988. For a useful discussion of these complexities in the context of research methodology, see Morgan, 1986.
[9] For a useful discussion of the constructed character of 'racial' and ethnic data, see Gordon, 1992.

is as a device for recognizing that people categorize and behave differently towards one another on the basis of assumed differences which do not exist. After all, biologists have shown that 'race' is not a category which picks out distinct groupings of human beings who display different patterns of human characteristics or behaviour (see UNESCO, 1969; Nei and Roychoudhury, 1983).

However, the concept of 'race' is less distinctive than this argument suggests: much of the thrust of research on gender has, of course, been concerned with denying some of the differences commonly believed to be associated with being male or female. While there is no suggestion that females and males do not differ biologically, there has been a denial that these biological differences are necessarily associated with the wide range of personal characteristics and behavioural dispositions which they are generally taken to be. And much the same applies to race: there is no denial that, for example, people's skin pigmentation differs across a range which can be crudely described as black to white. What is at stake are the implications of variation in skin colour, and in other physical features, for personal characteristics and behaviour (see Appiah, 1990). Here, as in the case of gender, what is significant is not physiological differences themselves (and these are in any case rather less biologically significant in the case of 'race' than sex) but how they are culturally interpreted.

For this reason, many researchers have concentrated on ethnicity rather than race, categorizing ethnic-minority students as, for example, Asian, Afro-Caribbean etc; or using more subtle ethnic differentiations. However, this too is by no means unproblematic: all manner of distinctions are possible, and some of them are politically contentious. Furthermore, it is often argued that this neglects the importance of *racism*. Thus, a feature of much recent discussion of inequalities in relation to 'race' and ethnicity is use of the category 'black'. Here, of course, the reference is not to skin colour itself but to a population whom, it is claimed, whites tend to treat as belonging to a different race (or to different races) than themselves. The aim is to gather together under one heading all those who are subjected to racism (with the latter term defined as 'racial' discrimination *by whites*). However, this usage has itself been criticized, on the grounds that it treats people as black who do not regard themselves as black, and because it overrides important ethnic differences (Modood, 1988; Mason, 1990). Some have sought to meet these criticisms by use of the phrase 'black and Asian', but this undermines the original rationale for the concept 'black' and retains a considerable neglect of ethnic variation.

The crucial consideration here, it seems to us, is the question of what any particular researcher is intending to measure. The answer to that question will have implications for the sort of categorization which should be adopted. Some writers (for example Bulmer, 1986) have argued that 'race' and ethnicity should always be categorized on the basis of people's own self-identity. However, even apart from the question of whether people operate on the basis of stable, trans-contextual ethnic identities (Barth, 1969; Moerman, 1974; Wallman, 1979), this fails to take account of the fact that very often what is of interest is how people are categorized *by others* and whether they are discriminated against on the basis of that categorization. To the extent that this is the focus, the aim should surely be to model the categorizations which these significant others employ. In other words, if the concern in research on educational inequality is with discrimination by schools, then the categorizations used by researchers should approximate those used by school personnel. If, on the other hand, the interest is in how variations in cultural background affect educational ability and aspirations, then a categorization system which takes account of significant cultural variations and their effects — such as religion, bilingualism, attitudes to schooling, etc. — may be appropriate. At the very least, though, the basis for the 'racial'/ethnic classification employed must be made clear.

Social Class

Social-class categories are notoriously problematic. There is a variety of class-ification systems designed to measure social class; and they are based on different interpretations of the meaning of that concept and on conflicting assumptions about the nature of modern societies (Marsh, 1986; Saunders, 1990). Most rely on occupational classification, but they group occupations in somewhat different ways; and while some represent a scale of social status others are intended to represent different relationships to the mode of product-ion or to types of market and work situation. It is not clear how divergent conclusions about educational inequalities are likely to be, based on these different classification systems. Indeed, some exploration of this would be useful (see Heath, 1984; Drudy, 1991). Alternative ways of collapsing classifi-cations into two or three broad categories are also of relevance here. For instance, the decision to rely on a manual/non-manual distinction, rather than, say, distinguishing among professional and managerial, intermediate, and working classes may affect the nature of the inequalities found.

There is another important problem with social-class categories. This is that most classification systems have been designed primarily with males in mind: they are not entirely satisfactory in dealing even with females in full-time paid employment, and they are wholly inadequate in relation to women engaged in part-time paid work and in unpaid work.[10] Very often, of course, researchers identify the social class of children on the basis of their father's occupation. Yet, the mother's occupation may be equally or more significant for the material circumstances of the home and for the socialization of the children. And, of course, there is a substantial number of families where a father is not present.

There is a deeper problem as well. To write of an accurate or valid divi-sion of students into social classes presumes that there is in the world some pre-existing structuring of phenomena which an accurate division of the

---

[10]   For a review of the debate about this and references, see Marshall *et al.*, 1988, Ch. 4.

population into social classes would match. There are, however, different views about the nature and basis of this structuring. One derives from general theorizing about societies and treats 'real' classes as features of an abstract model of social dynamics. From this point of view, categories composed on the basis of an index of occupations are typically regarded as only poor approximations to underlying structural realities. The debate around 'Wright classes' (Wright, 1985; Marshall *et al.*, 1988, Ch. 3) nicely captures the difficulties of finding the emanations of underlying structures in the messy, empirically observable world. A second approach is more pragmatic, and more closely confined to empirical work *per se*. It treats occupational classifications as indices of differences in what might be called 'clusters of life chances'. Thus, it is hoped that dividing people into categories according to the single criterion of occupation (or parental occupation) will result in categories the memberships of which are each internally similar in terms of life chances, and which differ from each other significantly.

Whichever approach is adopted, however, we need to recognize the probabilistic character of social-class categories. Assuming that they have been correctly constructed and operationalized, they tell us quite reliably about occupational positions, but much less reliably about all the other (and for most purposes much more significant) features we normally treat as part of (or as implied by) social class, such as: level of income and wealth, contractual conditions of employment (and risk of unemployment), working conditions, standard of housing, general health, political and social attitudes, cognitive skills etc. Almost whatever classification scheme we employ, we will find considerable internal variation in these respects within each social-class category, and substantial overlaps between categories.

Once we recognize that social-class categories are sets of probabilities, two things become clear. First, a social class referred to in one study may not be equivalent to 'the same' class referred to in another, in terms of the probability statements which may reasonably be made about them. For instance, the comparative study by Rutter *et al.* (1975) of London and the Isle of Wight shows that it is a rather different matter to be 'working class' in one area compared with the other; and this may have implications for educational achievement. Second, social class as such does not cause differences in educational performance. These arise as a result of the multiple factors associated probabilistically with occupational position.

Up to now, we have been concerned with the use of social-class classifications to map causes of inequalities in educational achievement that operate on children's abilities and aspirations. However, as with 'racial'/ethnic categorization, we may also wish to focus on direct and indirect discrimination, in which case what needs to be modelled is the social-class differentiation of students that is believed to underly teachers' treatment of them. We cannot assume that this will simply correspond to some definition of 'objective' social-class differences, though it may do so. There has been a considerable literature on social-class imagery (Ossowski, 1963; Bulmer, 1975; Roberts *et al.*, 1977);

but as far as we are aware little use has been made of this in understanding the orientations of teachers.[11]

Given these diverse interpretations of the social categories of students between which inequalities may be investigated, it is necessary for researchers to be explicit about which interpretations have been adopted and how these have been operationalized. Otherwise, it will not be clear among whom inequalities have been identified, or what their significance is. There is a further complication too. We have dealt with the three sets of social categories separately, but of course they cross-cut; and this can have a significant effect on educational inequalities and their explanation. There has been extended discussion of the interaction between gender and ethnicity (Fuller, 1980; Mac an Ghaill, 1988), and similar problems arise with interrelations among the other categories. This means that in any observation of differential treatment of students, some investigation may be necessary in order to identify the category, or set of categories, which is causally relevant in the cases studied.

Descriptive Adequacy

A second requirement which must be met in order for research to establish the validity of claims about inequality is descriptive adequacy. All research depends on descriptions, explicitly or implicitly. So, one of the main tasks in any assessment of research in this field is to consider whether inequality of the relevant kinds has been shown to exist in the situation being investigated.

We argued in the previous chapter that descriptive claims and the evidence accompanying them should be assessed on the basis of plausibility and credibility. Relatively little further needs to be added to what was said there about plausibility. It requires that the claims made or evidence provided are strongly implied by what is currently accepted as knowledge by the research community. In judging a claim in terms of this criterion, there are just two possible outcomes: that it is or is not sufficiently plausible to be accepted. It is rare for research findings to be sufficiently plausible to be accepted at face value; since if this were so they would have little newsworthiness by definition. However, *evidence* may well be offered which is acceptable on these grounds. Of course, judgments about plausibility are often open to reasonable disagreement, and may need to be revised as a result of further reflection and/or research; the rule ought to be that if there is any reasonable doubt claims must be treated as insufficiently plausible to be accepted. It is important to recognize that arguing that a claim is insufficiently plausible to be accepted is not the same as arguing that it is false. The implication is only that it is not convincing as it stands, in other words that further evidence is needed before it can be accepted. This brings us to the second standard for judging descriptive claims — credibility; and this requires much more discussion.

[11]   But see Nash, 1973; Goodacre, 1968 and 1971, and Sharp and Green, 1975.

Judging credibility involves an assessment of the likelihood that the production of the evidence has been seriously affected by one or more forms of
potential error.[12] We outline below the main types of these, beginning with
those which relate to observations by the researcher. Subsequently, we will
look at the problems involved where reliance is placed on informants' accounts.[13] Much of this covers familiar methodological ground, but we believe
that it is important to make explicit the basis on which our assessment of
research on educational inequalities will rely.

Observational Data Produced by Researchers

Errors in the Selection and Construction of Data

1   Errors of observation
All observation involves selectivity and inference. Neither of these is a source
of error in itself, but they can lead to error where what is relevant in a case
is not observed, or where behaviour that *is* observed is misinterpreted. There
are several possible problems.
   i) The question of what is relevant is not always easy to answer. Indeed,
this will often change over the course of a piece of research, as the focus is
clarified or even transformed; and it can change after data collection has been
completed, as a result of developments in the field. It is also an issue which
can be open to reasonable disagreement. These problems arise because, as we
noted earlier, judgments of relevance depend on value and factual assumptions. If there is change in those assumptions, then decisions about what is and
is not relevant to a particular research focus may also need to change. Moreover, relevance is a matter of degree, and as a result there can also be uncertainty and disagreement about what is the appropriate cut-off point; especially

---

[12]   One of the implications of this is that assessment depends to some degree on
background information about how the research was carried out. There has been a
growth in the provision of such information in recent years. In the field of educational
research, see Hammersley, 1983; Burgess, 1984, 1985a, b, and c, 1989; Walford, 1987,
1991, 1994.
[13]   We are assuming that there are just two fundamental kinds of data: researchers'
descriptions and informants' accounts. This is an unconventional way of thinking about
data sources, not least because it splits interview data in two. Sometimes interviews are
intended and/or used to provide data about the interviewee through inferences based
on responses made to questions. This is most obviously true with attitude inventories,
but it is also the case with some questioning in unstructured interviewing, where the
aim is to infer attitudes or perspectives from what is being said. In our terms, this comes
under the heading of observational data. Other interview questions are designed and
used to elicit information about the world which the informant has, either information
which would otherwise not be available to the researcher or that which is necessary
to check data from other sources. Here the informant is being used as a substitute
researcher, and the data take the form of an informant's account. Of course, the same
material can often serve as both kinds of data.

since, for the researcher, this involves balancing practical constraints against methodological requirements.

It is worth stressing, however, that decisions about relevance can have serious consequences for the validity of a study. It is not just that the picture may be incomplete, but also that what is omitted may affect interpretations of the evidence reported. Thus, where a researcher is investigating something which forms part of a set of related phenomena, it may be necessary for the whole set to be documented if misleading conclusions are to be avoided. For instance, if we were interested in inequalities in the frequencies with which different categories of student were suspended, these would probably need to be examined in the context of the various other strategies schools use for dealing with what they define as inappropriate behaviour on the part of students. This is because the relative frequency of suspension (of one type or another) is likely to vary with the use of other strategies, given that they are to some degree mutual substitutes. To omit these other strategies from the focus of the research would be to ignore something that is potentially crucial for any conclusion about the reasons for variation in suspension rates.

ii) Even when what is and is not relevant has been determined, there may be a failure to collect all the relevant data. This can result from unforeseen consequences of decisions about where and when to observe, or from restrictions placed on the data collection by gatekeepers and others, or from resource limitations. The aim must be to maximize the chances of observing what is relevant to the research, but this may not be achieved; thereby opening up the possibility of error.

Equally important, data-production methods vary in the degree of selectivity and inference that is built into them. As a result, they are differentially prone to the omission of relevant information. Video-recordings are at the bottom limit in this respect, though even they involve some element of selection in terms of what is and is not 'in shot', and what can and cannot be heard on the audio track. At the other end of the spectrum are highly structured modes of data collection, such as observation using a schedule which requires the observer to tick off or time the occurrence of instances of pre-specified categories of behaviour. With the latter, a great deal depends on the soundness of the decisions made about relevance in the formulation of the schedule: there may be little scope for subsequent correction.

Moreover, it is important to note that these contrasting modes of data collection involve interrelated costs and benefits. For example, the decision to use video-recording almost certainly reduces substantially the amount of observation which can be carried out (not least because considerable time has to be devoted to processing the data), and it may also restrict the locales in which observation can take place. In this way, the reduction of selectivity and inference in what is observed in any particular scene is often bought at the cost of increasing the danger that relevant scenes have not been observed. Social surveys and systematic observation studies, by contrast, involve the reverse trade-off, and its associated dangers.

2   Errors in recording and processing the data

Data can be recorded under a variety of conditions, and in a variety of ways. To different degrees, these will give rise to the possibility that what is observed is misrecorded in the data. Again, video-recordings minimize the dangers here — by contrast, for instance, with the recording of data by means of field-notes written some time after the events documented, or live unstructured or structured data recorded in busy surroundings. The positions are reversed, however, when we turn to data processing. The less selective modes of data collection are, the more processing the data require before they can be used; and this processing necessarily involves decisions about both the selection of what is relevant and the representation of what is recorded. For example, with video- and audio-recordings, error can be introduced in the process of transcription, since this necessarily involves interpretation (see Ochs, 1979; Atkinson, 1992).

3   Errors arising from unsystematic retrieval of data

Very often research involves the collection of very large amounts of data and not all relevant material may be found when a search is made. This means that, however successful the research has been in defining the focus and in producing the data, relevant material may still be overlooked, thereby distorting the findings. This is a particular problem with unstructured data, which cannot easily be summarized without considerable loss. And the problem is exacerbated in the case of exploratory research, where the research focus is developed over time. Before the availability of microcomputers, comprehensive searching of large qualitative data sets was tedious and prone to considerable error of this kind. However, even the use of appropriate software does not entirely eliminate this danger, since its effectiveness depends on the accuracy of the original data coding.

Errors of Inference from Data to Claims about the Case(s) Studied

All studies make claims about the particular cases they have investigated on the basis of the data which have been recorded. Various factors can endanger the validity of the inferences involved:

1   Reactivity

Most observation by researchers carries the danger that the behaviour observed will have been affected in relevant ways by the research process itself.

i) The very fact of observation can have an effect on behaviour. Where the people whose behaviour is being described know that they are being observed, they may adjust what they do in various ways, some of which may be relevant to the research focus. Similarly, there may be features of the organization of the research which have the effect of changing the environment in which the people concerned operate, in ways which lead them to behave in ways other than those they would adopt if the research were not taking place. An obvious instance is the presence of a video-camera, or even an audio-recording machine, where these are not usual features of the environment. We might call these sorts of effect *procedural reactivity.*

ii) The social and personal characteristics of the observer(s) may also have an effect on the behaviour of the people being studied. This is true even where research is being done by means of covert participant observation. It is excluded only where the fact that research is taking place is not known to the people being observed *and* where the observer is hidden; and this is very unlikely in research on educational inequalities.

The social class, gender, and ethnicity of the researcher are, of course, among the social characteristics which are likely to be particularly significant. These characteristics may affect what is said and done in the presence of the researcher, suppressing what might otherwise have occurred, or what would have been disclosed to a researcher with different characteristics. We can call this source of error *personal reactivity.*

2   Errors of sampling within the case

Very often, in studying a particular case the data employed relate to only part of it, yet generalization is made to the case as a whole. This involves generalization across a number of dimensions along which heterogeneity may occur. These include: time, people, and locales. As an example of the problem of time generalization, many studies rely on observations of a teacher at a single point in time, or over a short period of time, but make claims about general propensities or predispositions on the part of that teacher, implying that what was observed is typical of what he or she normally does. It is also common for observations of a small number of people to be used as a basis for generalizations about all the people, or all the people of a particular kind, within a case (for example all teachers or students within a school). Similarly, what happens on one or more occasions in a locale may be treated as routinely happening in that locale. All these forms of generalization within the case involve potential error.

3   Errors of operationalization

All research requires the operationalization of concepts or categories in the form of the assignment of instances to them. As a result, a variety of possible problems can arise:

i) The meaning of the concepts may not always be as clear as is necessary. We discussed this earlier in relation to the concepts of equality and discrimination and the social categories involved in inequality claims. However, there can also be problems about the meaning of concepts which play a more subordinate role in such claims.

There are two aspects to the meaning of a concept: intension (the concept's relationship to other concepts) and extension (its relationship to instances). For intension to be clear, other elements of the network to which the

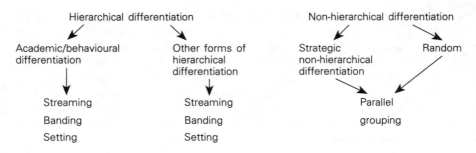

Figure 3.2: Modes of student grouping

concept belongs must be made explicit. Concepts get some of their meaning by forming part of a set of distinctions which is hierarchically organized. For example, the concept of differentiation employed by Abraham and others can be understood as contrasting modes of grouping students in school on the basis of academic/behavioural criteria with modes of grouping not based on such criteria. However, the latter include at least three relevant alternatives: random allocation, strategic allocation on the basis of a non-hierarchical set of criteria (for example, feeder school of origin, gender balance etc), and allocation on the basis of some *other* hierarchical set of criteria (these might include religious or ideological commitment, sporting ability, 'personality', wealth of parents etc). And the meaning of 'differentiation' varies according to which of these contrasts is being made. By making these distinctions explicit, we get a structure of concepts of the kind presented in Figure 3.2.

Lack of clarity about the network to which the central concepts of a piece of research belong can lead to ambiguities in the meaning of those concepts, and therefore in the findings of the research.

The second aspect of meaning, extension, concerns what instances do and do not belong to each category. In the case of qualitative research reports, it is not uncommon for there to be little direct information about how the categories were applied; and this may sometimes reflect a lack of clarity on the part of researchers about the basis for assigning data to categories. This need not matter where the categories are relatively concrete, though it is surprising how problematic in this respect even the most apparently straightforward concepts can be.[14] However, even where there are explicit coding rules, as in some quantitative research, problems can still occur: there may be a substantial number of ambiguous instances whose treatment cannot be based on the rules. In short, judgment is always involved and this can (though it need not) be erroneous.

A strength of qualitative research, in comparison with much quantitative work, is that particular instances of categories are often cited. This enables readers to gain some sense of the sort of events which have been treated as

[14] See Scarth and Hammersley's, 1986, discussion of the problems involved in identifying teachers' questions.

instances of each category. This is not possible on the basis of coding rules alone, so that such exemplification is of considerable value. However, it is no *substitute* for such rules.

ii) There may also be problems with the scaling of concepts. Very often, knowledge claims do not rely simply on the assignment of instances to categories, but involve a higher level of measurement: such as the frequency of events of particular kinds or variability in the intensity of different features, etc. For example, claims about unequal treatment in the classroom often suggest that more or less of some particular kind of teacher action (for example praise, blame, help etc.) is directed at a particular category of child or student. Where such an argument is deployed, some measurement system is required whereby different frequencies and/or degrees of treatment can be identified rigorously. Without this, there is a danger of judgments being made which might as legitimately be reversed, as in the case of the same container being both half empty and half full. Similar problems arise with judgments of frequency. As Sadler (1981) points out, in judging frequency qualitative researchers (like others) are liable to be unduly influenced by positive instances, by novel and extreme instances, and by patterns which occur early on in the period of observation (see also McCall, 1984, p. 273). It is not easy to devise accurate measurement systems for social phenomena, but where these are not employed (reliance being placed wholly on the judgment of the researcher) the danger of this type of error is heightened.

(ii) There may also be problems with indicators. Very often, evidence relating to the central concepts of a piece of research relies on indicators; in other words, on the assumption that there is a strong correlation between the features conceptualized in the knowledge claims and some more easily observable phenomena. For example, Abraham assumes a strong correlation between a negative attitude towards school on the part of students, on the one hand, and missed assignment and bad behaviour reports, on the other. Where indicators are used, an additional level of potential problems is introduced. All the issues we have already discussed apply to the indicators themselves. But, over and above this, there is the question of how strong the relationship is between indicators and concepts. Thus, while Abraham's reliance on these indicators is by no means unreasonable, there are various reasons why assignments may be missed or bad-behaviour reports given which have a weak or non-existent relationship to the student's attitude to school. It is also possible for a negative attitude towards school not to be manifested in terms of either of these indicators.

The problem of defective indicators is not one which only occurs with quantitative data. Qualitative data also often involve reliance on indicators. For instance, Abraham uses the negative attitude of students in lower sets towards 'boffins' as an indicator of the criteria underlying their selection of friends (Abraham, 1989a, pp. 70–1). Here again, though there may be other equally or more plausible interpretations of what has been observed than that presupposed by its use as an indicator.

Informants' Accounts

Up to now we have focused on the various potential forms of error involved in research making descriptive claims and relying on data produced by the researcher's own observations. The other sort of data on which descriptive arguments may rely is second-hand information provided by informants. All the same forms of error arise here, but they occur twice over. They arise first in relation to the informant: he or she may have had an impact on what was observed, may not have observed all relevant events, may use concepts which are insufficiently clear, may misdescribe what has been seen or heard, or made false generalizations etc. And such errors are probably more likely with informants than with researchers, because the former generally have less commitment to the research and frequently have other, more pressing, concerns. Moreover, informant accounts are often based on a blend of information, some of it from direct observation, some of it indirect or hearsay. To the extent that it consists of the latter, the potential for error is multiplied. There is also the problem that informants rarely systematically record what has been observed, so that what they can tell us is even more likely to suffer from distortion by memory and other factors than data recorded by the researcher.

Over and above these problems, however, the same kinds of potential error emerge again as regards the relationship between informant and researcher. For example, the researcher will have an effect on what information is reported by the informant as a result of procedural or personal reactivity, could misunderstand what is said, may record it inaccurately etc.

Sources and Types of Error

Being aware of these various threats to the validity of evidence provides us with a basis for judging the credibility of particular research findings. It suggests the sorts of error that are likely, given the particular methods used, and therefore what level and type of corroborative evidence might be necessary. Needless to say, it cannot give us any immediate conclusion about the validity or otherwise of any particular claim: judgment is always required. And what is being judged is not whether the conclusions drawn are actually true or false in some absolute sense; but whether or not they have been established as true beyond reasonable doubt, until further notice.

Various factors can increase the likelihood of the forms of error we have discussed: the social and personal characteristics of the researcher, difficult circumstances under which the research was carried out, inadequate resources, external pressures, bias (conscious or unconscious) on the part of the researcher etc. Here again information about the researcher and the research process can be important in the assessment process. However, it is necessary to emphasize that the operation of these causes does not in itself indicate the presence of error of the expected kinds. For example, the fact that a researcher has strong commitments or expectations about the phenomenon he or she is studying does not mean that the account produced is erroneous, even when it is consistent with the direction of likely bias. It only means that, in assessing the research, the possibility of error resulting from this source must be checked. The converse is also true: the absence of strong commitments does not mean that bias will not be present. It can arise arise from routine assumptions.

It is usual to distinguish between two *types* of error: systematic and haphazard.[15] The former involves a trend of errors in a particular direction, whereas with haphazard error the effects are not in a single direction and may tend to cancel one another out. The consequences of these two sorts of error are rather different, though both can result in claims and conclusions being seriously misleading. The consequences of systematic error are fairly obvious. It leads us to 'discover' descriptive features or explanatory effects which do not exist, or to overlook them where they do. The effect of haphazard error, by contrast, is indeterminate, but it can obscure evidence for the existence of a feature or effect (in the terminology of information theory, it introduces noise into the data) and will sometimes throw up spurious evidence.

Looking at the various forms of error we have identified, some are more likely to produce systematic error, others haphazard error. For example, the omission of relevant material from the data, reactivity, and errors of operationalization are all likely to produce systematic error. On the other hand, errors arising from unsystematic data retrieval and some kinds of observational error will often be haphazard in their effects.

Explanatory Power

Up to now we have been concerned primarily with the validity of descriptive claims, but very often research dealing with educational inequalities also has explanatory intent. Of course, where the conclusions of a study are explanatory, all of the forms of potential error discussed above apply here too, since explanations necessarily rely on descriptions or on descriptive assumptions. In addition, though, inferences about causal relations are involved in explanations; and it is widely recognized that there are special problems involved in validating these, especially when dealing with social phenomena. Some commentators even deny that causal relations operate in the social world: one of the rationales for social constructionism has been that it does not assume the operation of social causation. However, any substantive interest in educational inequality almost inevitably does assume this.

In the previous chapter we argued that explanations, like descriptions, are necessarily value-dependent. Explanatory factors are selected partly according to the purposes which the explanation is to serve, and the selection criteria involved need to be made explicit. Equally important, though, is to establish

---

[15] We use the term 'haphazard' because these errors are not necessarily strictly random, though the closer they approach to randomness the more easily they can be allowed for.

the causal power of the explanation proposed. Several problems arise here in the context of research on educational inequalities. One is that the causal processes being investigated are likely to be relatively complex, for example involving overdetermination, interaction effects, and feedback processes of various kinds. This makes them especially difficult to document. Another is that the most powerful method of investigating causal relationships, the experiment, is generally not available in such research.

There are at least two potential forms of error which threaten causal inferences. The first is spurious correlation. A correlation may appear to exist when it does not, being an artifact of the research process. This is a defect which is likely to result from descriptive errors, notably poor or inaccurate sampling within a case or across cases.

The second form of error is spurious causation. A correlation may exist between two variables, but causation may run in the opposite direction to that which is assumed; or a correlation may hold, but without indicating a causal relationship, because both cause and effect were produced by a third factor.

Given these problems, by what means can inferences about causal relations relating to educational inequalities be established? It seems to us that in order to justify explanatory claims the following procedure needs to be followed:

1 We must establish that the descriptions of, or descriptive assumptions about, all of the relevant phenomena are accurate, and that they match what the explanation claims. This usually involves comparative data, showing for example that the features which the explanation takes to be distinctive to the phenomena to be explained are not found elsewhere (or that, if they are, there is a sound reason for this).
2 Next, we must check the plausibility of the theory on which the explanation relies. Is it sufficiently plausible, on the basis of research evidence or commonsense, to be accepted?
3 We must also establish that the chronology of cause and effect is correct; though, of course, we may well have to allow for feedback processes.
4 Finally, plausible alternative explanations for the phenomenon being explained must be considered. We need to assess the relative strength of the evidence for these, in the respects already discussed: the match between alternative explanations and the descriptive data, the plausibility of the theories on which they depend, and the degree of fit with the chronology of cause and effect they have.

On this basis, we can try to determine which of the available explanations seems likely to have been operative in the circumstances. Sometimes, of course, competing explanations will not be incompatible; as, for example, with differentiation–polarization and cultural difference theories. Even so, we may be able to determine which was the most powerful factor in the case(s) studied; though this is unlikely to be easy.

Generalizability

Most, though not all, research makes claims, explicitly or implicitly, about cases beyond those which have actually been studied. In other words, it involves an element of generalizability. This can take two quite different forms, what we will call empirical generalization and theoretical inference. The former involves making claims about some larger, but finite, population of cases to which the case(s) studied belong. Potentially relevant populations are diverse, but they could include, for example, secondary schools in England and Wales, all English primary schools which employ vertical grouping, teachers in UK schools employing a 'formal' approach etc. Theoretical inference, on the other hand, is employed by studies concerned with developing and testing theories. The claim here is that what is true of the case (or cases) studied is also true of all other members of the relevant theoretical category to which they belong.

The distinction between empirical generalization and theoretical inference is not always recognized, and the two forms are often conflated. Thus, Abraham can be interpreted as employing both, and much the same is true of the main other studies on which he draws (Hargreaves, 1967; Lacey, 1970; and Ball, 1981). One of his primary concerns was with testing differentiation–polarization theory, or at least with clarifying its scope: showing that it applies not just to schools where there is streaming or banding but also to those where setting is employed. From this point of view, his conclusions rely on theoretical inference: he is claiming that the relationships among his key variables discovered in the school he studied would be found in any school where there was setting because differentiation–polarization theory is true and applies to such cases.[16] However, at the same time, he is also interested in explaining social-class differences in educational achievement in the British education system; and this requires empirical generalization from the school he studied to other secondary schools in Britain which are setted.

There are several potential problems arising in relation to these two sorts of generalizability.

Vagueness about the Type or Scope of Generalizability

As already noted, there may be a lack of clarity about what *type* of generalizability is being claimed: whether the study is offering support for a theory, or whether it is claiming that what is true of the case(s) studied is also true of some finite population. The distinction is important because the two types of generalizability require different kinds of evidence.

Empirical generalization demands evidence showing that the sample of

---

[16] He adds some qualifications: that the degree of academic pressure in the school and its social-class composition may be important factors which affect the relationship between setting and polarization.

cases studied is, or is likely to be, representative of the target population. The best known means of showing this is statistical sampling. However, this is not the only strategy available. One can also compare the cases studied with the population to be represented, where information is available about relevant features of the latter, for example in official statistics or in other studies in the literature. Also of value are multi-site investigations, where sites are selected by means of sampling decisions that are designed to represent relevant kinds of heterogeneity within the population.

Theoretical inference requires the selection of cases for study in such a manner as to test the theory concerned against rival theories. The most effective device for doing this, other things being equal, is the experiment. But, again, this is not the only method available. A sequence of naturally occurring cases can be investigated which allow at least partial control of theoretical variables. A good example of this is the set of studies investigating differentiation–polarization theory to which Abraham's work is the latest addition (see Hammersley, 1985).

There can also be lack of clarity about the *scope* of the generalization implied. In the case of theoretical inference, there may be vagueness about the character of the theory involved, for example about the conditions which have to be met for it to apply, or about the nature of the mechanisms by which cause is held to produce effect. With empirical generalization there may be a lack of clarity about the boundaries of the population to which generalization is being made. Indeed, it is not uncommon to find claims about typicality and representativeness made in research reports which lack any clear indication of the population with regard to which the cases studied are believed to be typical or representative.

Overgeneralization

Generalizations and theoretical inferences stated or implied in the conclusions of a study are not always supported with sufficient evidence. In the case of theoretical inference, the case(s) investigated may not be telling enough to allow inference to the validity of the theory in the way that the account suggests, even against the background of other studies which also support that inference. In the case of empirical generalization, there may be insufficient evidence to rule out a level of heterogeneity in the population which could render the findings in the case(s) studied unrepresentative.

Conclusion

In this chapter we have identified what we take to be the four requirements which research on educational inequalities must meet if its findings are to be accepted as valid: clarity of argument, descriptive adequacy, explanatory power, and generalizability. Whether studies meet these requirements is always a matter of judgment, but we have sought to outline the considerations which must be taken into account in making such judgments. In terms of clarity we argued that it is important for researchers to make explicit both the type of equality/inequality, discrimination etc. which is their focus, and how they have interpreted the social categories involved. In the case of descriptive adequacy we identified a variety of threats to credibility which need to be taken into account in assessing the descriptive findings or assumptions of any study. As regards explanatory power, we argued that explanations must be assessed against the background of the dangers of spurious correlation and causation. Thus, the plausibility of the theories on which explanatory hypotheses rely must be considered, along with the evidence needed to show that they are more convincing than any competitors. Finally, most research on educational inequalities involves claims about the generalizability of its findings. We considered the two forms which generalizability claims can take — theoretical inference and empirical generalization — and the requirements of each.

In the next chapter we will begin our assessment of research on educational inequalities by looking at work which has focused at the level of school organization.

Chapter 4

Inequalities at School Level

In Chapter 1 we noted how explanations for inequalities in educational achievement have shifted away from a focus on 'external' factors, such as the individual characteristics of students or the cultural environment provided by their homes, towards an almost total emphasis on processes occurring within schools and classrooms; albeit with these themselves sometimes treated as the product of wider social forces. Lacey, an early advocate of this move, saw it as opening up the 'black box' of the school in order to explore the micro-social mechanisms which mediate between educational inputs and outputs (Lacey, 1976, p. 68).[1] Indeed, school processes have increasingly been treated as themselves generating outcome inequalities (for example, Wright, 1986, 1992a; Mac an Ghaill, 1988; Troyna, 1991a; Measor and Sikes, 1992; Riddell, 1992). This research has operated at two levels. Some has focused on the organization of schools, being concerned with forms of selection such as streaming, banding, setting, option choice, etc. Other work has investigated differential treatment of students in the classroom. This chapter deals with the first of these areas; Chapter 5 will consider the second.

Almost all the research on selection processes in recent times has dealt with secondary schools; and it has usually relied on case studies of individual schools. Some of it has concentrated on inequalities in the operation of selection procedures themselves; other studies have explored the effects of allocation to different courses on students' subsequent school experience, and thereby on their levels of educational achievement. The arguments presented are often evaluative in character; but, for the reasons explained in Chapter 2, we shall be primarily concerned with their factual components.

The Main Claims

The Process of Selection

There are two main sorts of claim relating to selection procedures themselves. The first is characteristic of studies focusing on social class and ethnic-group differences, the second is more typical of gender-focused investigations.

[1] The concept of a 'black box' was originally derived from electronics, and specifically referred to situations where internal processes could not be opened up to direct investigation. See Ashby, 1956, Ch. 6.

1) *Discrimination in Allocation to Different Levels of Course*

Here it is argued that students from working-class or ethnic-minority back-grounds are more likely to be placed in lower-status groups: in lower streams, bands and sets, in non-examination groups, on vocational (rather than academic) courses, and in special units (see, for example, Hargreaves, 1967; Lacey, 1970; Tomlinson, 1981; Ball, 1981; Wright, 1986; Tomlinson, 1987; Abraham, 1989a; Troyna, 1991a, 1992; CRE, 1992). There are two main versions of this claim:

1 It is often argued that the allocation of students to different levels of course deviates from what would be expected on the basis of their ability, in such a way that working class or black students are more likely to be allocated to lower-status courses (Ball, 1981; Troyna, 1991a).
2 Occasionally it is explicitly claimed that the very concept of ability underlying allocation to higher- and lower-level courses derives from middle-class or white culture, rather than from a universally appropriate standard of selection; so that, in itself, it discriminates against working-class or black students (Mac an Ghaill, 1988, p. 35).

The first of these claims will be our focus here. Argument 2 will be given some consideration in the next chapter.

2) *Inequalities in the Distribution of Students across Courses in Different Subjects*

In the area of gender a number of studies have pointed out that where subject specialization occurs, notably at 13+ and 16+, boys tend to predominate in some subjects and girls in others: boys are in the majority on courses in subjects like mathematics, physics, technology and computer studies, and girls on courses in arts, languages, social science and home/parent craft (see Reid *et al.*, 1974; Hurman, 1978; Kelly, 1981; Grafton *et al.*, 1983; Pratt *et al.*, 1984; Whyte, 1986; Gillborn, 1990b; Riddell, 1992). These studies often argue that schools channel students into 'gender-appropriate' courses, directly or indirectly. Thus, it has been claimed that, despite legislation against sex discrimination, a minority of schools have policies which exclude boys and girls from particular subjects (Pratt *et al.*, 1984, p. 69). Generally, though, the channelling has been presented as more subtle and indirect in character. For instance, it is argued that in some schools option systems place constraints on students' choices which make 'non-traditional' choice less likely; that the way subjects are presented to students encourages 'traditional' gender-stereotyped choices; that there are subtle differences in the advice offered by teachers to girls and boys; and/or that teachers are reluctant to agree to non-traditional choices (Grafton *et al.*, 1983; Gillborn, 1990b; Riddell, 1992). These studies have also often suggested that schools do not play a sufficiently pro-active role in encouraging non-traditional choices and in supporting those students who make them.

The Effects of Selection Processes

The other main set of arguments about school-level processes concerns unequal *effects* of allocation to different courses on students' educational experience and achievement. Again, research dealing with social class and ethnicity has been concerned with allocation to different levels of course, while studies of gender have been preoccupied with imbalances across different subject courses.

1) Discriminatory Consequences of Allocation to Low-status Courses

Various processes are identified here which, it is claimed, discriminate against students on lower-level courses. And it is argued that, because working-class and black students are often disproportionately allocated to such courses, these processes also discriminate against *them*. There are three arguments of this type:

i) The most straightforward is the claim that being allocated to lower-level courses largely determines students' subsequent careers in secondary school, and affects the number and level of examinations for which they are entered at 16+ and beyond; thereby restricting their achievement in terms of educational outcomes (Ball, 1981 and 1986; Wright, 1986; Troyna, 1991a).

ii) It is also sometimes argued that the stigma of allocation to low-status courses has a negative effect on students' attitudes to school, on their motivation to succeed, and therefore on their educational achievement; while allocation to high-status groups has a positive effect in these respects. In this way, selection amplifies existing differences in achievement (Hargreaves, 1967; Lacey, 1970; Ball, 1981; Wright, 1986; Abraham, 1989a).

iii) Finally, it has been proposed that differential educational provision is made by schools for different levels of course, with lower-status courses receiving less resources or lower quality resources. This, it is claimed, has the effect of reducing the chances of educational success of students on those courses, compared with students on higher-level courses. For instance, it is said that low-status groups often receive a less demanding curriculum and less effective teaching (Hargreaves, 1967; Ball, 1981).

2) *Discriminatory Consequences in Relation to Subject*

There are two separate arguments here:

i) It is suggested that since school subjects form part of a hierarchy, with mathematics and science given higher status than humanities subjects, the fact that boys tend to take the former and girls the latter represents inequality which disadvantages girls. Furthermore, the claim is made that those practical subjects typically taken by girls are accorded lower status in school, and in society generally, than those typically taken by boys; because the former are related to occupational destinations, whereas the latter are seen primarily as preparation for home making.

ii) It is also sometimes argued that the types of educational experience offered on the different curricular routes typical of girls and boys encourage traditionally stereotyped gender attitudes and identities.

In the remainder of this chapter we will examine the evidence put forward by researchers for these various claims, and look at some of the methodological problems surrounding it.

Assessing the Process of Selection

Discrimination in Allocation to Different Levels of Course

A key element of much of research at school level has been the argument that the distribution of working-class or black, ethnic-minority students across levels of course is unequal in comparison with that of middle-class or white students, and that this constitutes discrimination against them. There is a small number of studies which have examined this issue, notably Ball's investigation of the allocation of working-class and middle-class children to bands at *Beachside Comprehensive* (1981, pp. 29–34) and Troyna's (1991a, 1992; CRE, 1992) analysis of the distribution of whites and Asians across sets in Jayleigh comprehensive school.

We must begin by considering the nature of the argument being presented in these studies, in terms of the framework we laid out in Chapters 2 and 3. It takes the form of a value-based description: it is a comparison of what *is* with how things *ought to be* from the point of view of some conception of equity. Given this, we need to know what principle of equity is being employed. This is not made clear in either of these studies, but we can identify several possibilities. One of these, analogous in many respects to what Jewson and Mason (1987) refer to as the 'radical conception of equality of opportunity', implies that members of the relevant social categories should be represented in different levels of course in the same proportions as they are in the whole school population. Here it is either assumed that ability is equally distributed across social categories, even across the relatively small samples of students present in a particular school, or that it is the responsibility of schools to equalize ability across social categories.

A second conception of equity is the idea that schools ought to operate in such a manner as to ensure that the distribution of students across levels of course is in line with *measured* ability. This seems to be the main definition of equality which Ball and Troyna use. However, there are two other principles which are also implicit in their work and/or in the selection processes they describe. One (the third conception of equity in our list) is the idea that in allocating students to courses teachers should only take account of ability, not of other factors; and that their assessments of student ability must not be influenced by the social class or ethnic membership of students. The final (fourth) equity principle we will consider is the argument that allocation should take account both of ability *and of other relevant factors;* but that, once again, judgments about these must not be affected by social class or ethnic stereotypes. We will look at the evidence about allocation to different levels of course in terms of each of these four assumptions.

The first, the 'radical' conception, is the least demanding of the four as regards the evidence which is needed to establish equality or inequality in selection procedures. It only requires information about the distribution of students from the different social categories across different levels of course; not about selection processes themselves, or even about student ability. Selection procedures are *defined* as discriminatory if outcomes are unequal.

Both Ball and Troyna provide evidence which shows middle-class or white students disproportionately allocated to higher bands or sets in the schools they investigated (See Tables 4.1 and 4.2).

The only major source of potential error in these data, as regards this definition of inequality, relates to operationalization of the social class and ethnic identities of students. There are conceptual and technical problems surrounding social class, as we saw in Chapter 3. Ball operationalizes this concept in terms of two categories — middle-class or working-class — on the basis of whether the child's father has a manual or non-manual occupation.[2] There are obvious conceptual questions here about whether the manual–non-manual distinction in fathers' occupation is the most appropriate one. Ball justifies his operationalization on the basis that previous research has suggested that 'in the majority of cases' there is a correspondence between the manual–non-manual distinction and 'the conventional social categories — middle-class and working-class' (Ball, 1981, p. 31). This is not a strong theoretical justification for the adoption of analytic categories, to say the least (Saunders, 1990, pp. 27–8). Moreover, there are some technical issues about the quality of the data he used. Information

[2] It is not entirely clear whether Ball used the broader category of head of household (Ball, 1981, p. 31); but it seems not, given that in the notes he indicates that the responses 'deceased' and 'I haven't got a father' were assigned to the 'unclassified' category (Ball, 1981, p. 293).

Table 4.1: The distribution of middle-class and working-class students across second-year bands in percentage terms: Beachside Comprehensive

	Middle-class	Working-class	Totals
Band 1	67.4 (60)	39.4 (54)	114
Band 2	32.6 (29)	60.6 (83)	112
Totals	89	137	226

Notes: We have omitted data for Band 3, since Ball makes little use of these, and for students whose social class was unclassified.
Source: Derived from Ball, 1981, Table N2, p. 293

Table 4.2: The distribution of Asian and white students across mathematics sets in percentage terms: Jayleigh School

	White	Asian
Sets A/AA	29.2 (35)	22.7 (10)
Sets B/BB	29.2 (35)	25.0 (11)
Sets C/CC	24.2 (29)	29.5 (13)
Sets D/DD	17.5 (21)	22.7 (10)
Totals	120	44

Source: Derived from Troyna, 1991a, Table II, p. 370

was derived from the students themselves, and there is clearly some scope for error here, as Ball recognizes; though it seems unlikely that this would be a major problem in terms of the manual–non-manual divide.[3]

There are also some questions to be raised about Troyna's use of the distinction between white and Asian students. As we saw in Chapter 3, such crude ethnic categories can obscure a great deal. In this case his failure to distinguish between Bangladeshi and Pakistani students may have produced misleading results, given that these groups often have different average performance levels (Kysel, 1988).[4] Troyna does not explain how he and his co-researchers distinguished between white and Asian students, but it seems likely that they relied on school records. These are rarely free from error, but this is probably not a significant problem here; indeed, it would have been a greater problem if they had adopted more precise ethnic categorizations.

There are some potential problems here, then. But for the most part they concern the theoretical significance and value relevance of the findings, rather than their validity. There can be little doubt that, given the operationalizations adopted by these authors, there is inequality in the cases they studied, on this definition. At the same time, we should note the *extent* of the inequality, which is relatively small by some standards. Thus, at Beachside, in order to produce

[3] Worse problems generally arise where reliance is placed on school records, not least in terms of incompleteness. Thus, Abraham (1989a, p. 53) was only able to obtain occupational information for sixty-one of the 145 fourth-year students he chose to study. And, as he notes, incompleteness of record may be related to social class.
[4] Pakistani and Bangladeshi students formed 12 per cent and 17 per cent of the fifth-year cohort at Jayleigh, respectively: CRE, 1992, p. 14.

full equality sixteen students in each social class would have to be relocated (out of totals of 89 and 137). This amounts to 12 per cent of working-class students misplaced; 88 per cent correctly placed. At Jayleigh the discrepancy is even smaller, 4 out of 120 white students would need to be demoted from the top two sets, and 4 out of 44 Asian students promoted to produce equality. In other words, 9 per cent of Asian students were misplaced, and 91 per cent correctly placed, in terms of this conception of equity.

Let us turn now to the second definition of equality we identified. This also focuses on outcomes, rather than on the process of allocation. But here what is crucial is the relationship between the actual distribution of students and what would be expected on the basis of measured ability. Again, since this is taken as *determining* the fairness or unfairness of the allocation decisions, no direct information about those decisions is necessary.

In his study of *Beachside*, Ball (1981) obtained information about students' performance on NFER tests of reading comprehension and mathematics from school record cards. He had this information for eighty-six out of 206 second-year students in bands 1 and 2 for whom he also had usable social-class data. On this basis, he compared the destinations of middle- and working-class students whose test scores were within the middle range (100–14). He argues that this evidence suggests a 'relationship between banding and social class at levels of similar ability', though he points out that this conclusion is dependent on the tests used, so that 'the researcher must be careful what he makes of [these results]' (Ball, 1981, pp. 32–4). In much the same way, in a study of allocation procedures in a multi-ethnic comprehensive school, Troyna (1991a; 1992) compared first-year mathematics and English-set placements of white and Asian students with information about primary-school assessments of these students' ability in each subject, obtained from secondary-school records. On this evidence he argues that 'Asian pupils were likely to be placed in lower ability sets than white pupils with comparable assessment profiles' (Troyna, 1991a, p. 371).

The problems with operationalizing social categories of student which we discussed earlier apply here too, but there are some additional sources of potential error. One relates to the operationalization of measurable ability.[5] Thus, Ball relies on *achievement* test results, and it could be argued that these do not accurately represent measured *ability*. In particular, the results may have been biased by differential opportunities in previous learning. In this respect, the results might underestimate rather than overestimate social-class inequality. Troyna is less clear about the ability measure he uses; though it appears that he only had the junior-school assessments rather than actual test scores. Given this, if there were a discrepancy between these assessments and the scores this could be a serious source of error in terms of this definition of equality.

---

[5]   It is important to note that in terms of this second definition of equality it is *measurable* ability not ability *per se* which is at issue.

It is also worth noting that measured ability will vary depending on which test was used and the conditions of administration. Ball employs the results of two tests, and this is certainly preferable to reliance on one. However, he does not tell us what the relationship was between the two sets of achievement data he presents (for reading comprehension and for mathematics). In other words, we do not know how much difference there was between the performances of the same students on the two tests. If there were discrepancies which placed a significant number of students in different result categories for these tests, then the variation between actual placement in bands and what would have been expected on the basis of test results may have been produced by these discrepancies. Indeed, such discrepancies would make it impossible for the teachers to avoid deviation from allocation on the basis of measured ability, judged by either one of the tests alone.

As regards the administration of the tests, in the case of both studies this was conducted in different primary schools, and thus in varying circumstances for different subgroups of children. If there were substantial differences in the social-class compositions of the feeder schools, this might be an important confounding factor. A related problem concerns the time elapsed between the primary-school assessments and the point at which selection occurred in the secondary schools. In neither case do we know very precisely when the testing was carried out. And, while it probably occurred in the final year of junior school, this leaves some scope for relative changes in measured ability before the point of selection. It is possible that this may have affected social-class or ethnic inequalities, though it seems unlikely to be very significant.

Another source of potential error concerns the use made of ability groupings by these authors. For example, in the case of Ball's analysis it is necessary to remember that the children in the 100–14 ability range do not all have identical scores. And this variation could be correlated with social class. Indeed, this is very likely given the sharp difference in the ability profiles of the social classes, as represented in Ball's data. Thus, at least some of the deviation from what would be expected on the basis of measured ability may have derived from differences in ability *within* that range, rather than constituting social-class differences over and above ability. This could be a significant source of error in Ball's results. In Troyna's case, it is likely to be less of a problem, both because he uses five categories of ability rather than three, and because the ability profiles of the Asian and white students in his data are much more similar than those of working-class and middle-class students in Ball's study.

Finally, there is the question of the size of the deviations from equality that were found by Ball and Troyna. In percentage terms they are substantial. (See Tables 4.3 and 4.4.) However, the relatively small actual numbers of students involved make these percentages misleading.[6] Thus, in the case of Ball's analysis, it would only be necessary to demote around four middle-class

---

[6] Ball does not employ percentages, presumably for this reason.

Table 4.3: Allocation to bands of working-class and middle-class students with the same scores (100–14) on the NFER reading-comprehension test, in percentage terms: Beachside Comprehensive

	Working class	Middle class	Totals
Band 1	38.5 (10)	85.7 (12)	22
Band 2	61.5 (16)	14.3 (2)	18
Totals	(26)	(14)	40

Source: Derived from Ball, 1981, p. 33

Table 4.4: Allocation to 1st year mathematics sets within each junior-school mathematics-assessment group, comparing whites and Asians, in percentage terms: Jayleigh School

	Ability groupings										
	Outstanding		Good		Average		Weak		Very Weak		
Sets	W	A	W	A	W	A	W	A	W	A	Totals
A/AA	67	0	60	46	25	22	0	0	0	0	45
B/BB	33	0	31	38	42	33	12	0	0	0	46
C/CC	0	0	9	8	27	33	48	60	11	0	42
D/DD	0	0	0	8	6	11	40	40	89	100	31
Totals	(3)	(0)	(35)	(13)	(48)	(18)	(25)	(10)	(9)	(3)	(164)

Source: Derived from Troyna, 1991a, Table II, p. 370

students to band 2 and promote four working-class students to band 1 in order to eliminate the correlation between social class and band. And in the case of the other test the modification required would be around three students. Using chi-squared, the difference is significant for the first test (at the 0.02 level) but falls just short of significance for the second.[7]

The deviation is also small, numerically, in the case of Troyna's data. For the mathematics sets it would be virtually eliminated by moving one to two 'good ability' Asian students up the set hierarchy at each level, plus one 'weak' and two 'average ability' Asians from C/CC to B/BB. With the English sets the differences are variable: among 'average ability' students Asians are underrepresented in top sets but they are overrepresented in the case of 'good ability' students.

With relatively small and variable numerical differences like these, the sources of potential error we have identified cannot be safely ignored. And this is exacerbated by the fact that both Ball and Troyna rely on samples of the respective year groups which cannot be assumed to be representative. Indeed, the sample of students for whom Ball had achievement data is significantly skewed in social-class terms, in comparison with the year group as a whole (see Gomm, 1994).[8]

---

[7] Our significance figures are slightly lower than Ball's because we have applied Yates' correction. Also, there are doubts about the application of significance tests to these data, since the samples are not random.

[8] It is impossible to assess the representativeness of Troyna's sample, even in terms of the relationship between ethnicity and set, because of a lack of information about base figures. See Gomm, 1993.

Thus, in terms of the second definition of equity, there is some evidence of inequality but it is of questionable reliability. And, as we have seen, Ball is circumspect about what conclusions can be drawn. While in the preface to his study he claims that 'social class differences are important in allocation to ability groups' (Ball, 1981, p. xv), in the conclusion to the book he describes the co-variation of test-scores and band allocation as 'inconclusive' (p. 283). By contrast, Troyna claims that his analysis provides 'clear-cut evidence of the way Asian pupils, at the time of the study, were denied equality of opportunity in the school' (Troyna, 1991a, p. 373). This is not a sound conclusion even in terms of this second definition of equity.

Let us now consider Ball's and Troyna's evidence from the point of view of the final two definitions of equity. Here, the relationship between the actual distribution and that expected on the basis of measured ability is used as an indicator of inequality in the decision-making processes which produced the allocations. Both Ball and Troyna seem to adopt this approach in places. The former states his concern as being 'the possibility of biases in teachers' recommendations', drawing a parallel between allocation to bands within the comprehensive school and allocation to different types of school under the tripartite system (Ball, 1981, p. 31). Similarly, Troyna (1991a, p. 368) claims that in the allocation of first-year children to English sets at Jayleigh, 'differential weighting was given to Asian and white pupils' performances in the last year junior school English assessments'.

All of the potential sources of error we have discussed so far apply here too, but there is also another important problem. This is that there are factors which could produce deviation of the actual from the expected allocations that do not imply social class or ethnic bias, as specified by these definitions.

One of these relates to the operationalization of 'ability'. With these last two equity principles, we are no longer concerned simply with *measured* ability but with ability itself. And, of course, this is a concept which is open to diverse interpretations. Thus, the teachers' conceptions of ability may well have differed somewhat from those enshrined in the ability data on which the researchers relied. Furthermore, in both studies the teachers' selection decisions actually depended on these ability data but also on additional information. In the case of Jayleigh, Troyna reports that allocation relied mainly on a common test given to all students after they had been in the school for around six weeks. The teachers reported that they relied heavily on this test for setting purposes because 'in their experience it provided a better indication of pupils' ability in mathematics and English than primary school assessments in these subjects'. However, the school did 'check pupils' test results with their primary school assessments' and 'if there was a significant difference' the latter could influence the sets in which a student was placed (Troyna, 1991a, p. 366).

Under the third and fourth definitions of equality, claims on the part of Ball and Troyna about discrimination in allocation decisions rely on treating their base-line ability data as a more accurate measure of student ability than teachers' judgments based on these and other data. Neither author provides a convincing argument in support of this. It could be claimed that test results are 'objective' and teachers' assessments 'subjective'. Indeed, this seems to be Troyna's position. Following Jenkins (1987), he draws a contrast between 'suitability' and 'acceptability' criteria in selection procedures. The former refers to past achievement, the latter to future potential.[9] Moreover, suitability criteria are 'formal, observable and accountable', whereas acceptability criteria:

> relate more to *perceptions* of a pupil's characteristics. They include a range of subjective, informal and less easy to codify set of (professional) judgments about the pupil's capacity to succeed in a given ability group or examination track. (Troyna, 1991a, p. 374)

The implication is that teachers' judgments are subject to ethnic bias whereas test results are not, or are less so. This is simply speculative, however; it relies on questionable assumptions about the objectivity of test measurements and the irrelevance of what is 'not easy to codify'. Even apart from this, though, as we noted earlier, what Troyna actually seems to be comparing are secondary-school teachers' and junior-school teachers' judgments of both suitability and acceptability. And it is not at all clear why the latter should be treated as the more appropriate or accurate measure of students' ability.

There are two other important sources of potential deviation of actual from expected allocations which may be relevant if we adopt the fourth definition of equity. One that neither Ball nor Troyna takes into account is practical restrictions on the number and size of bands and sets. These can affect a school's ability to distribute students across learning groups in such as way as to match differences in measured ability (where this is grouped). This problem can be illustrated with some of Troyna's data. He compared the allocation of white and Asian students from the five junior-school assessment categories to the four first-year mathematics sets (sets A/AA to D/DD) at Jayleigh. And, as we saw, he concludes that this shows Asian students being placed in lower-ability sets compared with white pupils of the same ability (Troyna, 1991a, p. 371). However, there is an obvious problem with the comparison being made here: that there are five ability categories but only four levels of set. Given fixed set sizes, however the school distributed the students across the sets, some of them from the same ability category would find themselves in different levels of set. This would not necessarily generate ethnic differences in allocation, but it has the potential for doing so.

To assess how far there is ethnic inequality when we have taken account of this 'decanting' problem we need some conception of what would be an equitable distribution across the four set levels. Troyna does not provide such a model, so we will have to construct one. One procedure would be as follows:

---

[9] It is worth noting that, in principle at least, reliance on past achievement is likely to result in assessments which reflect the effects of previous differential educational opportunity more than if academic potential were the basis of assessment.

It seems reasonable to argue that students in the 'outstanding' category should be allocated to sets A/AA (the top sets) first. There were three white and no Asian students in this category, so we would give these students 'priority' places. We might then argue that the remaining forty-two places in sets A/AA should be filled proportionately by ethnic category from students in the 'good' category. This would give the remaining top set places to thirty-one white students and eleven Asian students. This leaves four white and two Asian students unplaced from the 'good' category. They would then be given the first six places in the B/BB sets. And so on.

The comparative picture which emerges from allocating students on the basis of this conception of equity is presented in Table 4.5.

Table 4.5: Observed and expected figures for equitable distribution through mathematics sets, by ability and ethnicity: Jayleigh School

| | Whites | | Asians | |
	Observed	Expected	Observed	Expected
A/AA	35	34	10	11
B/BB	35	33	11	13
C/CC	29	31	12	11
D/DD	21	22	11	9
Total	120		44	

Here we have compared Troyna's observed figures for the distribution of white and Asian students across the four set groups with what we would expect to find had the above procedure been followed. There is still some ethnic inequality with whites overrepresented and Asians underrepresented, but the school actually comes very close to an equal distribution. Certainly the difference does not reach statistical significance. Indeed, the deviation between the actual figures and the ideal could be remedied by swapping just three Asian students from the bottom two bands with three white students demoted from the top two.

Other models of equitable distribution across fixed and variable size sets are possible, but all of them show only marginal inequalities (Gomm, 1993). If we examine Ball's data in a similar way, we find that the extent of social-class inequality in band allocations of students in the same ability category is reduced to very small, and statistically insignificant, levels once account is taken of the effects of allocation to bands of students in the higher ability category (Gomm, 1994).

Another possible cause of deviation of actual from expected distributions is that teachers' decisions may be based on judgments about other characteristics of the students than ability, for example about their level of motivation, the extent to which their 'behaviour' is troublesome etc. Once again, this factor might well be treated as relevant under equity definition four. It could be argued that students' motivation, as indicated by their behaviour, is important in deciding who will make the best use of, or are most deserving of, a scarce educational opportunity; that it is unfair on able, well-motivated students to have to suffer disruption caused by able, but poorly motivated, ones; that teachers need to consider the behavioural mix of teaching groups to ensure that students who are likely to engage in disruptive behaviour are not placed together etc. It would not be very surprising if teachers took such considerations into account. Ball and Troyna do not do so, however; they treat them as representing a deviation from what is equitable, and thus as a form of indirect discrimination. What is important to emphasize is that whether this is so depends on the conception of equity one adopts.

Of course, it may be that teachers' judgments of ability and/or of other relevant features of the students are affected by the latter's social class or 'race'. This would be defined as discrimination by all of the equity assumptions we have considered. However, the problem is that we have no way of knowing whether this was the case on the basis of the sort of evidence which Ball and Troyna provide. To determine this, it would be necessary to have information about the way that selection decisions were made, particularly those relating to students of similar ability but from different social categories. With such data it might be possible to identify the considerations taken into account by teachers, and the extent to which these were influenced by social class and 'race'; though this would be by no means straightforward.

No studies of which we are aware provide direct information about this; though Wright (1986) does offer indirect evidence about allocation procedures in her study of two comprehensive schools in the Midlands. She produces quantitative evidence which is claimed to show the over-allocation of Asian and the under-allocation of Afro-Caribbean students to top sets, with white students being allocated as expected. As regards the allocation to sets of Asian students, this is a rather different picture from that presented by Troyna for Jayleigh; but Wright's analysis suffers from all the problems we have documented so far, plus some additional ones (Gomm, 1991). However, Wright does provide data from interviews with several year heads, the deputy head, and an educational psychologist, as well as some from a 'Third Year Options' meeting, in one of the schools, with a view to explaining Afro-Caribbean students' underachievement (Wright, 1986, pp. 162–5). These data suggest that students' 'behaviour' (in terms of conformity to, or deviance from, school rules and norms) was taken into account when teachers were selecting students for places in high-status groups. She also reports data from school records — about suspensions, parental contact for disciplinary reasons, etc. — and from discussions with students, to suggest that Afro-Caribbean students were more likely to be judged as behaving badly in school. The evidence she supplies is not conclusive, but the claim that teachers take account of such considerations in allocating students to sets is quite plausible. Of course, whether this constitutes unequal treatment depends on which of the four conceptions of equity we adopt. It would do so from the point of view of the first three, but not necessarily from that of the last. Moreover, Wright's evidence does not relate to *ethnic* inequality in this respect, only to inequality in relation to those students who are judged able but ruled out on grounds of 'behaviour'; and she fails to establish convincingly that Afro-Caribbean students are disproportionately represented in that category. In other words, while it may be that the teachers' assessments of these students' behaviour involved 'racial' bias, Wright's evidence does not show this.

We have looked at evidence concerning the allocation of students to different levels of course in terms of four definitions of equity which might be used to define inequality in selection procedures. In terms of the first, and simplest, evidence of inequality is revealed, especially in Ball's data; though even here it is marginal by some standards, and there are conceptual problems surrounding the definitions of social class and ethnicity. In terms of the second definition, there is also inequality, but it is much smaller and subject to potential error that could well eliminate it.[10] As regards the other two definitions, the information provided in the studies discussed does not allow us to decide whether social class or ethnic inequality exists, even in the cases investigated.

The studies by Ball, Troyna and Wright provide more detailed information and analysis than some others which have argued that there is discrimination in the allocation of students to bands or sets. For instance, in his work with the 'black sisters', Mac an Ghaill (1988) makes claims about 'racial' bias in the streaming systems of three schools primarily on the basis of the retrospective accounts of nine ex-students. He reports that 'Afro-Caribbean students were concentrated in the lower streams and remedial departments', and that 'the division between the "high-achieving" Asian and white students and the "low-achieving" Afro-Caribbeans was further reinforced by the process of demotions to lower streams, with the latter group being disproportionately selected' (p. 15). Mac an Ghaill is even less clear than Ball and Troyna about the precise nature of the claims he is making, and the data he presents are totally inadequate as evidence in support of any interpretation of them.[11]

Inequalities in the Distribution of Students across Subjects

Several studies have pointed to gender differences in the numbers of students studying particular subjects, especially in the final two years of compulsory schooling and beyond. Many secondary schools have allowed students to choose some subject options at the end of their third year, and to select a small number of subjects from a fairly wide range in the sixth form. Most research has focused on the first of these two forms of course choice.[12]

---

[10]   However, it may be of significance that the departures from what would be expected on the basis of measured ability that have been found within and across studies, while small, tend to be always in the same direction. This indicates that more thorough investigation is justified.
[11]   He provides more evidence in his study of Kilby School, in the same book, but this still falls well short of the detail that Ball and Troyna offer.
[12]   The extent of choice at this point may have been reduced in recent years, as a result of the introduction of the National Curriculum.

Gender differences in subject choice have been revealed in statistical data in school case studies (Riddell, 1992), in larger-scale surveys (Pratt *et al.*, 1984), and in DES/DFE statistics. There is little doubt about the validity of these data. More controversial are claims that schools actively channel boys and girls along different curriculum tracks. Several types of claim are made here, supported by different kinds of evidence.

Direct Discrimination

It has been argued that some schools do not allow boys and girls to study certain subjects. These claims are made, in the main, in studies conducted in the late 1960s and early 1970s, before the Sex Discrimination Act came into effect (see, for example, DES, 1975). These often present documentary evidence of school policy, or direct observational evidence of school practice from teachers. Moreover, in some studies these claims relate to a relatively large, and probably broadly representative, number of schools; and therefore provide fairly strong evidence that this practice was widespread.

We know of only one more recent study in which this type of claim is made. This is a study by Pratt *et al.* (1984), which involved a postal survey of 199 secondary schools. A number of questions were asked about their policy on equal opportunities, such as whether they had a 'rotational craft timetable' and whether they taught subjects in single-sex groups. The researchers used this evidence to support their conclusion that in most schools students were not excluded from subjects on grounds of sex. However, they reported that 13 per cent of schools answered 'yes' to the question 'Are there any subjects taken by pupils [. . .] where allocation [. . .] is wholly determined by sex?' (Pratt *et al.*, 1984, p. 69). On this basis, they claim that in a minority of schools a policy of exclusion continues, primarily in relation to craft subjects. This could be so, but it is worth noting that the question is potentially ambiguous. It is possible that some schools interpreted it to mean: 'Are there subjects where students are of one sex only'. Given this, the figure reported may over-represent the degree to which there were restrictions by sex placed on student choice of craft subjects.[13] These authors also report some intra-subject restrictions, notably in relation to physical education and sport (see Pratt *et al.*, 1984, p. 153).

Such policies clearly represent an inequality, but while the value-basis on which it is selected for attention is one which is now quite widely shared, it should nevertheless be made explicit. After all, it was probably not commonly accepted thirty or more years ago, and is not even yet a matter of complete public agreement. What is involved here is a conception of equity to the effect that all subjects within the curriculum should be equally open to both sexes: that girls are as entitled as boys to take traditionally male subjects, and that

---

[13] It should be noted, however, that Grafton *et al.*, state that in the school they studied 'needlework was described (in the tutors' guidelines) as being taken by girls only' (Grafton *et al.*, 1983, p. 156).

boys are entitled to take traditionally female subjects. This conception depends, of course, on value and factual assumptions about the significance of
sex roles and of biological and other differences between males and females.

Indirect Discrimination via the Organization of Option Schemes

A more common claim in recent research on gender is that schools make non-
traditional option choices more difficult by the way they organize their option
schemes. It is suggested that such schemes place constraints on students' free
choice, and that these restrict non-traditional choices more than traditional
ones. This can be illustrated by considering the study by Grafton *et al.* (1983)
of option choice in a co-educational comprehensive school in south-west England. In this school option choice occurred in a limited way at the beginning
of the first year, when students chose either cookery/needlework or metal-
work/woodwork; but a more substantial range of choice was available at the
end of the third year, when students selected five options from a range of
around twenty-five courses, one from each of five blocks.

The authors suggest that, in the first year, students were more likely to
take gender-traditional subjects because most of them, and their parents, were
unaware that choice was available, and because 'special applications' had to
be made for non-traditional choices since 'practical facilities were said to limit
numbers' (Grafton *et al.*, 1983, p. 155). In addition, they claim that at the end
of the third year 'the grouping of subjects (in fourth-year option blocks) made
it less likely that boys and girls would choose a subject which was untypical'
(Grafton *et al.*, 1983, p. 158).

Clearly, there is an element of constraint in the way in which craft subjects
were organized in the first three years. For one thing, it was apparently not
possible to combine cookery with metalwork, needlework with woodwork,
etc. However, as regards the authors' suggestion that children and parents
were not made aware that choice was possible, this claim is based on only
'one teacher's opinion' (Grafton *et al.*, 1983, p. 155), and this is rather weak
evidence.

Grafton *et al*'s argument about the third-year option choice process is
supported by documentary evidence which shows the subjects available in the
five option blocks from which students made their choices. The authors point
out that, because some subjects only occurred in one block, and students were
restricted to one choice per block, some subject combinations were unavail-
able: 'needlework and commercial skills competed with woodwork and metalwork, [. . .] family and child, typing and commerce competed with motor
mechanics and technical drawing [. . .]' (p. 156). This evidence clearly dem-
onstrates that non-traditional choices were somewhat restricted by the option
system. However, it does not establish that these were any more restricted
than some traditional choices. Subjects were available to students irrespective
of gender (with the probable exception of needlework), and whilst some
choices involving a combination of a traditional and non-traditional option

were ruled out, so too were some combinations of traditional choices. For example, students could not study woodwork *and* metalwork, family and child *and* typing, motor mechanics *and* technical drawing, rural science *and* citizenship, or commercial skills *and* needlework.

In effect, Grafton *et al.*, are assessing the option-choice system in their study school by comparing it with a system which would give students a completely free choice. Yet, some constraint on the combinations of courses which can be chosen is inevitable in any option-choice system, given the logistics of organizing the timetable; and from some points of view such constraint is desirable, relating for example to the requirement that students experience a balanced curriculum.[14] Furthermore, it would be surprising if schools did not construct their option-choice schemes on the basis of assumptions about which combinations of subjects would be more and less popular. Indeed, assuming that their judgments about this are accurate, not to do so would increase overall the extent to which students found it impossible to opt for the courses they wanted.

In any case, the authors recognize that a completely free-choice system would not necessarily increase the likelihood that boys and girls would choose 'untypical' subjects. Indeed, they note Sweden's policy of compulsory allocation to courses, but suggest that even this is unlikely to achieve very much without substantial changes to the sexual division of labour in society at large (Grafton *et al.*, 1983, p. 168). There is an ambiguity here, then, about the basis on which the evaluative description of option-choice schemes is being carried out.

This ambiguity is also present in Riddell's (1992) study of option choice in two comprehensive schools. Once again, she argues that the schools claim to offer free choice, but actually do not do so.[15] Indeed, she describes free choice as 'a legitimating device for differing educational outcomes' (Riddell, 1992, p. 35). At the same time, she reports that 'in interviews the majority of pupils confirmed that they were able to study the subject they originally chose' (Riddell, 1992, p. 60). There is an apparent contradiction here; in effect she seems to operate on the assumption that students' choices cannot have been *truly* free unless they resulted in an equal distribution by sex across courses. Deviance from this is taken to reflect the influence of patriarchal assumptions (see also Deem, 1986, p. 180).

Once again, here we have an evaluative description without the value and factual assumptions on which it rests being made explicit. It is recognized and documented that students' choices are for the most part rather 'traditional', and that this reflects the orientations of many parents; but it is implied that schools must work to alter these preferences. Even aside from the ethical

[14] In another study of option choice, Tomlinson (1987, pp. 98–9) points to an inequality in the extent to which different ethnic groups study a 'minimum balanced curriculum'.
[15] This is a commonplace of sociological studies of option choice: see Hammersley, 1991.

issues involved here, there are also factual questions about whether 'free' choices on the part of students would ever produce equal proportions of each sex taking different subjects. Doubts on this score would, of course, arise from traditional views about biological differences between the sexes and their significance, but could also be derived from within feminism. Some feminists argue that there are fundamental differences between males and females in their life interests, whether these are socio-historical in origin or more permanent in character.[16] To the extent that such differences exist, one might expect to find contrasting attitudes towards subjects on the part of girls and boys which would be resistant to change by schools.

Indirect Discrimination via Course Presentation

Another claim sometimes made in research concerned with option choice is that subjects are presented in gender-biased ways to students: in documentary material or in teachers' oral presentations. For instance, Riddell (1992) argues that in the schools she studied the presentation of domestic craft subjects 'constantly emphasised their traditional feminine concerns', and gives the example of a CSE cookery course which was referred to in option material as 'hostess cookery', and that covered 'entertaining, personal grooming, clothes and fabric care' (Riddell, 1992. p. 51). She also argues that, in both schools, physics 'was characterised as an abstract, mathematical subject connected essentially with a mechanistic view of the world', and that no attempt was made to present its 'human and social dimension'. Moreover, it was portrayed as 'an important qualification for technical apprenticeships, medicine or engineering, all of which, with the possible exception of medicine, are likely to be regarded as male areas of work' (p. 50).

Riddell also provides an instance of gender bias from an options talk. Here a teacher encourages girls to take non-traditional courses, but the author argues that because he suggests that the girls underestimate their own ability the teacher is operating on 'a deficit model' of them, in which they are 'characterised as narrow-minded and conservative' (p. 63). In a more limited analysis, drawing on his study of a multi-ethnic secondary school, Gillborn also presents evidence of gender discrimination in a teacher's option talk:

Field notes:
3D's form tutor has arranged for Mr Flint (a physical science specialist) to tell the pupils what the course is about in the fourth and fifth year. As he begins, Flint shouts across at a group of girls sitting at the back of the class to stop talking. He has already succeeded in quietening them with 'I haven't got time to wait for you lot'. However, he continues very aggressively,

---

[16]   See Alcoff's 1988 discussion of 'cultural feminism'; and, for additional examples, see Gilligan, 1982 and Irigaray, 1985.

> *'One thing I hate and detest is ignorant females . . . and this*
> *school is lousy with them these days.* Suppose I better address myself
> to you lads. Don't want to see that ugly lot in my lab.' (Gillborn,
> 1990b, p. 168) (tape transcript)

Gillborn argues that the teacher's statement 'effectively exclude(d) all girls
from "his" subject'. He reports that such 'overt sexism' was rare, but claims that
'throughout the options process [. . .] teachers acted in ways which carried
similar (though implicit) messages about the gender-specific nature of certain
curricular areas' (p. 168).

As we saw in Chapter 3, even as a descriptive — though value-relevant
— category, indirect discrimination can be defined in different ways. Some
definitions would require evidence that subject presentations were motivated
by conscious judgments or unconscious assumptions about the differential
abilities or motivations of girls and boys. It is not clear whether the examples
discussed were intended to fit this definition, but they vary a good deal as
regards credibility in these terms, on the basis of the evidence offered.

The 'hostess cookery' example is a relatively clear case. The description
of the course explicitly assumes that girls rather than boys will take it, and it
seems reasonable to conclude that this was the assumption of whoever formulated the course description. The example provided by Gillborn might also be
taken to indicate that Mr Flint believed girls were 'ignorant' about physics.
However, there are some problems with this interpretation. Contrary to what
Gillborn claims, Mr Flint does not 'effectively exclude' all girls from physics.
He states that the particular girls in that class, or some of them, are not wanted
in his lessons. And, while he declares that he hates 'ignorant females' and that
the school is 'lousy with them', he does not claim that all females are 'ignorant', even as regards physics. Of course, there are also some important general
issues about the interpretation of verbal data here. Whether Flint's comments
can be taken to reflect his attitudes depends to some degree on their discursive
function. They could have been a 'jocular gripe' (Coser, 1959) and/or they may
have been an attempt to preserve some interest on the part of the boys in a
situation where he had concluded that the girls were not interested. This might
count against the idea that he was operating on the basis of a stereotype of
girls; though we should note that jokes often reveal underlying attitudes. Further evidence is required here, about this teacher's perspective and behaviour
in other circumstances, before we can come to any sound conclusion regarding whether this example represents indirect discrimination, in the sense of
being based on the assumption that boys are better at or more suited to
physics than girls.

This is also true of the example from a public options talk which Riddell
presents. A literal interpretation of what Mr Flint says about 'ignorant females'
would certainly imply that he operated on the basis of a deficit model of some
proportion of the girls in the school. In the case that Riddell cites, however,
a literal reading would not produce the deficit model she claims, since the

teacher is arguing that girls are capable of doing 'non-traditional' subjects and that any lack of confidence on their part can and should be overcome. Indeed, here we appear to have a teacher doing what is required by many equal opportunities policies: encouraging girls not to be restricted in their choices by gender stereotypes of subjects or by underestimations of their own ability. If his behaviour is to be described convincingly as premissed on a deficit conception of girls, a good deal more information about this teacher's perspective would be required; as well as clarification of what would and would not constitute evidence for a deficit model.

The other example cited by Riddell, relating to the presentation of physics in option booklets, does not seem to be a case of indirect discrimination in the sense we have been discussing. Nor does the author claim that the descriptions of physics were formulated on the basis of the assumption that the subject would be more attractive to boys than to girls. Instead, Riddell argues that these descriptions constitute indirect discrimination on the grounds that in practice they will have the effect of attracting boys and deterring girls. Once again, though, there are some interpretational problems. The author supports her claim by pointing out that physics is described in the options booklet as the study of 'heat, light, sound, electricity, mechanics, waves, radioactivity and atomic physics' (Riddell, 1992, p. 50). Yet it is not clear how this implies that the subject is abstract and mathematical, that it involves a mechanistic view of the world, or even that it has no 'human and social dimension'. There is an implicit comparison being made here with some alternative, and purportedly more appropriate, description; but this remains implicit.

There is also the problem of how far what is being questioned is the presentation of physics or the current nature of that subject (generally or specifically as taught in schools). So it may be that the issue is how far the subject should be changed in order to make it more appealing to girls. Other considerations would clearly be involved in any such decision; and these could not be overruled by an argument about the role of masculinist assumptions in physics, without some account of what is intrinsically masculine about the abstract, the mathematical, and the mechanistic. In any event, these are not matters which sociological research can resolve, in our view. What *is* important, though, is that the value assumptions involved in any account of the nature and/or presentation of subjects as discriminatory are spelled out. This is not done here.

Much the same problem arises with Riddell's criticism of subject presentations for linking subjects to particular occupations. Here what schools do is being evaluated on the basis of some notion of what would be the most effective strategy for attracting students to non-traditional options. Again, the evaluative standard remains implicit, and the validity of the criticism is by no means incontestable. It could be argued, for instance, that schools should be encouraging more girls to go into technical apprenticeships and engineering. If so, there may be nothing wrong with linking courses to these post-school destinations. And it also needs to be remembered that encouraging non-traditional choices on the part of students is not the only consideration teachers must take into account in presenting options. Another relevant one is attracting enough students for a course to be viable, and there are others too; so that there may be conflicting priorities here.

Irrespective of how 'indirect discrimination' is defined, claims about it must establish that there are differential effects on the relevant categories of student. There are two requirements here. First, it is necessary to show that the theoretical assumptions concerning the effects of a course presentation are reasonable. In the 'hostess cookery' and Mr Flint examples these are sufficiently plausible at face value, in our judgment. In both cases, there is the message that one sex, or some members of it, are not welcome to apply. However, the theoretical assumptions are more questionable in the other examples. For instance, Riddell's claims about the presentation of physics rely in part on the assumption that the girls in the schools she studied were less attracted to the abstract and the mathematical. This may be so, but it has not been convincingly demonstrated.

The second requirement is that the causal contribution of course presentations is shown in the cases studied. This is not a condition which is met very effectively in any of the examples discussed. Thus, while Gillborn, Riddell and others show that gendered patterns of subject choice prevail in schools, they do not establish that subject presentations make a significant contribution to these. Gillborn provides no such evidence, and Riddell offers it in only one case. In relation to the oral presentation which she claims was based on a deficit view of girls, she discusses the girls' reactions. She reports that:

> Reactions from pupils to these talks suggested that girls recognized the female deficit model which informed the school's conception of equal opportunities and resented it. For instance, after Mr Lill's talk Bernadette Coles commented: 'They don't make the boys do needlework, so why should we be made to do physics?' (Riddell, 1992, p. 63).

This is hardly convincing evidence, however. The girl's complaint does not seem to be about a 'deficit model' but rather about a perceived double standard. It is a reaction against attempts to dissuade her from taking the options she has chosen. Indeed, it could be taken to show the resistance of some girls to equal opportunities policies.

Most of the research in this area focuses primarily on the identification of messages in the presentation of subjects, making claims about discrimination on the basis of symptomatic, and sometimes questionable, readings of data about these presentations. It is largely assumed by the authors that the messages they identify are received by students, and by a substantial proportion of them; and that the latter respond by being 'turned off' some subjects and/or 'turned on' to others. This lack of attention to the links between subject presentations and students' choices is a major weakness. Discursive implications of subject presentations tend to be treated as if they were well-established effects. But, as Kress (1993) has argued, the critical analysis of ideology requires investigation not just of the text itself, but also of its production and its reception.[17]

Indirect Discrimination via Teacher Advice

Another claim sometimes made in the literature is that the personal advice about option choice given by teachers to students varies according to gender; or according to whether option choices are 'traditional' or 'non-traditional'. This claim is usually supported with evidence from the direct observation of teacher–student discussions. Riddell (1992, pp. 54–7), for example, observed all the interviews of students in two tutor groups, and presents summary data from eleven of these. She argues that there were subtle differences between the advice given to boys and girls, and that 'pupils' subject choices and educational and occupational aspirations were accepted unquestioningly when these were in line with traditional gender stereotypes' (p. 59). She concludes from this that 'some channelling by the school was taking place during the course of the option choice interviews'. However, she also notes that 'there was little evidence of parents or pupils resisting'. She explains this in terms of students having 'already effectively internalised the school's expectations of their future performance' (p. 60).

Unlike Riddell, Gillborn (1990b) gives an example of the treatment of non-traditional choices. He reports that one form tutor questioned the option choices of thirteen of the students in his class; and he claims that, in the two cases where the student's choice 'conflicted with gender stereotypes', 'the tone of the enquiry was noticeably harsher' and the statement "It's up to you"' (p. 169) was omitted.[18] He describes one of these cases in detail as an illustration of the way teachers commonly queried non-traditional option choices, thereby 'reinforcing gender stereotypes' (p. 168).

While Riddell claims that option choice interviews 'channelled' students (p. 60), she seems effectively to concede that the advice given by teachers did not make much contribution to the pattern of subject choice, that this had already been secured by previous socialization. Gillborn makes greater claims for such a contribution. Nevertheless, in both studies we are asked to rely on the researcher's detection of 'subtle differences', 'noticeably harsher tones' etc. And there is also the question of how far these differences represent systematic variation in teachers' responses to those making 'traditional' and 'non-traditional' choices. With relatively small numbers of cases, it is difficult to rule out the effects of other factors, and also to judge whether the examples discussed were representative of teacher advice in general in these schools. More

[17] Whitty (1985, p. 43) makes much the same point about research on school textbooks. On the rediscovery of 'reception' in cultural studies, see Morley, 1992.
[18] He suggests that this statement was designed to emphasize students' freedom of choice; though it could also be interpreted as 'be it on your own head', in other words as a renunciation of responsibility on the part of the teacher.

convincing would have been an investigation of substantial samples of students making traditional and non-traditional choices, and careful comparison of the advice offered in each case, as well as of students' interpretations of, and reactions to, such advice.

In effect, Gillborn tries to 'read off' the functioning of teachers' advice from its content. And the case which he discusses in detail is ambiguous. He assumes that the student had intentionally made a non-traditional choice; but he recognizes that the teacher believed that the student 'must have misunderstood the option pattern', and it should be noted that the response of the student is indeed compatible with just such a misunderstanding. Towards the end of the exchange the student says:

Ashley: Hang on a minute sir, I — No I want to do that.
Teacher: Woodwork?
Ashley: Yes sir.
(Gillborn, 1990b, p. 169)

Gillborn rules out the teacher's interpretation, perhaps because he finds it implausible, or perhaps on the grounds that any challenge to a 'non-traditional' choice amounts to sexism, whatever its overt motivation. As he notes 'discriminatory attitudes and actions are not always explicit; they may be part of an unconscious system of beliefs [. . .]' (p. 165). But he does not address the methodological problems involved in identifying such unconscious attitudes, and his interpretation of this incident is inconclusive without further information about the teacher's perspective (and also, of course, about the student's).

There is, of course, some research which has been concerned entirely with documenting teachers' attitudes, either regarding the importance of their subject to students of particular sexes, or towards equal-opportunities policies and their implementation. On this basis, it is often claimed that teachers see science and technical subjects as more important to boys (for example Spear, 1985, 1987) or that they are generally sceptical about equal-opportunities policies (for example Pratt, 1985). It is then suggested that such attitudes are an important influence on the way teachers present their subjects and on the advice they give to students.

Sometimes the data used to support these claims are quantitative, taking the form of the number or proportion of teachers in a sample agreeing or disagreeing with statements presented to them (Pratt, 1985) or giving particular ratings to certain subjects (Spear, 1985, 1987). The main problem with these data is that because of the method used they may tend to give a rather oversimplified picture of teachers' attitudes. That picture may be in large part a product of the questions asked, the way teachers interpret them, and the response categories available. For example, the survey reported by Spear (1985) (conducted as part of the 'Girls into Science and Technology' project) invited a sample of sixty-seven teachers to rate on a four-point scale the importance of technical subjects to the education of boys and girls, and asked a second sample of 103 teachers to rate the importance of a technical qualification to students' future careers. The survey concluded that the teachers tended to see technical subjects as more important to boys. However, there is a strong possibility that many teachers replied by describing what they thought the reality of education and careers for boys and girls actually was, rather than how they felt it should be. This reflects a general tendency in this type of research to confound teachers' descriptive and normative responses.

Some researchers have provided qualitative data, in the form of quotations from interviews or conversations, to support claims about teachers' attitudes. These data may provide a more detailed picture. However, there is a tendency in such work to report and highlight the views of a minority who express reservations about equal-opportunities policy and practice, or who express gender-differentiated views of subjects; and sometimes to generalize on the basis of this minority to a large number of teachers. In Gillborn's study, for example, the rather sexist view of one male craft teacher is the only evidence presented to support the claim that 'many teachers' in the school he studied had beliefs about the gender-specific nature of their subjects (Gillborn, 1990b, p. 168).

Moreover, on their own, both questionnaire and interview data of this kind provide rather limited support for the argument that teachers actually do give different advice or encouragement to boys and girls in their choice of subjects. It is entirely possible for individuals to have reservations about equal-opportunities policies (particularly those which stress positive discrimination) and yet to act in ways which do not channel students along traditional subject routes. Teachers may even have strong views that certain subjects are more appropriate for boys or for girls, and yet not offer differentiated advice; or they may not be in a position to offer such advice. In short, teachers' attitudes are not a strong indicator of their actions and of actual school processes; though they are a relevant form of evidence, and sometimes constitute an essential complement to observational data.

We can conclude this discussion of the extent to which schools channel boys and girls into different curriculum tracks with some more general points. First, while most of these studies treat the gender imbalance in option choices as representing 'male and female curricula' (Riddell, 1992, p. 10), as preparing each sex for quite different futures (Measor and Sikes, 1992, p. 71), what is actually involved is two substantially overlapping distributions; with most, if not all, girls taking a majority of courses which boys also take (and vice versa). Considerable exaggeration of the differences in the curriculum presented to girls and boys by schools is frequently involved.

Second, it is important to notice that while researchers in this area typically claim that discriminatory actions channelling students into gender-stereotyped courses are frequent, the instances they cite are few in number. Questionable generalizations are involved even *within* the cases studied. This is a serious weakness given the nature of the claims made. There is also the question of the relative causal contribution of school processes, compared with that of other factors operating on students' choices. It seems likely that students' conceptions of what they are good at, what they like etc. are among the most important factors shaping their choices. This is easily forgotten when reading the research we have been discussing. It is thoroughly obscured, for example, when Riddell declares that her 'central focus is the way in which option choice is used by the school to bring about traditional gender divisions in the curriculum' (Riddell, 1992, p. 21).

Of course, we can treat students' option preferences and judgments about their own abilities as themselves shaped by various influences, including school experience; and this is what Riddell and Gillborn do. But in this they are adopting a particular evaluative standard as a basis for explaining option choices, one that needs to be made explicit, since it is by no means the only reasonable one. Moreover, it is unclear how powerful a role schools do or could play in shaping student preferences; in comparison with home background, peer-group influence, the impact of the mass media etc.[19]

Finally, it is important to notice that the claims made by these authors, as with those discussed in the previous section, are evaluative not just factual. Thus, Riddell (1992, p. 17) frames her central research problem as 'why girls and boys apparently consented to a process which would be to the long term detriment of many, and was likely to be particularly damaging to working class girls'. And, in answering this question, she claims to describe 'the way in which the process of option choice was managed by the schools in order to promote an ideology of free choice and open access whilst at the same time selecting pupils on to particular courses on the basis of sex, class and achievement'. According to her, 'both schools [. . .] attempted to nod in the direction of equal opportunities', but '[. . .] the messages conveyed reveal a weak understanding of the issues, and amount to no more than tokenism.' (Riddell, 1992, p. 37). These evaluative conclusions are presented as if they were merely factual ones, with no argumentative support provided for the value judgments involved. Indeed, the specific assumptions about equity on which they rely are not even stated. This is despite Riddell's claim to 'adhere to the principle of reflexivity, making explicit my political and theoretical position and their impact on the process of data collection' (Riddell, 1992, p. 17).

To summarize this discussion, a variety of claims have been made about the ways in which school processes channel boys and girls along distinct curriculum tracks, these being supported by varying degrees and kinds of evidence. In general, though, there has been a failure to make explicit the value principles on which the descriptions and explanations are based, and to establish that discrimination was involved in the examples discussed and that

---

[19]   The best evidence about this comes from the GIST project, suggesting that changes in school procedures have a rather limited impact, and are not likely to bring about the sort of dramatic transformation, desired by the authors discussed here (See Whyte, 1986). However, this is certainly not to suggest that such changes in procedures are not worthwhile.

it occurred on a large scale. There has also been a tendency to move to evaluative conclusions as if these were based entirely on the empirical data or the theoretical analysis provided.

Assessing the Effects of Selection Processes

As we noted earlier, besides arguments about inequality in the process of selection itself, there are also claims about unequal *effects* of allocation to different levels and types of course.

Discriminatory Consequences of Allocation to Low-level Courses

There are three routes by which differential allocation to levels of course has been claimed to influence students' chances of educational success: through determining subsequent school careers and examination entry; through effects on student motivation; and through the consequences of unequal resource allocation for student learning. In all three cases, what is put forward is a mechanism or process which reinforces or amplifies social class or ethnic inequalities in selection procedures.

Allocation to Different Levels of Course as Determining School Careers and Examination Entry

Here the streaming, banding, or set system in secondary schools is presented as largely determining the subsequent careers of students, so that once they have been assigned to a lower level of course there is little chance of them later being promoted. And this is consequential, it is suggested, because at the end of secondary schooling entry for examinations (in terms of number and level) is decided in large part on the basis of students' band or set placement.

Thus, Ball (1986, p. 85) argues that 'the separation of pupils into streams or bands or sets has as powerful a predictive effect on their school careers and post-school opportunities as did earlier separation into grammar and secondary modern schools'. He claims that this predictive effect arises from the 'phenomenological power' of streaming, banding and setting; that stream, band, or set membership affects teachers' perceptions of students, and thereby their treatment of them in the classroom and their decisions about the levels of fourth- and fifth-year courses which they are allowed to study.

However, while Ball (1981) establishes that teachers at Beachside do have very different conceptions of the typical student in each band, he does not show that these typifications are inaccurate or that teachers rely entirely on them in their treatment of students. He certainly does not establish that they are 'preconceived' or that they 'represent powerful limitations on the sorts of social and academic identity' to which students can achieve or aspire (Ball, 1986, p. 85).

Troyna (1991a) provides a further example of this argument. He claims that at Jayleigh, once the children had been allocated to sets early in their first year, their educational futures were largely determined because of the rigidity of the set system. He argues that there was little movement of students among the sets between the first and third years, and that allocation to fourth- and fifth-year sets was largely determined by students' position in the lower-school set system. And, finally, set position determined entry for examinations, in that those in the lower sets in the fifth year were not entered.

Each of the elements of this argument requires evidence. First, the rigidity of the set system needs to be established. As with initial allocation to sets, this can be assessed on the basis of several different principles. For example, we could define rigidity in terms of absolute amounts of movement between sets, or in terms of the degree to which movement would seem to be warranted by changes in students' relative achievement levels. In relation to movement between sets in the first three years at Jayleigh, Troyna relies on the first of these principles (perhaps because the data were not available to apply the second); though without indicating that it is not the only criterion. He reports that: 'some 79 per cent of pupils were in the same mathematics set in year 1 as they were in year 3'. How one interprets this depends on what scale one adopts, in other words on what counts as rigidity.[20] But, whatever scale is used, it seems to us to be misleading to describe a system in which there is movement on the part of around 20 per cent of students over the three years as 'almost inflexible' (Troyna, 1991a, p. 369); especially when it appears that around 80 per cent of students were 'correctly' allocated to sets if junior-school ratings are taken as the benchmark.

As regards allocation to fourth-and fifth-year sets, Troyna adopts a different approach, using performance in the end of third-year examination as the base-line. Thus, he notes that 'some pupils in set D/DD performed equally well as their counterparts in higher ability sets [but] were not permitted to move up in the fourth year to set 6 or higher; a move which would have enabled them to sit English at GCSE examination level [. . .]'. And he concludes from this that:

> results in the third year examination in English were used selectively. That is to say, they were used to strengthen existing categorisations of pupils in the hierarchy of sets rather than as a means of modifying these groupings. (Troyna, 1991a, p. 369).

Much the same issues apply here as in our earlier discussion of allocation to sets on the basis of ability. In particular, the question arises as to whether examination results are a better measure of ability than other sources of information about students. There are arguments in support of this, especially when

---

[20]   The problem of scaling involved here is similar to that involved in assessing the level of social mobility; see Saunders, 1995.

what is being predicted is GCSE examination success. But there are also arguments against it, to do with coursework elements in assessment, the differences between external and internal examinations etc. And even if we accept that examination results are the most accurate predictor, what Troyna is pointing to as evidence of discrimination is an unspecified number of marginal cases where students' scores were equal but allocation to sets differed. As we saw earlier, this may often result from constraints on the size of sets, as well as from other considerations that would be defined as discriminatory under some conceptions of equity but not others.

Troyna presents much the same picture, in much the same way, in relation to mathematics sets: 'pupils in set D/DD in year 3 who obtained the same scores as pupils in higher year 3 mathematics sets did not move up to higher sets in [. . .] year 4'. And he concludes from this that 'set placement in year 3 was the pre-eminent criterion in determining who was "capable" of sitting the GCSE examination in mathematics' (p. 371). Yet his conclusion does not follow from his premiss. Once again, without justification, he is reading off bias in the allocation process on the basis of evidence about outcomes.

A second important component of Troyna's argument is the claim that examination entry was determined by set position. Here what he claims seems simply to be false. While he refers to the top six sets as 'the GCSE sets' and the others as 'the non-GCSE sets' (p. 369), it appears that some students from the lower sets did take GCSE. So, while placement in such sets may have reduced the chances of taking GCSE, it did not eliminate it; and it reduced it less for Asians than for whites (Gomm, 1994, p. 213). Over and above this, though, a crucial assumption of Troyna's analysis is that some proportion of those not entered for GCSEs would have passed them. Yet he provides no evidence that would allow us to judge this. For all these reasons, his claim that the set system denied the chances of GCSE success to some significant number of students is unconvincing.

Finally, there is the question of how far the operation of the set system amplified ethnic differences. Troyna does not provide complete data about the effects of movement among sets on the proportions of Asians and whites in the top sets. However, it is clear from the data he does present that the lack of movement of those in lower sets who scored the same as those in higher sets applied to both white and Asian students, and that most of the mobility there was between third- and fourth-year sets involved South Asian students moving upwards, presumably because of their performance in the third-year examination: 28 per cent of Asian students were upwardly mobile as against 18 per cent of whites (Gomm, 1994, p. 83). Little or no amplification of whatever ethnic inequality Asian students suffered seems to be involved here; indeed the effect may even have been the reverse.

In general, then, studies making this first type of claim about the effects of differentiation have not been effective in establishing that students' subsequent school careers have been determined, and in such a way as to reinforce social class or ethnic inequalities.

Differentiation as Producing Polarization in Student Attitudes

The argument here is that the stigma of allocation to low-status courses has a negative impact on students' attitudes to school and level of motivation, and thereby on their educational achievement. This is argued most strongly in the case studies conducted by Hargreaves (1967), Lacey (1970), Ball (1981) and Abraham (1989a). These researchers investigated a streamed boys' secondary modern and grammar school, and mixed banded and setted comprehensives, respectively.[21] They claim that, in these schools, students who were denied academic status in the formal system of differentiation created anti-school, and in Hargreaves' case 'delinquent', subcultures that allowed them to gain status in non-academic ways. And it is suggested that this, in turn, reduced their levels of academic achievement from what might otherwise have been expected.

The key descriptive component of this differentiation–polarization theory — that students on low-status courses have more negative attitudes towards school than those in high-status groups — is supported in these studies by data which compare the attitudes and behaviour of students across streams, bands, and sets. For instance, Hargreaves provides data about fourth-year students in four streams at Lumley; Ball compares the students in a band 1 and a band 2 form in the second year at Beachside; Lacey provides observational and quantitative data over the five years of Hightown students' careers; while Abraham compares fourth-year students from different 'set-score bands' (which he worked out by summing students' set number for English and Maths and dividing students' scores into three bands).

Hargreaves provides the most substantial amount of data, both quantitative and qualitative, to demonstrate the contrast in attitudes and behaviour. This evidence gives convincing support to his claim that, at Lumley, students in low-status groups tend to be less committed to school and to academic work than those in high-status groups; a claim that is, in any case, fairly plausible. He also shows how these polarized attitudes structure the friendship groups and the informal status hierarchies within each stream.

The other authors provide less comprehensive evidence about contrasting attitudes within any particular year-group, but still present enough to make a convincing case; with the possible exception of Abraham. He offers two main types of evidence. First, responses to a questionnaire completed by 127 fourth-year students, showing that students in higher set-score bands tended to spend more time on English and Maths homework. Second, there is evidence, obtained from the school records of 119 of these students (covering years one to four), that those in the lower bands were more likely to be reported for missed assignments and for bad behaviour, but less likely to be reported for good work or behaviour. Abraham also notes a significant correlation between the

---

[21] Hightown Grammar moved to a set system during the course of Lacey's research, though it retained an express stream. Beachside changed to mixed-ability grouping while Ball was studying it.

number of missed assignment reports and the number of bad behaviour notes received by students.

Abraham himself recognizes the problems with these indicators. He points out that his data on homework refer to only two subjects, and that variations in the amount of time spent on homework may be as much an indicator of differences in the homework teachers set as of student attitudes. He also notes that some of the variation in the number of missed assignments and bad-behaviour reports may be produced by differences in teachers' reporting policies rather than differences in students' attitudes. Nevertheless, he assumes a fairly strong relationship between these indicators and student attitudes. This seems probable, but more direct evidence of students' attitudes would have been welcome.[22] So, while Abraham's data point in the same direction as those of Hargreaves, Lacey and Ball, they give rather less convincing support for differentiation–polarization theory, particularly as regards whether setting has the same effect as streaming. Abraham himself suggests that the effect is likely to be weaker (Abraham, 1989a, p. 76), and this implies that more comprehensive and detailed data would be required to detect it.

The second element of the argument presented by these authors is causal or explanatory in character: it is claimed that these polarized student attitudes are the result of the denial of status and of consequent 'status frustration' induced by differentiation.[23] This claim does have some theoretical plausibility. Much sociological literature has highlighted the importance of the pursuit of status in human societies and the tendency of those treated as low status to reject the values on which status allocation is based. Moreover, social psychology has suggested that people sometimes tend to adopt the attitudes of others towards them and to behave accordingly.[24] It is certainly possible that the message communicated by allocation to low-status groups could reduce students' commitment to school values and motivation to succeed, and that allocation to high-status groups has the opposite effect (though it is worth remembering that people do not always react in these ways).

At the same time, we must recognize that there are other plausible explanations for the polarization of students' attitudes. One possibility is that students with negative attitudes tended to be placed on lower-level courses, and those with positive attitudes in the higher groups; and that over time movement

---

[22] He does provide some questionnaire data on attitudes for a small sample of students.

[23] The authors do not always restrict themselves to differentiation–polarization theory as a basis for explaining the polarized attitudes they found. Hargreaves, in particular, uses a variety of explanations (see, for example, Hargreaves, 1967, pp. 165–75). However, we will concentrate on differentiation–polarization theory here.

[24] It ought to be remembered, though, that the findings of research in this area are rather mixed, see Rogers, 1982, Ch. 2. It is quite common to find appeal being made in the literature to Rosenthal and Jacobson's (1968) study, without any attention to the results of subsequent experimental and quasi-experimental studies; see, for example, Wright, 1992b, p. 12. For a critical assessment of the role of teachers expectations in the underachievement of Afro-Caribbean students, see Short, 1985.

between streams, bands, or sets increased these concentrations of students with contrasting attitudes. In other words, it could be argued that students' attitudes were the *cause* of their allocation to high- and low-status courses, rather than the effect. This might have happened directly, if such attitudes were taken into account when teachers decided group allocations; or it may have occurred indirectly, because students' attitudes influenced their academic work and performance.

This alternative explanation poses the strongest threat in relation to Hargreaves' study. He provides little evidence with which to assess whether the causal relationship implied by differentiation–polarization theory may actually have operated in the opposite direction. Indeed, in his penultimate chapter he reports that:

> there is a constant movement of boys between streams. Those with positive orientations towards the values of the school will tend over the four years to converge on the higher streams; and those with negative orientations will tend to converge on the lower streams [. . .] (so that) boys with similar values and attitudes are drawn together by the selective process. (Hargreaves, 1967, p. 169).

He treats this as one factor contributing to the process of subculture formation, but it is an explanation which is potentially in competition with differentiation–polarization theory.

By contrast, Lacey's study provides the strongest evidence for this theory. The students entering the school seem likely to have been very committed to academic success and to school values. For the most part, they had been the top students in their primary schools, and Lacey reports that their commitment was visible in their enthusiastic participation within the school as first years (Lacey, 1970, pp. 50–2). This suggests that the subsequent polarity in attitudes between streams which Lacey documents was not the product of pre-existing differences in attitude. Moreover, he provides evidence to support the chronology of cause and effect assumed by differentiation–polarization theory, documenting polarization over time from the point of differentiation.

Another explanation for polarization in attitudes which competes with differentiation–polarization theory is that differences in students' attitudes are caused by external cultural influences, though these would need to have an increasingly differential effect as students move through their secondary-school careers. In this way, some students (perhaps mainly working-class) might become more hostile to school and/or others (perhaps mainly middle-class) might become more positive. If this were so, to the extent that working-class students tend to be concentrated in lower-level courses and middle-class students in higher-level courses, this would produce a process of polarization over time. Given our knowledge of the impact of social-class culture on student attitudes to school this theory has some plausibility. Additional data to those provided by the studies we have discussed would be required to show what contribution, if any, this makes to the polarization in attitude towards school which they found.

Overall, then, these studies provide quite strong evidence, not just for the existence of polarized attitudes but also for the operation of a differentiation–polarization effect; at least in the context of streaming and banding. The quality and variety of the evidence provided here represents a sharp contrast with that which is characteristic of most other research on educational inequalities in schools. So too does the care with which arguments are developed and presented.

Differential Educational Provision

The other route by which allocation to different level courses is claimed to have an unequal effect is through variation in educational provision: it is often suggested that students on higher-level courses receive more and/or better resources than those on lower-level courses. In this way, the educational achievement of lower-status groups is restricted, whereas that of high-status groups is enhanced. This argument features in several of the studies we have mentioned.

Hargreaves (1967), for example, argues that the educational experience of lower-stream classes was very different from that of the top stream. He supports this with several types of evidence. He presents details from the school timetable showing that fourth-year C and D stream classes were more likely to be taught by younger teachers with poorer qualifications, less experience and lower status in terms of allowances, whom he claims were 'less competent', notably in having weaker discipline (Hargreaves, 1967, pp. 96–8 and 102). Hargreaves also provides a summary comparison, which appears to be based on teacher and student interviews, of the treatment of 4A and 4D students in the third year. 3A, he claims, were encouraged to develop 'strong group loyalties' and a 'wish to excel', whereas 3D were 'subjected to depressing and inhibiting forces' (p. 99). This differential treatment is illustrated by a description of the form teacher of 3D who wasted considerable time locking equipment away and getting it out again. Furthermore, this teacher's approach in mathematics:

> was based on the correct assumption that most of the pupils in 3D were far from expert at the theory or practice of simple mathematical calculations, and had not fully memorized the multiplication tables. His method was thus to take each pupil back to the most basic mathematical computations and allow him to progress from that point. This meant that few of the pupils were doing the same work at the same time, whereas in 3A the slow boys were forced to keep up with the rate the teacher imposed. Most of the boys worked from text books which gave endless lists of repetitive exercises. Any mistake was penalized by repetition of the page of work. Thus, one slight error

> would lead to a considerable delay in the boy's progress. It is hardly
> surprising that most of the boys failed to make progress, became
> bored and tried to undermine the lessons. (Hargreaves, 1967, p. 99)

Hargreaves provides further support for this by quoting the accounts of students who claim that this teacher 'let us sit there without doing our work', went over material they already knew, and required them to repeat the work if there was any error, and that they 'learnt nowt' from him (p. 100).

Hargreaves concludes by arguing that teachers tended to respond to the difficult discipline problems posed by low-stream groups by adopting either a strategy of 'withdrawal', in which chaotic class discipline was accepted, or 'domination', where 'a completely rigid discipline' was imposed (p. 104). In both cases, he suggests, little constructive teaching took place.

Ball (1981) also puts forward an argument about differential provision for different bands in his study of Beachside Comprehensive. He claims that there were significant differences in the educational experiences of band 1 and band 2 students which included 'curricular differences, syllabus differences, pedagogical differences and relational differences' (p. 281). These claims are supported by differing types and amounts of evidence.

On curricular and syllabus differences Ball points out that band 1 students were introduced to a second language in the third year, whereas band 2 were not; that different textbooks were used in French and this subject's aims differed for the 'more gifted', 'average', and 'less able'; that in mathematics students in different bands followed different courses and used different textbooks; and that 'in Music band 2 were not taught major scales and in Chemistry they were not introduced to atomic structure' (Ball, 1981, p. 281).[25] Ball also claims that there were 'informal syllabus differences', which meant that some teachers left out topics from band 2 work or took them more slowly and therefore failed 'to cover the whole syllabus' (p. 282). On pedagogical differences he claims that 'discussion' was used more in band 1 lessons, but 'board work and exercises' in band 2, and that teachers 'spent longer talking' and 'less often felt the need to reiterate basic principles' (p. 282) in band 1. Finally, on relational differences, Ball argues that difficulties of classroom control with band 2 classes meant that 'the relationship between teachers and pupils tended to be set in a regulative rather than an instructional context' (p. 282). And, in support of this, he gives a small number of quotations from interviews and conversations with teachers suggesting that discipline problems were greater in band 2 classes, and presents information showing the higher numbers of detentions received by band 2 classes. He also reports his observation of twenty-four lessons using Flanders Interaction Analysis Categories in which he found that in band 2 classes 12.5 per cent of teacher time was spent 'criticizing or justifying authority' in comparison to 1.5 per cent in band 1 classes. And he complements this with four detailed descriptions of parts of the lessons of a band 1 and a band

---

[25] Presumably the implication is that band 2 students were not taught even the most common scales, rather than that they were only taught minor ones!

2 class illustrating the type of classroom interaction which he claims was common (Ball, 1981, Ch. 2).

In addition, Ball argues that teachers' negative stereotypes of band 2 classes meant that they devoted 'less care and energy to the preparation of (band 2) lessons' (p. 46), had lower academic expectations of band 2 students, and transmitted a 'lack of enthusiasm for band 2 teaching [. . .] in their classroom-management techniques, their organization of learning and their mediation of the syllabus' (p. 47). Again, some evidence is presented in support of these claims. He gives a general summary of the types of stereotype teachers had of the different bands. More specifically, he supports the first claim with a quotation from one year tutor who says that 'Band 2 kids are often neglected and their lessons are the least prepared of the week' (p. 46). And he grounds the second with a quote from another teacher who states that 'some teachers don't expect much from second-band forms, they accept anything for the standard of work' (p. 47).

While evidence is provided by both these authors in support of their claims about differential provision, it is less comprehensive and detailed than that offered in support of differentiation–polarization theory. As a result, their accounts are rather less convincing. Taking Hargreaves' claims about variation in the quality of teaching received by the different streams, there is a leap of inference involved in concluding that teachers who are younger, have lower qualifications and less experience are more likely to adopt strategies which worsen the progress of students. There is not necessarily a strong relationship between a teacher's qualifications and length of experience and the extent to which he or she is able to achieve classroom control or to teach constructively. Indeed, Hargreaves himself recognizes this at one point (Hargreaves, 1967, p. 97).

Moreover, the observational evidence which Hargreaves uses amounts to a practical evaluation, one which is by no means beyond dispute. And if we assess what he writes in factual terms, as a claim about the strategies employed by 'low-stream teachers', the evidence presented is even less conclusive. Thus, he mentions at one point that 'all the 4th year boys shared the same teachers for half their periods' (p. 97), so that what we have here is a difference of degree rather than a complete separation in the teachers experienced by higher and lower forms.[26] Moreover, the observational and informant evidence which Hargreaves provides relates to only one teacher, and is itself subject to problems of interpretation. Above all, it does not establish the link between this teacher's strategies and a lack of progress on the part of the students. Time wasted in getting out and putting away equipment may well have an effect on students' learning; though this is, of course, a response to the behaviour of the students, as Hargreaves notes. More questionable is the suggestion that taking

[26] It may be, of course, that the 'high-stream' teachers behaved differently towards low-stream students when they taught them, in a way that reduced the latter's progress compared to what it would have been if they had treated them the same as high-stream students; but Hargreaves does not establish this.

the students back to basic mathematical computations with which they are having difficulty, rather than 'forcing' them to keep up with the rate imposed by the teacher, damages their progress; different theories of learning would lead to different conclusions about this. Nor is Hargreaves able to establish what contribution the differences between the teachers allocated to higher- and lower-streams made compared to other factors, given the data available to him.[27]

Ball's account suffers from similar problems. For example, he relies heavily on comments from single teachers, these often generalizing about their colleagues; and this is rather weak evidence given the problems associated with informants' accounts. However, there is also the difficulty that the equity principles on which his descriptions of differential provision are based remain implicit, and are not always the most obviously justifiable ones. For instance, his portrayal of curricular and pedagogic differences as inequalities seems to rest on an equity principle which requires that all students be taught the same syllabus in the same way. Yet, it could be argued that students learn more effectively if what is taught, and the teaching techniques and materials used, are closely related to their current level of achievement; and, since bands are likely to differ in this respect, it would follow that they should not to be treated the same in this sense.

Furthermore, like Hargreaves, Ball provides little evidence about the effects of differential provision on students' subsequent educational careers. Some of the causal relationships involved are very plausible. For example, to the extent that lower-level courses are taught generally by teachers who have difficulty in establishing classroom control or have less understanding of the subject, this is likely to amplify the differences in achievement between students on those courses and those in higher-level groups. Other, causal claims are less plausible, though. Thus, Ball points to the effects of curriculum differentiation in the early years of secondary education on the level of course that students can take later. But, as with Troyna's argument about the effect of early set placement on entry to examinations, there is an important counterfactual condition involved here, concerning the chances of students succeeding at higher levels if there had been no curriculum differentiation. Some assessment is required of whether, or to what extent, any achievement differences are the product of differences in the treatment of the groups, as opposed to other factors.

This represents a general problem with arguments about the amplification of differences in student achievement by school processes. On most interpretations, a large proportion of the variation in achievement between students in different streams, bands etc. is likely to be caused by differences in ability. We therefore need to know whether differences in achievement occur over and above those expected from ability differences, and how great these are. Yet,

[27] Hargreaves' argument regarding 'quality' of teaching experienced by higher- and lower-stream students overlaps with the differentiation–polarization effect he discusses elsewhere, given that much of his argument relates to the relationships between teacher and students.

many studies do not even supply information about achievement levels. And those that do are not able to provide any basis for assessing the relative contribution of school processes.

To conclude, support for claims that the allocation of students to different status groups has a differential impact on their educational achievement is variable. Troyna fails to establish that the set system at Jayleigh determines students' subsequent school careers. Hargreaves, Lacey, Ball and Abraham provide rather stronger evidence for the operation of a differentiation–polarization effect. Those authors who have argued that differential provision of educational resources disadvantages low-status groups have supplied some important evidence, but it is difficult to judge from their work how significant a factor this is. In the case of all three explanations, convincing evidence would seem to require longitudinal studies of reasonably large samples of school students in which achievements and attitudes to school could be monitored before, and on several occasions after, allocation to different levels of course, movement of students between groups being recorded, and the treatments received by the different groups examined in depth. Whether such studies are likely to be funded in the foreseeable future remains to be seen, but they would offer an complement to research currently available.

Readers may be wondering, after all this discussion, what has happened to the variables of social class and ethnicity. It may be recalled that a key claim in this research is that it is the educational achievements of working-class and ethnic-minority students which are adversely affected by their allocation to lower-status groups in schools — that social-class and ethnic-group differences in educational outcomes are, in part at least, a product of such processes. The answer is that in most studies these variables tend to get backgrounded in discussions of the complex causal chains involved.

Ball's work is a case in point. As we have seen, he makes claims about the differential allocation of students from different social classes to bands, but he subsequently focuses his attention on the differences in attitudes between all students (both middle- and working-class) allocated to different bands, and the treatment of these bands. The relationship of social class to differences in attitude, treatment and achievement tends to fade from view as his study progresses, only to re-emerge towards the end of the book; for example in the conclusion, where he draws attention again to the predominance of middle-class students in the band 1 classes, and of working-class students in the band 2 classes (p. 281). In effect Ball implies that, because middle-class students were more likely to be in the band 1 classes and working-class students in the band 2 classes, achievement differences between students from the different social classes were widened by the effects of selection. And, elsewhere, he has argued that his own work and that of others (including that of Hargreaves and Lacey) has 'demonstrated the strong and enduring relationships between streaming and social class differentiation' (Ball, 1986, p. 84). However, neither his own work nor these other studies have provided such a demonstration.

Abraham adopts a similar strategy. He makes the claim early in his report that working-class students are more likely to be placed in lower sets than their middle-class peers, but then concentrates on the impact of differentiation on all students, only returning to the issue of social class in his conclusion. Here he argues that:

> Since working-class pupils tend to be placed in the lower sets and middle-class pupils in the top sets it follows that streaming also becomes a form of social class differentiation in symbiosis with the dominant values of the sets. Thus streaming by sets, as with streaming by forms, is likely to accentuate social class differences in academic performance at school. (Abraham, 1989a, p. 77)

None of the studies discussed here provides any specific documentation of widening social-class differences in attitude or achievement. Rather, researchers infer this from the operation of the processes they describe. This is unsatisfactory; and much the same is true when the argument relates to ethnic inequalities, as in the work of Wright (1986; Foster, 1990b).

Discriminatory Consequences in Relation to Subject

The final argument concerns the discriminatory consequences of girls and boys predominating in different subjects. We have relatively little to say about this. There is no set of research studies which has focused specifically on this issue. Instead, assumptions are made in much writing on gender about the relative status of different subjects, and about links between differences in the educational routes travelled by boys and girls and the gender attitudes they come to hold. For example, at one point in his discussion of 'curricular "choice" ' at City Road school, Gillborn claims that 'sexism characterises the entire process' (p. 165), and that 'as a consequence of some subjects' gender-related images, girls tended to study a curriculum of less academic standing than many of the boys' (p. 166). Given the way that he formulates this, as a comparison of an unspecified subset of the boys with all the girls, this is not a very significant claim. However, he does indicate that girls were less likely to take five or more subjects recognized for university entry than boys (p. 166).

There are undoubtedly status differences between subjects within secondary schools; indeed, these are reflected in the level of financial resources allocated to them. However, there is not complete agreement among teachers about the relative importance of different subjects; not least because of their own subject commitments. Furthermore, it is not at all clear that there is any close correspondence between the subjects in which girls predominate and the attribution of lower status. Domestic science has low status in many eyes, but the status of woodwork and metalwork hardly seems much better. English, foreign languages, and history are not generally regarded as low-status subjects, and girls tend to predominate in these, especially at the sixth-form level. However, part of the argument here relates to assumptions about the differential value of subjects in occupational recruitment. This is an issue which we leave for discussion until Chapter 6.

The other argument under this heading is that the educational experience of girls in the subject areas they study encourages traditional views of femininity and women's roles, and that the experience of boys in the subjects in which they predominate encourages traditional views of masculinity and men's roles. This has been the subject of some empirical research relating to the nature of curriculum content in different subject areas. We will discuss this work in the next chapter.

Conclusion

We began this chapter by trying to clarify the types of argument pursued in research about inequality in selection processes within schools. There are considerable similarities between claims made about the experiences of working-class students, in research conducted in late 1960s and 1970s, and those made in more recent research about the experiences of ethnic-minority students. It is argued that both groups often face discrimination in their allocation to different levels of course, with negative consequences for their educational achievement. Claims in the area of gender are somewhat different. Here researchers focus on school processes which, they argue, channel boys and girls along different curriculum tracks, with consequences for the knowledge, skills and qualities learned, and for future occupational opportunities.

In both cases researchers have tended to make evaluative as well as factual claims. They have implied or stated that inequalities of treatment are inequitable, though justifications are not provided for the value components of these claims. Indeed, this research has generally failed to make explicit the conceptions of equity which have been used to identify inequalities. Instead, the inequalities documented have been presented as if they were simply facts about the world, implicitly denying that other value interpretations are possible. In addition, the scale and significance of the inequalities reported have often been exaggerated; and there has been a tendency to neglect important sources of potential error, and thereby to draw conclusions which are of very questionable validity. Indeed, some of the interpretations of the data presented are little more than speculative, and there are also questions about the generalizability of the conclusions drawn, even within the schools studied. Of course, these criticisms apply unevenly across the various studies we have discussed, but taken overall this body of research fails to establish that discrimination against working-class and black students occurs on any scale in the allocation of students to courses or through the effects of this allocation. As regards gender differences in the distribution of students across subjects, there is no doubt that such differences exist, and they constitute inequalities on some interpretations. However, claims about the role of schools in 'channelling' students into gender-appropriate courses are not supported effectively by the evidence provided. In general, there seems to be considerable over-interpretation of the data available in this literature, and this occurs fairly constantly in the direction of questionable claims about inequalities which disadvantage working-class, ethnic-minority, and female students.

Chapter 5

Inequalities in the Classroom

The research we examined in the previous chapter concerned school-wide processes. In recent years, however, there have also been many studies which have adopted a more micro-focus, concentrating on what goes on at classroom level. Key topics have been the differential treatment of students by teachers, the nature of the values operating in classrooms, and the images of different social categories and groups presented in the curriculum. Inequalities in these respects have typically been viewed as undesirable in themselves, but above all because they are believed to have consequences for educational outcomes.

Our task in this chapter is to examine and assess this classroom research. We will adopt the same procedure as in Chapter 4, first outlining the main types of claim which are made, and then considering the nature of the evidence which is presented to support them. Once again, we will treat these claims as factual ones: as descriptions and explanations, not as practical evaluations. We will illustrate the discussion by reference to a number of widely cited studies.

The Main Claims

There are four main sorts of claim about inequalities in classroom process. These broadly parallel those applying at the level of school organization. They are as follows:

1) Unequal Distribution of Classroom Resources

Some studies argue that important educational resources are distributed un-equally in the classroom. Generally, the focus is on the amounts and types of teacher attention received by students from different social categories. The most common claim is that female, working-class or ethnic-minority students receive a smaller amount of teacher time and attention than their male, middle-class or ethnic-majority peers (Sharp and Green, 1975; Spender, 1982; Stanworth, 1983; French and French, 1984; Croll, 1985; Whyte, 1986; Crossman, 1987; Morgan and Dunn, 1988; Wright, 1992a and b). A similar argument is that these students receive less of those types of attention which are assumed to be more conducive to educational success — for example, praise or encouragement — or less of the time or opportunities needed to develop key skills like public speaking or independence of thought; or that they receive more of what are seen as negative types of attention, such as reprimands, criticism, or hostility (Green, 1983; Wright, 1986, 1992a and b; Swann and Graddoll, 1988; Merrett and Wheldall, 1992; Mirza, 1992). It is also sometimes suggested that teachers respond differently to the same behaviour on the part of students from different categories. In particular, it is argued that teachers respond more negatively to Afro-Caribbean students even when they are behaving in the same way as Whites, or more negatively to assertive or aggressive behaviour from girls than from boys (Clarricoates, 1980; Gillborn, 1990a; Wright, 1992a and b).

These inequalities in classroom treatment are often explained as the product of teachers' distinctive attitudes towards, or low expectations of, female, working-class and ethnic-minority students.

2) Inequalities in School Knowledge and Values

Claims of the first type effectively take as given the value of the education that is offered in schools, along with the nature of school achievement and how it is judged. However, some studies argue that what is valued in the classroom — the knowledge and skills taught and the norms of behaviour applied — are systematically biased in favour of particular categories of student.

It is claimed, for example, that the content of the school curriculum, or of the most influential parts of it, is based around the knowledge, skills and concerns of middle-class, white, and/or male students. And, as a result, such a curriculum is more meaningful and motivating for these students, so that assessment in terms of it will automatically place them at an advantage (St John-Brooks, 1983; Bentley and Watts, 1987; Dubberley, 1988a; Mac an Ghaill, 1988; Moore, 1993). There are two component claims here. First, that working-class, ethnic-minority or female students have different background knowledge, skills, and interests from their middle-class, white, male peers; and, second, that schools value only (or value more) those of the latter.

A related claim is that school rules and teachers' conceptions of the 'ideal client' are based on middle-class, white, and/or male norms of behaviour, so that teachers' judgments about students in terms of these conceptions are inevitably biased against working-class, ethnic-minority and/or female students (Tomlinson, 1981; Mac an Ghaill, 1988; Gillborn, 1990a). Again, there are two component claims. First, that these categories of student have different norms and ways of behaving from their middle-class, white or male peers; and, second, that the norms which teachers enforce conform to those of the latter.

According to these arguments, even if we ensure that different categories of student receive an equal allocation of resources, some are still being treated unequally because the whole culture of the classroom discriminates against them.

3) Socialization into Inequality

In the area of gender, especially, there have also been claims that the curriculum presents images of different categories of person which portray inequality as normal. For example, it is argued in a number of studies that curriculum materials portray men and women in traditional gender roles, or that curriculum materials in subjects which have been regarded as traditionally male involve mainly men, and those in subjects regarded as traditionally female involve mainly women (Lobban, 1975; Walford, 1980; Buswell, 1981; Northam, 1982; Whyte, 1986; Abraham, 1989b). Similar claims are sometimes made in research on ethnicity. It is suggested that curriculum materials often either neglect ethnic-minority people altogether or else present them in negative ways (see, for example, Hicks, 1980; Prieswerk, 1980). It has also been claimed that the hidden curriculum — the social relationships in the classroom, school staffing structures, and the like — socialize students into accepting inequality (Kelly, 1987; Riddell, 1992).

4) The Effects of Differential Treatment on Students' Self-esteem and Motivation

As with research at school level, it is often argued that unequal treatment does not just affect students' levels of educational achievement directly but also indirectly, via students' self-conceptions and levels of motivation (Green, 1983; Stanworth, 1983). Here too, it is suggested, there are processes which amplify differences in educational achievement, and thereby inequalities between different categories of student.

In the remainder of this chapter we will examine the kinds of evidence offered in support of these claims, and their cogency.

Unequal Distribution of Classroom Resources

As we noted, much of the research in this area has been concerned with the unequal distribution of teacher attention, or of types of teacher attention. Studies making this sort of claim take a variety of forms. Some adopt an ethnographic approach, others employ discourse analysis or 'systematic observation', and a few rely entirely on informants' accounts.

An early example of ethnographic work in this field is the study by Sharp and Green (1975) of a 'progressive' infants school. They identify what they refer to as a 'paradox' or contradiction between the ideals and the practices of teachers in this school. They argue that the teachers 'claim[ed] to be supporters of the egalitarian principle that all pupils are of equal worth, having an equal right to receive an education appropriate to their needs', whereas 'in practice there was a marked degree of differentiation of pupils in terms of the amounts and kinds of interaction they had with their teachers' (p. 115). In terms of the progressive-teaching ideology to which these teachers were committed, to one degree or another children's learning is controlled by their level of development, and occurs primarily through engagement in activity rather than by direct teaching. Thus, children were to be kept busy, to get on with various activities independently. Yet, Sharp and Green claim, the teachers tended to interact more frequently with, and more directively towards, those children they saw as intellectually able: they 'paid closer attention to their activities, subtly structuring and directing their efforts in ways which were noticeably different from their relationship with other pupils less favourably categorized' (p. 115). As a result, the authors suggest, these children learned more about the teachers' conceptions of 'development' and 'readiness', and thereby about what they had to do to be successful in these classrooms. Thus, existing differences in achievement among the children were amplified by the teachers' actions: 'whilst the teachers display[ed] a moral concern that every child matters, in practice there [wa]s a subtle process of sponsorship developing where the opportunity [wa]s being offered to some and closed off to others' (p. 218). Furthermore, Sharp and Green argue that teachers' assessments of children were heavily based on assumptions about the kind of home backgrounds from which they came. And the authors conclude that, as a result, this progressive school operated in such a way as to reproduce the social-class structure (p. 221).

As with other accounts of the generation of educational inequality, in assessing Sharp and Green's argument we need to begin by identifying the evaluative standard which is being used. Several are referred to here. One, mentioned in the first quotation we gave, is that resources should be allocated according to individual need. A second, implied in the continuation of that quotation, and the one which Sharp and Green actually apply in their study, is that classroom resources should be equally distributed across social categories of student. This second equity principle is probably the most common standard employed by researchers in this area of research, whether applied to the distribution of teachers' attention as such or to different types of teacher attention.

It is worth emphasizing that these two principles will often give rise to quite different ideal distributions of resources. Indeed, those distributions would only be the same if needs were equally distributed across the relevant social categories. This is fairly implausible even in general terms, and is very unlikely to be the case in any particular school class. We have a potential conflict here, then, in terms of what would count as equitable treatment.

A third evaluative standard which is implicit in Sharp and Green's account is that classroom resources should be distributed in such a way as to ensure equity of opportunity. In other words, children from different social classes should be given the same opportunities to learn and gain educational success. The authors seem to treat this as identical with the other two principles. But, once again, it seems likely to imply a different distribution of resources; though what this distribution would be depends on value assumptions about the appropriate response to differences in ability and aspiration, and on factual assumptions about the likely effects of different sorts of teaching on educational outcomes.

As we noted, for the most part Sharp and Green concentrate on the second of these three evaluative standards, arguing that children from what the teachers considered to be higher social-status backgrounds received more teacher attention, and a better quality of attention, than those seen as coming from lower-status homes. They base this claim on qualitative data collected by three observers (themselves and an additional researcher) in three classrooms over the course of an academic year. Much of these data document the perspectives of the headteacher and of the three teachers whom they studied. The account of these perspectives provides an essential context for subsequent discussion of the classroom behaviour of the teachers. However, the authors present relatively little observational evidence. They illustrate their argument with a series of child case studies from each teacher's class (four from one class and three from each of the others); but, these consist of descriptions, derived from interviews and conversations, of the teacher's perceptions of each child, and summary accounts, based on the researchers' observations, of the ways in which the teachers' interactions with these children differed from their interactions with others.

It is important to recognize that Sharp and Green's claims about differential treatment of children from different home backgrounds are fundamentally quantitative in character: they concern variations in the *amount* of teacher attention, and of the *frequency* of different types of attention, given to different categories of children. For this reason, the observational data they provide are inadequate. The authors' generalized *qualitative* descriptions are likely to be subject to all the well-documented problems of impressionistic judgment of frequencies (Sadler, 1981; McCall 1984, p. 273). This is especially so given the absence of explicit operationalizations of 'teacher attention', and of different types of teacher attention. These concepts were probably applied in different ways on different occasions, and differently by different observers, resulting in substantial error, systematic and haphazard. Furthermore, the lack of precision in the claims made about inequalities of treatment, and the relative absence of specific supporting illustration, makes it very difficult for the reader to assess them. We are faced with having to make judgments solely in terms of plausibility; and, as a result, for the most part no reasonable conclusion can be reached about their validity, one way or the other.

There are also problems with Sharp and Green's argument that the differential treatment of the children reproduced the social-class structure. One is that we are given little evidence to show that there was a correlation between teachers' judgments of the ability of the children and social class; and it is not at all clear how Sharp and Green operationalized that concept. While such a relationship is not implausible, and it is clear that the teachers understood differences in the children's behaviour partly in terms of social-class imagery, a systematic assessment of this relationship would be necessary to establish the claim. Moreover, any attempt to document this relationship would be complicated by the social composition of the school. Sharp and Green describe it as located 'on a large, new local authority housing estate', whose inhabitants 'were mainly working class with very few non-manual workers'. They suggest that this 'renders the school particularly interesting given the frequently found preoccupation with somewhat crude comparisons between social classes rather than within them [. . .]' (Sharp and Green, 1975, pp. 36–7). However, the limited range of social-class differences represented in the school means that, at best, data from it can only establish the reproduction of social differences *within* the working class.

Another problem with Sharp and Green's argument that the behaviour of the teachers reproduced the social-class structure relates to the link between the differential treatment by teachers of different categories of child and their subsequent levels of educational achievement. The authors offer no specific evidence about levels of achievement. Nor do we have any way of assessing what contribution the teachers may have made to the learning rates of the children, as against the various other factors which would be operating on these.

This problem of causal analysis is thrown into relief if we compare Sharp and Green's findings, and their interpretation of them, with those of Tickle (1983). He investigated art and design lessons in a middle school. On the basis of data that were rather more detailed (but no more systematic) than theirs, he concluded that the children judged least able by the teachers were given the *most* attention, and were subjected to *closer* structuring of their learning. Yet, despite this contrast in findings, his conclusion about the effects of differential treatment is much the same as Sharp and Green's: that it benefitted the able children. He argues that there were, effectively, two curricula operating in these classrooms, one for the 'less able', involving the imposition of basic skills, and one for the 'more able', which allowed 'the opportunity to engage in creative work' (p. 123). In this way, 'restricted chances for some ran side by side with afforded opportunities for others to fulfill creative potential'. And he locates this within the context of a clash between contrasting views of schooling as maximizing personal development or as 'anti-creative, inegalitarian and stultifying to the individual' (p. 124). He suggests (with Bowles and Gintis, 1976) that there is a sense in which both views may be true, but for different groups of students. Of course the conclusions of Tickle, on the one hand, and Sharp and Green, on the other, are not logically contradictory. But the fact is that neither study provides empirical evidence to establish the effects of the differential treatment claimed. Instead, they simply assume opposite effects, presumably relying on different learning theories.

A more recent example of ethnographic research dealing with unequal treatment by teachers of different categories of child is a study by Wright (1992a and b) of four multi-ethnic primary schools. She argues that, on the surface, the schools were characterized by a pleasant and caring atmosphere which took account of the needs of different groups of children; but that her classroom observation 'revealed subtle differences in the way white teachers treated black children' (1992a, p. 26). She claims that Asian children received the least attention from the teacher in the classroom, and that teachers frequently responded negatively to them when linguistic or cultural differences created problems for classroom management or teaching effectiveness. She also argues that the teachers had negative expectations of Afro-Caribbean children, who were 'always among the most criticised and controlled group in the classroom' (Wright, 1992b, p. 19). 'Rastafarian' children, Wright suggests, were 'particularly prone to experiencing prejudice' (p. 23). Finally, she claims that the teachers' efforts to encourage multi-culturalism in the classroom often backfired, because of their lack of confidence and understanding, this resulting in the embarrassment of black children.

Wright presents a good deal of qualitative data to support her arguments, but once again there are some serious problems. Often, she relies on general qualitative description of what *typically* occurs. This is true, for example, of her claims that Asian children were given less teacher attention than other groups and that they were rarely encouraged to take part in classroom discussion. She reports that 'they were generally observed to be excluded from the discussions because of the assumption that they could not understand or speak English'; and that when they *were* included the teachers 'used telegraphic language' and 'when this strategy failed to get any responses the teachers would quickly lose patience with the children and would ignore them' (Wright, 1992b, p. 16). With such generalized description, the reader is in much the same position as with Sharp and Green's analysis. Given that these claims are not sufficiently plausible to be accepted at face value, judgment must be suspended about their validity.

Even where more detailed evidence is provided, this is often inadequate. One problem is that, as with Sharp and Green, we have qualitative data offered in support of quantitative claims about the differential attention given to, and differential frequency of teacher actions directed at, various categories of child. As in the case of Tickle, what are provided are descriptive accounts of particular classroom incidents which, Wright suggests, are indicative of broader patterns. For the reasons outlined earlier, such data are not sufficient; especially when, as she notes, 'most of the incidents witnessed in the classroom were not as clear cut as the ones cited [. . .]' (Wright, 1992b, p. 27).

There are also doubts about Wright's interpretations of some of her data. For example, she reports an incident in which a teacher has problems conveying instructions and the meaning of a word to an Asian child, and so asks another Asian girl to translate. The second girl does not speak or help, a response which seems to irritate the teacher and leads to a reprimand. Wright interprets this as an instance of teachers' annoyance that 'the Asian children's poor English language skills interfered with their teaching' (Wright, 1992b, p. 16). Yet this teacher's annoyance seems much more likely to have been a response to what she saw as the second girl's refusal to help. Indeed, the teacher tells the child: 'you're supposed to be helping' (p. 17). Wright's interpretation hinges on the girl not being *able* to help, but no evidence is provided about this and the teacher clearly assumed that she was capable of helping.

There are also problems with the interpretations Wright makes of some of the teachers' comments in interviews. For example, one teacher describes the difficult behaviour of two Afro-Caribbean boys, and Wright interprets this as a statement about the poor behaviour of Afro-Caribbean boys *in general* (Wright, 1992a, p. 44). It *may* be that the teacher was operating on the basis of an ethnic stereotype, but these data do not establish that claim. Rather, it seems that Wright is employing a stereotype of these teachers to interpret her data, in the sense that she assumes that any differential treatment of children from different ethnic groups must stem from racism. This is further illustrated by her analysis of teachers' logs. She claims that these 'showed a tendency for some teachers to direct their frustration at the Afro-Caribbean children' (Wright, 1992b, p. 45). Yet the examples Wright gives relate to individual children not to Afro-Caribbean children generally. She does not even show that the positive and negative comments in the logs are distributed unequally between white and Afro-Caribbean children. She simply infers that the teachers were primarily oriented to the 'racial' characteristics of the children: here, and elsewhere, she seems to assume that comments made about particular Afro-Caribbean children can be taken to indicate a general attitude on the part of the teacher to all Afro-Caribbean children. While in the interview data reported the teachers do sometimes make generalizations about ethnic categories of student, these are qualified rather than being presented as universal generalizations (pp. 43–4). Nor are we told the nature of the questions to which the teachers were responding, and these may have specifically requested such generalizations.

Wright is no clearer than other authors in this field about the evaluative standards she is employing in constructing her account of classroom inequalities. Much of the time she seems to be operating on the basis of the second of those we mentioned earlier, contrasting what occurred with what would be expected on the basis of an equal distribution of attention and of types of attention across ethnic categories of student; though, like Sharp and Green and Tickle, she also seems to have equity of opportunity in mind, without specifying what this would involve. At one point, though, she employs a rather different evaluative standard: that teachers ought to respond to the same behaviour in the same way, irrespective of the ethnicity or 'race' of the children concerned. She reports that Afro-Caribbean children were often 'singled out for criticism even though several pupils of different groups were engaged in the same act or behaviour' (Wright, 1992a, p. 52). Thus, she describes a teacher-led discussion in a nursery class, in which she reports that an Afro-Caribbean boy called Marcus was reprimanded by the teacher for shouting out when others in the group were also shouting out (Wright, 1992a, pp. 30–2).

Even if we take this evaluative standard at face value, however, there are problems of interpretation here. Once again, Wright treats this as an instance of the teacher responding more harshly to Afro-Caribbean children in general, when the data relate only to the treatment of one particular Afro-Caribbean boy on one occasion. Thus, we are given no information about the proportions of children of different ethnic origins in the class or of the frequencies with which differential treatment of 'the same behaviour' occurred. Furthermore, it is difficult to tell from Wright's description whether Marcus's behaviour actually was the same as that of the others who were not reprimanded. He may have shouted out more often than they did, or his shouting out may have been more extreme. These are possibilities which need to be excluded, since minor variation in the immediate context can have a considerable effect on teachers' responses to student behaviour. Furthermore, identifying what does and does not constitute 'shouting out' is by no means straightforward, since in classrooms speakers can be nominated by nonverbal as well as by verbal means.

Beyond this, though, there is an important conceptual issue about what 'the same behaviour' means. In particular, there may be a difference between the temporal contexts in which an observer and a teacher place particular incidents; over and above any differences in orientation that derive from their respective roles. Especially in primary schools, perhaps, teachers do not respond to children on the basis solely of what the latter do at any particular moment, but also on the basis of what they know about the children from past experience.[1]

We are faced here with much the same choice of evaluative standards as with the research on allocation to different levels of course discussed in the previous chapter. We could define 'the same behaviour' in a temporally restricted way, as Wright seems to do, and describe any difference in treatment in these terms as itself constituting ethnic bias. However, this is not the only evaluative standard which could be adopted, and it does not seem to be the one which Wright herself actually applies. Rather, she treats difference in treatment, defined in this restricted way, as an indicator of ethnic bias in the teachers' interpretations of children's behaviour. She recognizes that the teachers' treatment of children is based on knowledge about them, but seems to assume that this necessarily involves ethnic stereotyping or racism if differential treatment is involved. This could be so; but evidence is required to show that it is. Wright claims that Marcus was treated differently because of the teacher's 'expectations of bad behaviour' (Wright, 1992a, p. 30) from Afro-Caribbean children. But it could have been caused by her 'expectation

---

[1] There is evidence to suggest that this is also true in secondary schools. See Hargreaves *et al.*'s (1975) detailed analysis of secondary-school teachers' interpretations of student behaviour and the role of typifications in their classroom decisions.

of bad behaviour' from Marcus; an expectation which may or may not have been well-founded.[2]

Like a number of other researchers who claim to document differential classroom treatment, Wright makes only a perfunctory attempt to understand the perspectives of the teachers.[3] While she quotes some teachers explaining their point of view, in general these accounts are not analysed, but 'read' in a largely speculative way as evidence of ethnocentrism. In other words, she largely ignores the immediate content and function of what teachers actually say, concentrating instead on what she believes can be inferred from their accounts about their underlying attitudes towards different ethnic groups. This is a far from satisfactory mode of analysis in general terms; but it is particularly unfortunate given her claim to document a contradiction between teachers' 'genuine' commitment to ideals of educational opportunity (Wright, 1992b, p. 15) and their classroom behaviour.

At one point Wright does touch on the problem which seems to be pre-eminent for the teachers: that of classroom control. She comments that 'it would be crude simply to dismiss these teachers as "bad" and racially preju-diced' (Wright, 1992b, pp. 30–1); and, echoing Foster's analysis (Foster, 1990a, pp. 157–8), she suggests that they were experiencing a 'survival threat'. Yet, the source of this threat is left unspecified. The teachers' own explanation, that it arose from the behaviour of the children, is ruled out by the very rhetorical structure of Wright's account. But it is left unclear whether she believes, for instance, that this sense of threat was itself a product of the teachers' ethno-centrism or that it resulted from their mode of teaching being inappropriate for the children they faced.

In effect, Wright treats 'racially' discriminatory behaviour on the part of the teachers as a matter of simple empirical observation. Yet it is not so straightforward. As we saw in Chapter 3, identifying discrimination relies on some conception of equity, and it can take different forms. Moreover, provid-ing convincing evidence is not unproblematic even if one treats discrimination as differential treatment of 'the same behaviour' defined in overt terms. There are problems of measurement, and systematic evidence is required to establish that there is a *pattern* of discrimination. It is even more complex and difficult, however, if (as seems to be the case with Wright) discrimination is defined as action on the basis of ethnic stereotypes. Here, evidence that teachers have such stereotypes, and that they routinely act on them, is also required. Wright's account does not meet these requirements.

Similar problems arise with much research on gender inequality in the classroom, where it is often claimed that teachers' responses to the same behaviour vary according to whether girls and boys are involved; though here the argument is generally not just that this is inequitable but also that it plays

[2] Wright reports that he was considered by the teachers to be 'very able', 'active', and 'boisterous', and to display 'behaviour which often bordered on being "potentially distruptive"' (Wright, 1992b, p. 19).
[3] There is a considerable contrast in this respect with the work of Sharp and Green.

a central role in the differential socialization of the sexes. Thus, Clarricoates (1980) claims that teachers in the four contrasting primary schools she studied held stereotypes about the behaviour of girls and boys, and that this led them to react to that behaviour in different ways. In establishing this claim in relation to Dock Side, a working-class school, she reports that the teachers believed that girls are better behaved while boys are louder and more aggressive. This is documented by means of brief quotations, but two of these are not directly related to the claim and all of them are unattributed, so that it is unclear how many teachers are represented (Clarricoates, 1980, p. 30). Clarricoates implies that these teacher beliefs are, at the very least, not entirely accurate, claiming that: 'the girls were as verbally aggressive (particularly in terms of swearing) as the boys'. She also notes that the teachers explained the sources of the differences between boys and girls in terms of parents' differential expectations and treatment of them in the home. She comments that:

> this did not prevent these same teachers from going right back into the classroom and reinforcing the sex-role stereotypes by their expectations and toleration of different standards of behaviour between the sexes, instead of trying to eradicate the previous conditioning.

> Craig, a five-year-old, spent a good deal of his time in harassing his classmates. He took a great delight in breaking up their games, bombarding any hapless child who happened near him with marbles, and was a constant source of irritation to the girls, whom he maliciously attacked — either verbally or physically — and all this within the confines of the class and to the non-reaction of the teacher. On the other hand, Sarah was prone to outbursts of temper, either screaming or letting loose a barrage of insults at her offender. I was present at a time when she let fly a quantity of paint at Lynsey, who promptly burst into tears. Sarah's behaviour was met with severe rebuke in public by the teacher: 'Little girls do not do that,' amongst other things; and thereafter she was nicknamed the 'paint-dauber'.

The teacher then proceeded to justify her own behaviour by telling me how Sarah was a problem child; for example, annoying her classmates. It seemed to escape her attention that this was the very same behaviour that Craig was allowed to get away with. Not only were different standards of tolerance applied, but also the same behaviour was categorized differently depending on the sex. Many times I observed children involved in play, and in many instances I was aware of the use of this double standard:

> Craig and Edward were involved in a game of Plasticine and both are seized with a fit of laughter. They are allowed to

carry on. But, parallel to this, when two girls were caught up in a similar game and became noisy the teacher classed it as 'giggling hysterically' and told the girls to 'calm down'.

And yet in this particular instance there was no real distinction between the girls' and the boys' behaviour. It can be seen that there is a subtle interaction between the teachers' observations and the teachers' beliefs. (Clarricoates, 1980, p. 31)

Here, then, Clarricoates begins by questioning one aspect of the teachers' beliefs about the differences in the behaviour of the girls and boys; though without providing any evidence in support. This opens up the possibility that any differences which do exist might as easily be the product of differential treatment in school as of sex stereotyping at home. Evidence is then presented to support this. But her interpretation of these data involves similar problems to those we raised in relation to Wright's analysis. Once again, the data concern a very small number of children; these being treated as exemplars of the relevant social categories. And we are presented with generalized description of their behaviour interspersed with one or two more specific examples involving questionable interpretations of what is 'the same behaviour'. Furthermore, we have no investigation of the teacher's interpretation of the incidents, of why she reacted differently etc. Here too discriminatory behaviour on the part of teachers is treated as if it were a purely factual and easily observable matter.

In Clarricoates' work, as elsewhere, it is assumed that teachers can and should act consistently in such a way as to achieve equity of treatment. Yet there are different conceptions of equity, and these often do not prescribe the same behaviour on the part of the teacher. Distributing attention equally may not be compatible with responding to the same behaviour in the same way, if there are behavioural differences between categories of child. More than this, though, there are other considerations which we might reasonably expect teachers to take into account, of both a valuational and a practical kind. For instance, they will be concerned with the value of the education being provided as well as with its equitable distribution. And, since they are not in a position of total control in the classroom, they are likely to take account of different children's likely responses to 'the same treatment'. This will stem in part from the fact that children's definitions of what is equal treatment may differ from those of teachers (and even from those of researchers).

Up to now we have concentrated on research relying primarily on ethnographic observation. An example of work employing more structured observational evidence is a study by French and French (1984) of gender imbalance in the distribution of teacher attention in primary-school classrooms. They audio-recorded teacher–student talk and tried to measure systematically the amount of teacher attention received by boys and girls, in terms of the number of turns at talk in whole-class discussion. They claim that boys in the lessons they observed received more teacher attention than girls. In support of this they provide detailed evidence from one of the lessons, which they argue is 'richly representative' of others, showing that boys took far more interactional turns than might have been expected given their number in the class. The thirteen boys in the class took fifty out of the 188 turns, whereas the sixteen girls took only sixteen turns.

Here the focus is more modest than with the previous studies we have discussed; and the sort of evidence provided is potentially more effective in documenting quantitative variation. Even so, there are several problems with French and French's argument. One concerns whether 'number of interactional turns' is an adequate measure of the amount of teacher attention received by the children. Not all of what the authors count as turns seem to involve teacher attention. For example, they include shouted out comments by students which the teacher appears to ignore, and student responses to questions which the teacher seems not to have heard, given that he asks for repetition. There is also the question of whether duration as well as number of turns should have been measured. Some student turns are much longer than others in the data cited, and this no doubt varies in the rest of the data as well. This might have an effect on measurements of the relative amount of teacher attention received; though all of these problems seem unlikely to result in any substantial altera-tion to the authors' account of the different overall participation rates of girls and boys in the lesson investigated.

More significant is that French and French only provide quantitative data for the lesson they examine in depth, not for other lessons involving the same teacher and children. And, related to this, the research focuses on turns at talk in whole-class discussion; but it seems likely that this does not measure the distribution of teacher attention in primary classrooms very effectively, given that much interaction there will be with small groups or individual children. It may be that the distribution of teacher attention is different in such interaction compared with more 'public' classroom sessions.

Another problem is that the authors focus simply on differences in the *amount* of teacher attention received by girls and boys, with no attempt to distinguish between different *types* of attention. To the extent that they are concerned with equity of opportunity, the differential allocation of types of teacher attention seems more likely to be of significance than sheer differences in its amount. This has been the assumption of the other researchers whose work we have discussed, and it seems a reasonable one.

Finally, it is important to note, as French and French themselves point out, that the gender imbalance in interactional turns in the lesson they analysed is produced by a small number of boys. The authors provide data on the number of turns taken by each student in the class. This shows that three of the thirteen boys take 41 per cent of the total number of turns (and 74 per cent of the number of turns taken by boys), while five of the boys do not participate at all, and two only once. On the basis of qualitative analysis, the authors argue that this imbalance was produced by a minority of boys employing attention-seeking strategies which led the teacher to respond in ways which gave them further opportunities for participation. At the very least, this suggests that there were other factors than gender at work in producing the differential participation rates in this lesson. The authors note that there were examples of girls using attention-seeking strategies in their corpus of data, but report that it was more common among boys; though they do not provide evidence about this, and their data do not even establish that the boys who dominated the lesson they analysed did the same in other lessons. The authors argue, quite rightly, that more broad-ranging longitudinal work is required.[4]

Another study which adopts a more structured approach, this time employing 'live' systematic observation, is Green's (1983) research on teacher–student interaction in the multi-ethnic classrooms of seventy middle- and junior-school teachers. He used Flanders' Interaction Analysis Categories to record the interaction of teachers with 'West Indian', 'Asian' and 'European' students. He claims that there were significant differences in patterns of contact between these students and teachers who, on the basis of questionnaire responses, were classified as ethnically 'highly tolerant' or 'highly intolerant'. And he suggests that in the classrooms of the twelve highly intolerant teachers West Indian students received less of the teaching categories 'accepts feeling', 'praise or encouragement', 'acceptance/use of pupils' ideas', 'direct teaching', but more 'criticism or justification of authority', than their European and Asian peers. Also, West Indian students were less likely to initiate contributions and to respond to their teachers. By contrast, in the classrooms of the twelve highly tolerant teachers European students received less of the categories 'accepts feeling' (boys only), 'praise or encouragement', 'acceptance/use of pupils' ideas', 'asks questions', and 'giving directions' than their Asian or West Indian peers; and they were also less likely to initiate contributions and respond to their teachers.

Like French and French, Green tried systematically to measure differences in teacher interaction with different categories of student. However, his study contrasts sharply with theirs in its level of ambition. For example, he attempted to distinguish between different *types* of interaction received by different groups; and he examines a much larger sample of teachers than most studies in this area, as well as seeking to distinguish amongst these teachers in terms of their attitudes.

Partly as a result of the sheer breadth of focus, his work suffers from a number of major weaknesses. Some of these concern the measurement of the many variables he includes in his analysis. Take, for example, his use of Flanders' observational schedule to measure classroom interaction. This schedule is not usually employed to assess how much of the different interactional categories are devoted to particular groups, so that Green had to modify the coding to record the ethnicity of the children to which each type of interaction was directed. This will have worsened a problem with the use of this schedule

---

[4] See Hammersley, 1990a for a more detailed analysis.

which is widely recognized: that it requires quite complex decisions about the functions of teachers' utterances to be made very rapidly (usually every three seconds); with no facility for subsequent review and correction of the interpretations involved. This is especially problematic given the fact that the categories themselves, and the coding rules associated with them, are rather ambiguous. Furthermore, Flanders' schedule was designed to code public teacher–student interaction. It is not well suited for use in classrooms where teachers interact with students in small groups or individually, and these types of interaction are very common in many junior and middle schools (Walker and Adelman, 1975).

There is also a problem with Green's presentation of his data. This is that he does not provide results for individual teachers. Instead, he groups his data — in terms of the twelve highly tolerant and twelve highly intolerant teachers — calculating the total amount of each type of interaction received by students of different ethnic groups in the classes of all twelve teachers. We do not know, therefore, whether the patterns he identified were characteristic of each teacher's lessons, or were produced by a small number of teachers who interacted with their students in particularly extreme ways.

There is also doubt about Green's explanation for the differences in interaction patterns he claims to have discovered: in terms of differences in the 'ethnic tolerance' of the teachers. Setting aside the issue of the accuracy with which he has measured teachers' attitudes, there is the question of how far the differences in the teachers' behaviour that he recorded were caused by other factors than by differences in their attitudes; for example by variations in the behaviour of the students to which they were responding. Green could not, of course, control this variable, but this threatens the validity of his explanation.

Against the background of the other work we have discussed, Green's study highlights the severe difficulties faced by social researchers in this area (and in others). On the one hand, multiple variables are involved, and even Green was not able to cover all of them. Yet, lack of attention to some of these leaves open the possibility that the explanations presented are spurious. On the other hand, in the absence of much greater resources than are currently available, and a more effective division of labour amongst researchers, the attempt to cover a large number of variables forces researchers to rely on relatively crude measures, so that there is considerable potential for error. There is a dilemma here which is not easily resolvable, at least not without major changes in the organization and funding of research. Nevertheless, it is essential that researchers recognize and make explicit the implications of these problems for the validity of their findings.

Up to now we have concentrated on the use of observational data, but some of the studies we have discussed have also drawn on informants' accounts. For example, Wright uses the views of welfare assistants to support her argument that the teachers she studied behaved differently towards children from different ethnic groups. She cites one as saying:

> They [white teachers] have got this way of talking to them [Asian children] in a really simple way . . . cutting half the sentences 'Me no do that' sort of thing . . . and that is not standard English. And they've [teachers] got this way of saying words 'That naughty' and they miss words out and it really does seem stupid . . . I feel that it's not my place to say 'Well that's a silly way to speak to children . . .' I worry about what it tells the white children who think that the Asian children are odd anyway. (Wright, 1992a, p. 27)

Such data are useful as a complement to observational evidence; though they cannot compensate for the kinds of deficiencies in such evidence which we identified earlier. At the same time, as we noted in Chapter 3, informants' accounts involve all the potential errors associated with observation, plus additional ones. In the case of the account cited above, we have a generalization about the way in which all the white teachers (in one of the schools) speak to all Asian children. The reliability of this generalization is uncertain — for instance, we do not know the range of observations on which it was based. It is also evaluative, but the basis for this is left implicit and is thereby treated as the only one appropriate. Nor are the conditions under which this account was elicited indicated, so that it is difficult to know what role these played in producing it and how they might have affected its validity.

There are a few studies concerned with the unequal distribution of classroom resources which have relied entirely on informants' accounts. A widely cited example is Stanworth's (1983) research into gender differences in teacher–student interaction in the humanities department of a college of further education. She argues that this is a critical case because gender inequality is least likely to occur in such a 'liberal setting'. The implication is that, if it can be found here, it is likely to be widespread. And, indeed, Stanworth claims to find marked inequality in the treatment of male and female students. She concludes that 'the sexual distribution of interaction appears decisively weighted in favour of boys' (p. 51), since boys received more total attention than girls; and more of certain types of attention, such as questions, involvement in discussion, and praise. It is also claimed that their relationships with the teachers were more positive. On this basis Stanworth claims that girls were relegated to 'the margins' of classroom life.

The student accounts on which this study relies were elicited during interviews with a sample of male and female students in seven 'A' level classes. In the course of these interviews students were asked questions like: 'Which of these pupils does the teacher pay most attention to?' (p. 37) or 'Who does Mr Hurd most often direct questions to in this group?' (p. 39). As far as we can tell, Stanworth then worked out the frequency with which boys' and girls' names were mentioned. She reports that, on the basis of students' accounts, boys are:

> Slightly more likely to be the pupils for whom teachers display most concern.

Twice as likely to be asked questions by teachers.

Twice as likely to be regarded by teachers as highly conscientious.

Twice as likely to be those with whom teachers get on best.

Three times more likely to be praised by teachers (and slightly more likely to be criticised).

Three times more likely to be the pupils whom teachers appear to enjoy teaching.

Five times more likely to be the ones to whom teachers pay most attention.
(Stanworth, 1983, pp. 37–8)

Stanworth also presents eight extracts from interviews in which students describe, in more detail, specific instances in which they felt male teachers were 'substantially more sympathetic or more attentive to the boys' (p. 38).

Stanworth's research is of value for its attempt to provide a picture of classroom interaction from the students' perspective. But she seems to treat their experience as corresponding to reality. While she declares at one point that 'the objective was not to produce a description of events in the classroom as they appear to an impartial observer, but rather to capture the quality of classroom life as currently experienced by the pupils themselves' (Stanworth, 1983, p. 23), as we have seen she nevertheless makes claims about the behaviour of teachers, not just about students' experience of it. Yet students' accounts, particularly those relating to judgments about general patterns of interaction, are likely to be subject to substantial error. They will have been shaped by the contingencies of their own experience, as well as being subject to memory distortion. We cannot assume that the students had observed representative samples of each teacher's behaviour; or that, if they had, their accounts were based on all the data. And a high level of inference was involved in some of their descriptions. Students were asked, for example, to speculate on which other students 'teachers appear to enjoy teaching' and which ones were 'regarded by teachers as highly conscientious'.

Furthermore, here again reliance on accounts involves additional threats to validity besides those characteristic of observation, stemming from the interaction between informant and researcher. We need to ask, for example, how far Stanworth's questioning of the students may have stimulated certain sorts of answers and discouraged others. It is worth remembering that she was carrying out research in the college in which she taught, so that the students may already have been aware of her views, and this may have affected what they said.

A final problem is that there seems to be a significant difference between the data Stanworth collected and the way she presents it. As we have explained, she asked students to name other students in their class whom 'the teacher pays most attention to', or 'most often directs questions to', etc. This would have given her information about the number of students of different sexes that students felt received most attention, most questions, etc. It would *not* have told her what proportion of the teachers' attention or of teachers' questions went to boys or girls in the classes concerned, or even what proportion of boys received more than an equal share of attention or questions, in the students' eyes or otherwise. Yet Stanworth presents the data as showing that, according to the students, 'boys receive the lion's share of teacher's attention and regard' (p. 37). Even taken at face value, her data cannot support such a claim.

Before concluding this section we want to discuss a further problem which is common to most of the research in this area. This relates to the generalizations made within the cases studied. There are at least two dimensions to this: generalization over time, and across other members of the same category of actor. French and French's research is weak in both these respects: given that the data relate to only one lesson, we do not know how typical the patterns were of other lessons involving the same teachers and children, or of those involving other teachers and other children. While the authors assure us that the data were typical in relevant respects, they do not provide information about the whole corpus of data from which the lesson was drawn, and this is needed if we are to assess *its* representativeness of classroom interaction in the school studied.

The other research we have discussed draws on data from larger samples of interaction, but it rarely establishes its generalizations very effectively. Thus, the ethnographic studies typically provide observational evidence relating to fairly small samples of teachers and children; and it is difficult to know how representative the behaviour and experience of these teachers and children is of that of others. Wright (1992), for example, makes generalizations about typical patterns of behaviour on the part of teachers in the four schools she studied, but these are based on data relating to only a few of them. And though Clarricoates gives more attention to the differences and similarities between the schools she investigated, the observational evidence presented in relation to each school is weak in this respect. Green's work avoids these problems by investigating and reporting the behaviour of quite a large number of teachers. However, partly as a result of this, he was only able to observe each teacher's lessons for one day. As with much systematic observation research, there is a problem here about how representative the observations were of each teacher's behaviour.[5]

To summarize, then, these studies make several different types of claim about inequality in the distribution of classroom resources. However, they are

[5] Both Berlak *et al.* (1975) and Ball (1983) have raised the problem of temporal variation in the study of teachers' behaviour.

not very clear about the nature of these claims, and the evidence they present is subject to some serious methodological problems. Interpretation of particular incidents is often questionable, and support for claims about quantitative variation in the treatment of children from different social categories is generally weak. Moreover, where quantitative evidence *is* provided, there are doubts about the adequacy of the indicators employed. Finally, we noted that much of this research fails to establish the validity of the generalizations it makes, even within the cases studied.

Inequalities in What is Valued in the Classroom

Some research on classrooms has been concerned not so much with inequalities in the distribution of resources as with inequality in what is treated as valuable knowledge and proper behaviour. This type of claim is often made in theoretical or polemical work where little or no empirical evidence is provided. Such evidence is not always necessary, however. For example, the claim that ethnic-minority students often have distinctive linguistic knowledge and skills which are given less value by schools than the language of the ethnic majority is so plausible that it does not require evidence to support it.

However, many other claims of this type are not sufficiently plausible. For example, the argument that working-class students have different background knowledge and interests in the area of humanities or the arts, but that schools value mainly those of the middle class; or that there are distinctively feminine forms of knowledge and interest in science, but that schools place more value on masculine types; or that the behavioural norms of ethnic-minority students are significantly different from those of ethnic-majority students, but that schools only value those of the majority. These *do* seem to us to require supporting evidence.

Where evidence is provided it usually consists of researchers' observations of the content of the school curriculum and the way it is taught (in the case of claims about inequality in the knowledge valued by schools), or of teachers' responses to what is argued to be the culturally different behaviour of students from particular social groups (in the case of claims about inequality in the behaviour valued). However, there has also been some use of informants' accounts of schools' curricular and behavioural norms.

An example of a study which focuses on the curriculum and the way it is taught is St John-Brooks' (1983) research in a secondary-school English department. She claims that the English teachers in this department had developed a very close-knit subject subculture which rejected a rationalist/basic skills approach, and found expression in an English curriculum which emphasized the personal development of students through the discussion and analysis of literature. She argues that they deliberately tried to adopt an egalitarian approach in the classroom, teaching in mixed-ability groups wherever possible and eschewing favouritism and negative labelling. However, she claims that the subject content of English, and the way it was taught, left many less able students, who were more often than not working-class, 'bewildered on the outside' (p. 44). St John-Brooks argues that the teachers often failed to recognize the difficulties faced by these students, and that those who gained most were those from the middle class who 'already possess the background and experience — the cultural capital, in fact — to intuit what kind of response was implicitly demanded' (p. 44). The result was that 'the experience and achievements of pupils did tend to divide along class lines' (p. 55).

St John-Brooks bases her claims about the departmental subculture among English teachers on summary accounts of her observations of the teachers' behaviour (in and outside the classroom) and on short extracts from interviews and conversations with three 'core' members of the department (Mr Rogers, Mr Anderson and Mr Davies).[6] These indicate their views of English as a subject and of the aims of English teaching. Her claims about the English curriculum are supported by a list of the literature most commonly used, and case studies of the classroom practice of Mr Rogers and Mr Davies, these being illustrated by observational accounts of parts of a small number of their lessons (three of the former's and two of the latter's). She also provides evidence about the responses of some of the students to these teachers' lessons, which were collected during interviews.

Despite the variety of evidence used here, as with the other work we have examined, there are a number of problems in drawing the conclusions St John-Brooks does on the basis of the evidence provided. For example, this gives little support to her claim that less able, predominantly working-class students found the English curriculum less meaningful, and less rewarding, than the more able, middle-class students. The interview data reported show that a small number of students found some parts of the English curriculum taught by Mr Rogers and Mr Davies stimulating and enjoyable, whereas others found them mystifying and said they gained little from them; but it is not clear how many students fell into these categories. And it is also unclear whether the views quoted are representative of these students' views about other aspects of the English curriculum, or whether they were representative of those of other students taught by these teachers, or of students' views of English teaching generally. Furthermore, it is not established that this difference in response reflected social-class divisions; nor does St John-Brooks tell us how she operationalized social class.[7] Moreover, some of the evidence she provides seems to run counter to her claim that what occurred was the inclusion of 'more able' and the exclusion of 'less able' students. She reports that:

> The alienation of some pupils in the upper-band fourth year group might lead one to expect disaster with the lower band, but quite the reverse was true. Mr Rogers tempered his insights and enthusiasms

[6] A good deal more information of this kind is provided in her thesis, see St John Brooks, 1980.

[7] In fact, she recognizes that there is by no means a perfect correlation between social class and the possession of cultural capital (St John Brooks, 1980, p. 282).

with some awareness of his pupils' possible limitations, taking care to relate texts to their own lives. His group was small, with a couple of lively and articulate members willing to interrupt, and Mr Rogers took their contributions seriously, which was appreciated by pupils unused to such consideration. (St John-Brooks, 1983, pp. 48–9)

As with many of the other researchers whose work we have discussed, St John-Brooks engages in practical evaluation of the work of the teachers. And, like them, she does not make her evaluative standards explicit. Moreover, the standard seems to vary during the course of the analysis. At one point, despite the primary emphasis on social-class inequalities, the author reports that most of those who found the lessons 'boring and alienating' were 'quiet girls, who in class otherwise appeared interested and compliant'. And she comments that 'Mr Rogers' strong interest in elevating the less able, so it seemed, had carried in its wake an unanticipated and unrecognized sexism, differentiation of response between boys and girls respectively, to the detriment of the latter' (St John-Brooks, 1983, p. 47). Here it seems that at least one of the teachers succeeds in working against 'excluding' the less able, but the response of the researcher is to find fault on the grounds of sexual inequity; though, once again, no systematic evidence is offered in support of this.

An example of a study which examines the behavioural norms valued in a school is Gillborn's (1990a) research in a multi-ethnic comprehensive. He claims that the teachers in the school held conceptions of the 'ideal client' which were based upon the values and norms of their 'white experience and culture' (p. 27); and that, as a result, they tended to make negative, ethnocentric judgments of the behaviour of their Afro-Caribbean students. He argues that '[. . .] in the day-to-day life of the school almost any display of Afro-Caribbean ethnicity was deemed inappropriate and was controlled [. . .]' (p. 29); that the students' ethnicity was 'devalued'; and that this created tension and conflict between teachers and students.

Gillborn presents very little evidence which specifically supports these claims. We might reasonably have expected examples of teachers' conceptions of the 'ideal client' derived from interviews or conversations with a representative sample of them, together with an analysis of the ways in which they could be considered ethnocentric. We could also have expected Gillborn to present observational data on a range of displays of Afro-Caribbean cultural behaviour on the part of students, with examination of the teachers' interpretations and behavioural responses to these. But this aspect of Gillborn's study rests almost entirely on a description of one example of a teacher's negative response to an Afro-Caribbean boy's 'way of walking': the student was 'called out from a line of pupils entering the assembly hall and ordered to "Stand up straight" and "Walk properly." ' (p. 28). Gillborn argues that this way of walking, 'with seemingly exaggerated swinging of the shoulders and a spring in the step', was distinctively Afro-Caribbean. And he claims that the teacher's response on this occasion was typical of the way teachers in the school routinely responded to this cultural form. 'It was', he claims, 'always interpreted as in some way inappropriate by members of staff' (p. 28). He also argues that teachers' responses to this way of walking were typical of their responses to other displays of Afro-Caribbean culture amongst the students, and 'reflected a more general tendency among the staff to devalue anything which did not conform to their own (white) expectations and experience' (p. 29).

There are obvious problems with this evidence. First, one example is insufficient to support the generalizations that Gillborn makes. Indeed, one of his generalizations would have been impossible for him to establish: he claims that this student behaviour was 'without exception interpreted by the teachers as being inappropriate to school' (p. 29). Yet he could not have witnessed every instance of this behaviour in the school. And if what he means is that every instance in his sample was treated by teachers in this way, we need information about the nature of the sample. Moreover, there is some evidence which raises questions even about this much more restricted claim: on the previous page he mentions another example of a student walking in this way *following* a reprimand, and no teacher response is reported.

We also need to consider Gillborn's assumption that this way of walking was a display of Afro-Caribbean culture. Treating particular forms of behaviour as expressions of ethnicity raises serious theoretical problems; indeed, it can amount to cultural essentialism (see Sharrock, 1974). Moreover, people's behaviour is rarely just an expression of *ethnic* culture. There are multiple cultural influences on it, including those deriving from gender, social class and generational factors; and this way of walking seems likely to have been subject to all of these other influences. Furthermore, behaviour is rarely just a product of culture. It often involves strategic action, where cultural characteristics are used in different ways on different occasions to achieve different ends. In examining and assessing teachers' responses we would need to take account of how this way of walking was *used* by Afro-Caribbean boys. Indeed, Gillborn points out that it was sometimes adopted by these students as 'a strategy of resistance' (p. 28). Yet he fails to consider that the teacher he described might have interpreted it in just this way, as a challenge to his authority. Here again Gillborn provides no evidence about the teacher's perspective — indeed he declares that such evidence is 'unimportant' (p. 29). From the point of view of some evaluative standards this may be so. It could be, for example, that Gillborn believes that attempts to control students' ways of walking are outside the legitimate authority of teachers and schools. This is certainly the view of some students (see Werthman, 1963; Willis, 1977), and there is a case to be made for such a view. However, it is not the only value judgment which could be used as a basis for describing this incident, and the question of the scope of teachers' authority is not a matter about which we believe researchers can come to any conclusion, given the limits of *their* (intellectual rather than practical) authority.

Finally, we need to ask whether the teacher's response was simply a reaction to the student's way of walking. Here again the possibility arises of different interpretative definitions of the same behaviour. We are given very little information about the context in which this incident occurred. As a result, we do not know whether Gillborn has presented all the relevant features of it. Indeed, because he does not spell out the evaluative standard he is employing we do not know what he would and would not count as relevant. Instead the nature of the incident is treated as obvious and as an unproblematic indicator of this teacher's and others' ethnocentrism and racism.

Another study which claims to document inequality deriving from the cultural differences between the school and students is Dubberley's research on a comprehensive school located in a Yorkshire mining community (Dubberley, 1988a). He claims that there was a major culture clash between the middle-class staff and the working-class students. He argues that the majority of teachers regarded working-class culture as 'deficient and parochial' (p. 181) and sought to impose middle-class linguistic and cultural norms on the working class students. He claims that they saw those students as 'thick' and 'inferior' and provided them with a 'second rate form of education' (p. 184). Moreover, they added insult to injury by blaming the students and their culture for their failure in school. Dubberley goes on to suggest that the students saw through and resisted this process of 'cultural hegemony', though only in part: they tended to blame, and react against, individual teachers — those whom they perceived as weak or disrespectful — rather than the system itself. He suggests that, ironically, this reaction served to reinforce their failure.

Dubberley supports these claims primarily on the basis of informants' accounts, though he also occasionally provides generalized description of classroom interaction based on his own observations. The informant accounts provided are of two main types. First, there are extracts from interviews conducted with two groups of 16-year-old working-class, bottom-stream, students: the 'lads' and the 'lasses'. In three of these extracts students complain about the teachers correcting their speech and in one they object to a teacher's over-elaborate explanation of the meaning of a word and what they see as the more favourable treatment of 'posh people', that is of higher-stream students. Second, there are extracts from interviews with, and conversations between, some of the teachers. For instance, a small number of teachers comment on what they see as negative aspects of some students' social backgrounds (four teachers), their frustration with some of the students' attitudes to school (two teachers), their strategies for dealing with less able groups (two teachers), and the lack of social-class awareness of some of their colleagues (two teachers).

This research suffers from similar problems to other work relying primarily on accounts. A small number of teachers and students are quoted, and there must be considerable doubt about the representativeness and accuracy of their views. In the case of the students, as with other studies (including that of Willis, 1977), a particular group of students is treated as representative of working-class students in general, with no supporting evidence for this and the strong probability that they were unrepresentative in important respects.

In addition, in several cases there are questions to be raised about the interpretations Dubberley makes of his informants' accounts. Take, for instance, the following discussion between Dubberley and one of the teachers:

Mr Marshall: I'd like to teach fishing next year if the boss OK's it.
Me: With everybody?
Mr Marshall: No — with the 'Duggie Diggers' — have you heard of them?
Me: I've heard of them but who are they?
Mr Marshall: They're of very low ability. There t'hardest group I have . . . I take them for rural studies and duggie is the local term — it means 'thickie'. They call themselves that — 'Duggie Diggers'.
Me: Why not fishing across with the 'O' level group?
Mr Marshall: Well you try to give the kids what they need. They need this.

Dubberley claims on the basis of these comments that the teacher 'implicitly accepted the notion of IQ and culture deficiency when describing the kind of curriculum the students should be following' (p. 196). It seems to us that no such acceptance is implied. The teacher refers to the students' 'ability', but does not mention IQ, and what he means by this term is unclear on the information provided. He makes no reference to cultural deficiency, nor is there anything said from which views about this could reasonably be inferred. A more generous interpretation of the comments would be that the teacher wished to provide a relevant and meaningful curriculum experience for this group of students. Of course, whether such treatment is equitable depends on the version of that principle we adopt. The important point here, though, is not equity, or even the charity with which we should interpret informants' accounts, but rather recognition that competing interpretations are possible. Dubberley shows no sign of this: he treats the validity of his own interpretation as obvious and not in need of supporting evidence; and this is characteristic of the way he interprets the accounts of the teachers.

Dubberley's interpretation of the teachers' accounts contrasts markedly with his tendency to accept unquestioningly many of the students' complaints about the teachers' behaviour; translating them into his own language of class-cultural oppression. Here again, alternative interpretations are often available, but they are not considered. For example, he accepts the students' criticism of a teacher's attempt to explain the meaning of a word by referring to its origins, and 'whether it is an adjective or a noun' (pp. 182–3), as implying that they are stupid. This could be interpreted, however, as the teacher treating bottom-set students in the same way as top-set students, rather than treating them differently. Dubberley simply accepts these students' claim that the teacher does not behave the same way towards 'the "snobs", "wi money", "whose parents have got a good job" ' (p. 183). Moreover, here and elsewhere, Dubberley makes no attempt to spell out the evaluative standards that either he or the students are using. Instead, different ones are employed on different occasions, in such a way as to reveal what he takes to be endemic discrimination against working-class students.

Another major problem with Dubberley's work is that, throughout his account, he makes little attempt to explain what he means by middle-class or working-class culture. There is no information about how social class has been operationalized. Furthermore, it is not clear what Dubberley takes to be the middle-class 'linguistic and cultural norms' which the teachers are imposing, or how he feels working-class cultural forms differ from them. Indeed, doubt is thrown on the conflict between the local working-class culture and the 'middle-class' knowledge and behavioural norms purveyed by the school when it emerges that (much to Dubberley's dismay) the local community was in favour of the re-introduction of a grammar school (p. 186; see also Dubberley, 1988b, p. 121).

In summary, then, there are serious problems with much of the research which makes claims about bias in the knowledge, skills and norms of behaviour valued in schools. The underlying evaluative standards are often not made explicit, and researchers generally fail to establish that the curriculum they describe appeals more to the interests and background knowledge of dominant social groups, or that norms of behaviour devalue the culturally different behaviour of subordinate groups. Furthermore, interpretations of data are often presented as if they were incontrovertible, when they are patently open to question; and there are frequently doubts about the representativeness of the examples provided.

Socialization into Inequality

There is also research which is concerned with the images of different categories of person transmitted in overt and hidden curricula. It is often argued that these portray inequality as normal, and thereby reinforce it. This is typically supported by two types of evidence. Some studies provide data about the gender or ethnic images contained in the content of curriculum materials, especially of school textbooks. Others present evidence from researchers' observations of the messages conveyed in teachers' classroom strategies.

An example of the first approach is a study by Walford (1980) of 'sex bias in physics textbooks'. He argues that the physics textbooks in use at the time of his research presented a masculine image of the subject. This resulted from the fact that in text and illustrations male characters appear more frequently, and males are shown in 'more leading and active roles', that physics problems are related more often to 'typically masculine pursuits such as football or boxing', that the questions which students are asked are 'usually about "a man" or "a boy" ' (p. 222).

To support these claims Walford presents the results of a content analysis of some popular physics textbooks (two series containing several volumes and nine other books). He focuses on the illustrations and presents data about the number in the books showing males, females or both. He also presents a series of examples of the sort of traditional roles that women are shown play-ing in these illustrations. He notes that a few show 'women taking an active part in an experiment or occupation', but he argues that they 'are far more likely to be seen in passive roles or in traditional feminine roles rather than as active participants in the world of physics' (p. 223).

Many of Walford's claims are quite plausible in themselves, and his evid-ence shows convincingly that in these textbooks males are predominant in illustrations, and that women tended to be shown in traditional roles. It offers less support for Walford's other claims, or for the proposition that physics textbooks generally present a male-biased image of the subject. This is be-cause his analysis is confined to illustrations. He does not give any data about the text in these books, or about the nature of physics problems or ques-tions for students. Of course, it might be argued that illustrations are the most influential aspects of textbooks in shaping students' perceptions of sub-jects. Walford claims that they have 'immediate impact' (p. 222) but he does not provide evidence that they are the most influential feature. This relates to a wider problem: that textbook analysis does not tell us how materials are actually used in the classroom; and thus whether the supposed images are actually received by students, or how they interpret them. There is also the question of how representative these textbooks are (or were) of physics text-books used in schools. This is difficult to know for certain, though it seems probable that they were representative of those in common use in schools at the time.[8]

An example of research which is based mainly on a researcher's observa-tions of the *hidden* curriculum is contained in Riddell's (1992) study of gender inequality in two comprehensive schools, part of which we discussed in the last chapter. She devotes a section of her book to the study of 'gender codes in the classroom', and claims that the teachers' coping strategies 'transmitted traditional conceptions of masculinity and femininity' (p. 146). More specific-ally, she argues that teachers controlled boys by giving them most attention, by orientating the content of lessons to their interests and, in the case of male teachers, by using physical violence or creating 'an atmosphere of male cama-raderie based on sexual joking' (p. 150) which sometimes 'involved the dero-gation of women' (p. 151). She also argues that some female teachers controlled girls by drawing on 'a culture of femininity' (p. 151) of a 'traditional' kind.

In the main, Riddell supports these claims with illustrative examples con-sisting of qualitative descriptions based on her lesson observations. For exam-ple, she provides evidence for her argument that teachers allowed boys to monopolize their attention by means of a description of an art lesson where

---

[8]   A method adopted by Hicks (1980) in a study of geography textbooks was to survey a sample of schools to ascertain which textbooks they used and to base the content analysis on these books.

the teacher appears to respond to the demanding, and sometimes deviant, behaviour of a group of boys by giving them more attention. And she supports her claim that the teachers utilized traditional notions of femininity in handling girls with a description of a textiles lesson in which girls were engaged informally in making floor cushions and clothes. 'The atmosphere of this lesson,' Riddell comments, 'as girls tried on clothes and talked about boys, parents, friends, and teachers, was more like a cosy chat in a bedroom than a school lesson' (p. 152). She also uses a small number of informants' accounts to support her arguments. For example, she offers evidence for her claim that male teachers used 'sexual joking' to control boys by quoting a woodwork teacher who explains that he sometimes uses 'a dirty joke' in teaching all-boys groups, whereas this is not possible with all-girls groups.

Riddell's study suffers from most of the problems we have already discussed. She uses a very small number of examples which, though useful in themselves, cannot establish her claim that the strategies she describes were typical of lessons generally in the two schools. Indeed, she does not tell us how many lessons or teachers she observed; though it is clear that the observations in both schools took place over a considerable period (Riddell, 1992, p. 242). More importantly, she does not make clear in what proportion of the lessons the particular coping strategies were observed, or how often they occurred in particular lessons. Instead she relies upon vague generalizations such as that 'in many lessons the masculine bias was fairly subtle' (p. 150) or that 'the content of lessons was often shaped to hold the attention of potentially disruptive boys' (p. 148).

Riddell's work also displays considerable conceptual ambiguity. She is unclear, for example, about what she means by the term 'coping strategy'. She appears to use it to refer to teachers' behaviour which is orientated to 'maintain(ing) their authority in the classroom' (p. 143). But how such behaviour was recognized and distinguished from other forms of teacher behaviour is not made explicit; and this is likely to be problematic given the multi-functionality of much teacher behaviour (Doyle, 1977). This raises questions about whether some of the behaviour Riddell describes can be legitimately placed under this conceptual heading. For example, the textiles lesson mentioned above is presented by her as an instance of teachers drawing on 'a culture of femininity to win girls' cooperation in the classroom' (p. 151). Yet, it seems possible that the content of the lesson and the teaching techniques adopted were selected not merely to 'win girls' cooperation', but because the teacher wished to transmit particular knowledge and skills in the most effective way.

There are also problems regarding how Riddell decided whether or not the coping strategies she observed 'transmitted traditional conceptions of masculinity and femininity'. Certainly, there are doubts about some of the instances she presents. For example, she describes a history lesson in which a teacher talks about the violent deaths which occurred in the trenches during the First World War, arguing that the lesson content was selected to 'hold the

ntion of potentially disruptive boys' (p. 148), and noting that a girl com-
ained that she did not want to hear about this, but that boys 'made a great
now of enjoying these accounts' (p. 149). But it is not clear from Riddell's
description what conceptions of masculinity or femininity are being transmitted here, or that the material was selected or functioned as a 'coping
strategy' in this case. And in many of the other examples Riddell gives there
are similar questions about whether a gendered image is being transmitted,
and if so what the nature of that image is.

Finally, here too there are questions about the causal contribution made
to students' attitudes by whatever picture of gender relations may have been
contained in the curriculum. Riddell does document these attitudes, but she
does not provide any rigorous assessment of the effect of schools on them.

The argument that classroom processes socialize students into an acceptance of inequality is by no means well established, then. Claims are sometimes
based on analysis of only limited aspects of the curriculum material, there are
doubts about how representative the materials analysed are of the curriculum
which is actually taught in schools, and there are questions about the actual
impact of the features identified. Those studies which focus on images contained in the hidden curriculum often fail to clarify the phenomena which is
their real focus of concern, or the nature of the images they claim are presented. And, where they highlight particular instances of bias, they present
little evidence to support their claims that such bias is common and has a
significant impact on students.

Effects of Differential Treatment on Self-esteem

A small number of studies have explored some aspects of the link between
unequal treatment and students' self-concepts and levels of motivation. One is
the study by Green (1983) discussed earlier. Green not only claimed that 'West
Indian' students were treated less favourably than their 'European' peers in the
classrooms of the twelve ethnically 'highly intolerant' teachers he studied, but
also that this treatment resulted in these students having lower levels of self-
esteem than European students.

Green's claim has some theoretical plausibility. If we accept his account
of the particular nature of the unequal treatment received by West Indian
students (especially boys), involving high levels of criticism and low levels
of praise, it would not be surprising if this had a negative effect on these students' self-esteem. Such an argument has some support in psychological theories which emphasize how a person's self-image is influenced by the way
significant others behave towards them; it is central, for example, to symbolic
interactionism, as epitomized by Cooley's concept of the 'looking glass self'.

However, we have already expressed doubts about the validity of Green's
measurement of classroom interaction; and there are problems too with his

assessment of levels of students' self-esteem. He measured this variable by adapting three existing scales — the Bledsoe Self-Concept Scale, the Coopersmith Self-Esteem Inventory, and Waetjen's Self-Concept as a Learner scale. The students, some of whom were as young as 7, were asked in a classroom situation to indicate, by placing a tick or cross next to an appropriate serial number, whether or not they thought various short descriptive statements applied to them. The Bledsoe Scale included thirty statements (such as 'I am friendly', 'I am obedient', 'I am honest') on a variety of personal qualities. The Coopersmith Inventory contained twenty-five statements (such as 'I'm a lot of fun to be with', 'I give in very easily', 'I can't be depended upon'), again dealing with a variety of qualities. The Self-Concept as a Learner scale included fifty statements of a similar style focused on four dimensions of learning: 'motivation, task orientation, problem solving and class membership'. The descriptive statements were read out to the students by the researcher and, at regular intervals, they were reminded that they had to indicate whether or not the statement described them. Following this, as the students' papers were collected, 'they were sorted unobtrusively into ethnic groups' (p. 75). In each scale responses which indicated a positive self-concept were given a score of one, and the student's total score was calculated by summing his/her score on the three scales.

There are at least two problems with this measurement strategy. First, Green combined three different measures of self-esteem. Two of these relate to self-esteem on a variety of different dimensions, such as friendliness, obedience, sociability, dependability, and so on. In other words they were general measures of self-concept. Only the third relates to what we termed earlier 'academic self-esteem'; though there were more statements in the third scale, so that his measure was weighted towards this dimension. There is also a question about Green's conceptualization of levels of self-esteem. Using his measure students were seen as having low self-esteem if their views of themselves were less positive than the views of other students about themselves. Yet, it could be argued that of greater relevance was the degree to which students' views of themselves were lower or higher than their actual academic capabilities. Green did not consider levels of self-esteem in this sense.

The second problem is that the measures of self-esteem may have been influenced significantly by reactivity. Given that many of the students were quite young, that the exercise was conducted in the classroom, and that students were asked to put their names on their replies, it seems possible that they may have adjusted their answers to fit how they thought others (perhaps the researcher, their teacher or possibly their peers) felt they should see themselves.

Furthermore, even if we accept the validity of Green's data about unequal treatment and self-esteem, there are problems with accepting his conclusion that the differences in self-esteem he documents were the product of differential classroom treatment. First, his data about both refer to the ethnic groups in the classes of the two sets of twelve teachers, not to individual children. For instance, we are only given information about the total number of instances of criticism directed to West Indian students compared to European and Asian students, and about the mean self-esteem scores of each group. Thus, we do not know whether those particular West Indian students who experienced high levels of criticism (or other aspects of unequal treatment) were the ones who also had low self-esteem scores. For Green's explanatory claim to be convincing we need this sort of evidence.

It is also possible that the causal link actually worked in the opposite direction to that which Green assumes — that the low self-esteem of West Indian students caused the unequal treatment that he identified, rather than the reverse. It would not be surprising if low levels of self-esteem resulted in poor motivation amongst students. This, in turn, could have caused them to behave disruptively in the classroom, and teachers could have responded with high levels of criticism, lower levels of praise, etc. Whilst Green points out that the correlation he discovered does not necessarily imply causation, the whole tenor of his presentation suggests that unequal treatment causes low self-esteem on the part of West Indian students.[9]

Stanworth (1983) also argues that unequal treatment has an effect on students' self-esteem and motivation. She claims that the dominance of boys in classroom interaction results in girls under-estimating their own academic ability, and in boys over-estimating theirs. We have already reviewed Stanworth's claims about unequal treatment in the classroom. To support her argument about the effects on students' estimation of their own abilities she reports the results of an exercise in which teachers and students ranked each member of their class 'according to their success in the subject'. She explains: 'In the nineteen cases out of twenty-four where pupils' rankings were different from those of their teachers, all of the girls under-estimated their rank; all but one of the boys over-estimated theirs' (p. 44).

The problem here, though, is that we do not know how representative the twenty-four students who completed the ranking exercise were of the students in the department as a whole, nor do we know how many teachers were involved, or what their relative rankings of boys and girls were. Moreover, Stanworth does not tell us how many of the nineteen whose self-rankings differed from their teachers were male and how many female, or by how much their rankings differed.

As regards Stanworth's explanatory argument, like Green's it has some theoretical plausibility. It is certainly possible that boys' high profile, and girls' lack of prominence, in classroom interaction conveys an implicit message that

---

[9]   It is also worth noting that the large corpus of research on self-esteem and ethnicity is contradictory in its findings; or, to put matters another way, while some studies find students of a particular group to have lower self-esteem than their peers, others do not. As Verma and Bagley (1982, p. 225) write: 'it is unwise to conclude that one ethnic group has poorer self-esteem than another. Self-esteem is part of a complex identity structure and has different groundings and different meanings in different ethnic groups'. See also Tomlinson, 1983, Ch. 9.

boys are more capable than girls.[10] But, of course, there are other equally plausible explanations for these differential judgments of self-worth. Differences in self-esteem between different categories of student may also be due, for instance, to factors relating to the differing socialization of boys and girls outside the classroom. And, as with Green's study, it is possible that, if there is a causal relationship here, it works in the opposite direction — that girls' under-estimation of their own capabilities causes them to be more reticent in the classroom, and boys' over-estimation results in their greater participation. Stanworth seems to select one explanation from a range of plausible ones, without showing that it is more credible than its competitors.

These studies also assume, of course, that there is a causal link between self-esteem and educational achievement — more specifically that low levels of academic self-esteem lead to low achievement. In fact, though, the psychological literature does not give strong support for this view. It seems to be the case that the interaction between students' beliefs about their competence and what they actually achieve varies under different circumstances (see Moreland *et al.*, 1981; Bachman and O'Malley, 1986; Marsh, 1990; Skaalvik and Hagtvet, 1990; Eshel and Kurman, 1991). Given this, it is dangerous to make any broad generalizations about the relationship between self-esteem and achievement. However, what evidence there is suggests that students with high levels of performance often have relatively low levels of academic self-esteem, in the sense of underrating their ability, whilst students who achieve less often overestimate their ability. This might be taken to suggest that low self-esteem (in this sense) may be more conducive to educational success than high-esteem. At the very least, the causal question about the relationship between unequal treatment and lower educational achievement, via depressed levels of self-esteem, requires considerably more evidence than these studies provide.

Conclusion

In this chapter we have examined a variety of arguments about unequal treatment by teachers in the classroom of students from different social categories, and the effects of this. This research has gone some way to charting a complex and important area, but there are significant problems with much of it. Conceptual issues about the value principles on which evaluative descriptions and explanations are based have been almost totally neglected. Instead, descriptions and explanations have been presented as if they were founded solely on factual considerations; even though evaluative conclusions have often been drawn on the basis of them.

[10] For a rather different explanation, in terms of causal attributions of failure, see Licht and Dweck, 1987. They suggest that it is not that teachers have lower expectations of girls but that girls interpret those expectations differently to boys. In fact, they argue that girls are disadvantaged by the effects of teachers' greater criticism of boys for their classroom behaviour.

There are also some serious problems with the evidential base on which descriptive claims about differential treatment rely. Sometimes no evidence at all is presented, even though the claims are insufficiently plausible to be accepted at face value. And when evidence *is* provided it is often of a kind which cannot effectively support the sort of claim made: for instance, one or two examples are offered to establish the differential frequency of particular sorts of teacher action in relation to different categories of student. Moreover, many of the interpretations made of data are questionable. And, whilst the explanatory claims made in this area have some theoretical plausibility, most of them lack adequate empirical support. Despite this, they are often presented as if they were well established, little or no attention being given to alternatives. In short, the difficulties involved in establishing claims about unequal treatment in the classroom have been grossly underestimated.

Differences in treatment of the kind discussed in this chapter and the previous one are sometimes presented as inequitable in themselves. However, a central concern in most of this research is inequity of opportunity. This involves additional claims about the effects of these inequalities on educational outcomes. It is to this issue that we turn in the next chapter.

Chapter 6

Inequalities in Educational Outcomes

In the previous two chapters we examined a wide range of research reporting inequalities in schools, both at the level of school organization and at that of classroom interaction. Our primary focus there was on how effectively these studies had established that unequal treatment of students from different social categories had occurred. However, most of this research has been concerned not simply with the fact of differential treatment, but also with its effects on educational outcomes. Indeed, as we saw in Chapter 1, this work emerged as part of a movement which rejected earlier explanations for inequalities of outcome, in terms of differences in home background, in favour of an emphasis on the role of school processes. In this chapter, then, we will consider the explanatory validity of research on inequalities in schools; in other words, we will assess how effectively it explains differences in the educational outcomes achieved by different categories of student.

In Chapter 3, we outlined a procedure for assessing explanations, and we will follow it fairly closely here. The first step of that procedure is to establish the nature of what is to be explained. So, to begin with we need to address the character and extent of social class, gender, and ethnic differences in educational outcomes. Subsequently, we will consider some of the problems involved in interpreting outcome data, and then review the evidence for a causal relationship between unequal treatment in schools and outcome inequalities.

Inequalities in Educational Outcomes

Many studies of inequalities in the organization and functioning of schools discuss the outcome inequalities they are seeking to explain in only the briefest of terms. Thus, in the preface to *Beachside Comprehensive*, Stephen Ball confines himself to locating his work in the tradition of studies concerned with explaining 'the disappointing performance of working class pupils' (Ball, 1981, p. xv); echoing the rationale provided by Lacey ten years earlier (Lacey, 1970, p. ix). Similarly, in the terms of its subtitle, Paul Willis's influential book *Learning to Labour* is concerned with 'how working class kids get working class jobs' (Willis, 1977, pp. vii and 1). Much the same summary treatment of what is to be explained is also found in an article by Bruce Carrington which argues that extra-curricular involvement in sport constitutes a 'side-track' that facilitates 'West Indian academic failure' (Carrington, 1983, p. 41). And, in their review of research on gender and schools, Measor and Sikes (1992, p. 2) identify one of the central concerns of such work as the fact that 'girls and more specifically working class girls', along with black pupils, 'significantly underachieve in British schools'; in that they leave 'unqualified or inadequately qualified'. In many studies of school and classroom processes, then, the existence and nature of the outcome inequalities which those processes are held to explain are treated as sufficiently well-known and unproblematic in character as to require only the sketchiest of outlines. Indeed, sometimes outcome inequalities are not even mentioned but are simply assumed, as for example in some studies of gender imbalance in classroom participation (Hammersley, 1990a).

However, a few researchers have given rather more detail about their explanatory focus. Thus, in her book on sexual divisions in the classroom, Michelle Stanworth begins with a discussion of social-class inequalities in educational outcome, expressing what has become the standard conclusion in this area:

> [. . .] those who hoped that the reforms which followed the 1944 Education Act would ensure a society in which selection was based on merit rather than social position have been disappointed; neither educational expansion nor educational reform has ushered in an era of equal opportunity. (Stanworth, 1983, p. 9)

And in her book she extends this conclusion to gender inequalities as well. She reports that although girls have overtaken boys in some aspects of school achievement, nevertheless a higher proportion of boys than girls leave school with three 'A' levels, and fewer girls gain suitable qualifications for university entry. She also emphasizes the differences in achievement between female and male students across subjects, arguing that this damages the occupational prospects of women. She comments:

> The oft-cited fact that similar proportions of women and men now gain two 'A' levels is cold comfort when we consider the majority of women [. . .] who, lacking any marketable qualifications, end up combining unskilled and poorly rewarded occupations with the responsibilities of housework and child care. (Stanworth, 1983, p. 10)

Similarly, in his book *'Race', Ethnicity and Education*, Gillborn also devotes considerable discussion to outcome inequalities, providing one of the most substantial discussions of the differential examination performance of ethnic groups (Gillborn, 1990a, Ch. 5). His main conclusion on the basis of this is that 'as a group Afro-Caribbean pupils are not leaving school with qualifications which match those of certain other groups at the highest levels' (p. 140); and he notes that this is also true of Bangladeshi and Turkish students. Both he and others have argued that teachers' attitudes towards and treatment of Afro-Caribbean and other ethnic-minority students, coupled with the effects of school-based selection processes, explain their relatively poor educational attainment. Indeed, great emphasis has recently come to be placed in this field on the causal significance of intra-school processes (Troyna, 1991a and b; Gillborn, 1995, pp. 41–7).

In this section we will look briefly at some of the information which is available about educational outcomes, dealing separately with social class, gender, and 'racial'/ethnic differences. As we shall see, there is a great deal more information about some sorts of outcome than about others.[1] Most of the research we have examined in the previous two chapters was carried out in the 1960s, 1970s and 1980s. As such, it relates to educational outcomes from the late 1960s onwards, so we will restrict our focus to that time period.

Social-class Differences

As we noted in Chapter 1, until relatively recently interest in the question of educational inequality was largely restricted to a concern with social-class differences in educational achievement. The main landmarks in post-war educational policy were all partly justified by reference to the goal of increasing educational opportunities for working-class students. Not surprisingly, therefore, differential educational outcomes between the social classes were a major preoccupation of researchers in the 1950s and 1960s (see, for example, Little and Westergaard, 1964). Since then, however, rather less attention has been given to this topic.

The major source of more recent data is the Oxford Mobility Study (Halsey, Heath and Ridge, 1980; see also Goldthorpe, 1980); and even this only provides information about the early section of our period and about males. Halsey, Heath and Ridge examine the fortunes of four cohorts of men born at various points during the twentieth century, tracing their routes through the education system and into the occupational structure. Using a three-class model — which distinguishes service, intermediate, and working classes — they argue that there are significant social-class differences in examination results at 16+ and 18+. However, they suggest that these are to be accounted for almost entirely in terms of differential survival rates in secondary school (Halsey, Heath and Ridge, 1980, p. 141). Table 6.1 shows the information they provide about survival rates to 16 and beyond, for the cohort of students born 1943–52, the latest one for which they have data (see Table 6.1).

Here we have clear social-class differences in the proportion of boys staying on at school; and even sharper differences are to be found among

---

[1] We will focus on *school* outcomes rather than on those of the education system as a whole; and we will not even discuss all the types of school outcome which have been given attention in the literature. The main omission is delinquency levels, on which see, for example, Rutter *et al.* 1979 and Reynolds, Sullivan and Murgatroyd, 1987.

Table 6.1: Percentage staying on until 16 or after

Father's social class	
Service class	78.6
Intermediate class	48.5
Working class	31.6

Source: Derived from Table 8.10, Halsey, Heath and Ridge, 1980, p. 136

Table 6.2: Attendance at university

Father's social class	%
Service class	26.4
Intermediate class	8.0
Working class	3.1
All	8.5
N	(2246)

Source: Based on Halsey, Heath and Ridge 1980, Table 10.8, p. 188

those staying on until 18 or later (Halsey, Heath and Ridge 1980, p. 140, Table 8.11). Moreover, as might be expected, social-class inequalities are greater still in terms of attendance at university (see Table 6.2).

This research reveals substantial social-class differences in educational outcomes, then; and these increase the higher the level of outcome considered. Indeed, Halsey, Heath and Ridge suggest that, because of this, the process of qualification inflation may well lead to class differentials persisting indefinitely (Halsey, Heath and Ridge 1980, pp. 140–1).

It is important to note that this study does not allow us to draw conclusions about the effects of comprehensivization and other changes since the early 1970s. The youngest cohort Halsey, Heath and Ridge studied went through the school system while comprehensive schools were still in a minority, and in their early stages of development (Halsey, Heath and Ridge, 1980, p. 21).

There are a few other sources on which we can draw for information about more recent trends, but what they offer is rather limited. The Youth Cohort Study provides national data about social-class differences in 16+ examination results, relating to both girls and boys (Drew and Gray, 1990). Figure 6.1 presents a comparison of the examination performance of students from manual, intermediate and professional backgrounds who formed part of the largest sample in this study. These students reached the minimum leaving age in the mid- to late-1980s. A rather similar picture is given for all maintained schools in Nottinghamshire in 1991 by Jesson *et al.* (1992).

These data reflect the fact that the school-leaving age has been increased since the time of Halsey, Heath and Ridge's final cohort, and that the proportion of students entered for 16+ examinations has risen dramatically. However, differences in educational performance still persist between social classes at

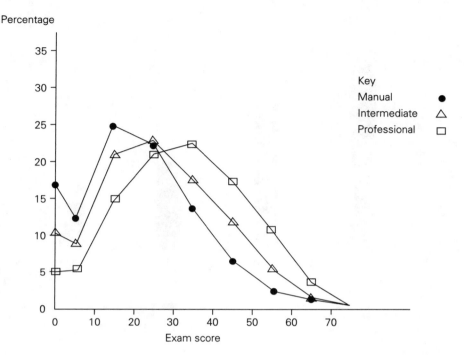

Percentage

Figure 6.1: Distributions of examination scores, by socio-economic groups
Source: Drew and Gray, 1990, Figure 3, p. 113
Note: Exam scoring system: 'O' level grades receive the following points: A = 7, B = 6, C = 5, D = 4, E = 3. CSE grades: grade 1 = 5, grade 2 = 4, grade 3 = 3, grade 4 = 2, grade 5 = 1. Ungraded results in both exams are scored as zero.

this point, and it is likely that they are greater at 18+; though it is not possible to assess changes over time in precise terms.

Sex Differences

Information about many educational outcomes is easier to obtain in relation to sex, as compared with social-class differences; since DES and DFE statistics often include separate figures for the two sexes. We will look at data for 16+ and 18+ examinations, and for entry to university, from the early 1970s to the most recent data available.

Figures 6.2 and 6.3 provide an indication of trends in examination performance at 16+ over the period from 1970–84. In 1970 approximately equal proportions of boys and girls gained at least one higher-grade pass (GCE A–C or CSE grade 1) at 16+, and gained multiple qualifications in English, mathematics, science plus a modern language. Girls underperformed compared to boys in mathematics, while outperforming them in English. Several

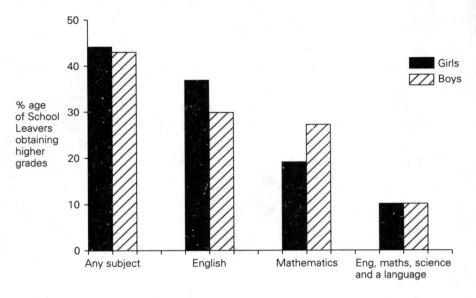

Figure 6.2: Percentages of male and female school leavers obtaining higher-grade scores at 16+ (GCE/CSE) by subject 1970/71
Source: Derived from DES *Digest of Statistics*, England, 1985 (Source: 10% Sample School Leavers Survey)

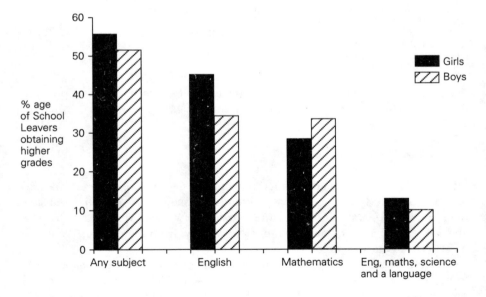

Figure 6.3: Percentages of female and male school leavers obtaining higher-grade scores at 16+ (GCE/CSE) by subject 1983/4
Source: Derived from DES *Digest of Statistics*, England, 1985 (Source: 10% Sample School Leavers Survey)

changes had occurred by 1984: a higher proportion of girls than boys now achieved at least one higher-grade GCE/CSE pass; and the gap between boys and girls in mathematics was reduced substantially; while that in English had increased. There was also a slightly larger proportion of girls than boys obtaining multiple qualifications in English, mathematics, science plus a modern language.

If we look at the situation at 18+ we find even sharper differences between the performance of girls and boys in different subjects, but similar trends towards a reduction of the disparity in mathematics and an increase of that in English (see Figures 6.4 and 6.5).

The picture presented by the most recently available data for performance at 16+ and 18+ is found in Figure 6.6. This shows that, overall, girls are now outperforming boys at both GCSE and 'A' level. If we look at performance at 16+ we find that girls generally outperform boys, apart from in mathematics and physics; and even here the gap has been reduced (see Figure 6.7). At 'A' level, substantial subject differences remain (see Figure 6.8). Here there is a clear imbalance between girls and boys across subjects, with girls dominating the humanities, and boys predominating in mathematics and the sciences (with the exception of biology). However, the gender gaps in all the science subjects have narrowed, in the context of a contraction in the overall number of passes (reflecting a reduction in the number of entries).

Finally, if we look at entry to university, we find that there has been an increase over time in the number of women gaining access. Indeed, in terms

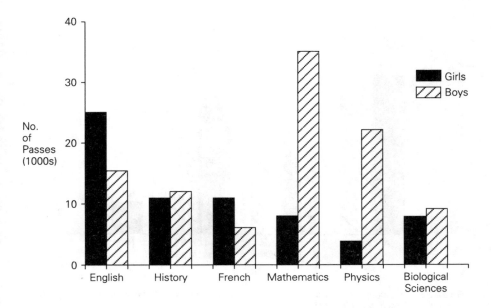

Figure 6.4:   Numbers of passes at 'A' level in various subjects by sex (1970)
Source: Derived from DES *Statistics of School Leavers CSE and GCE,* England 1980, Table 32

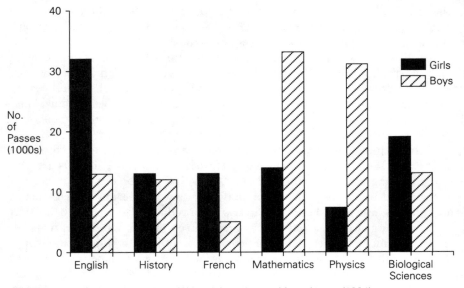

Figure 6.5:   Numbers of passes at 'A' level, in various subjects by set (1984)
Source: Derived from DES *Statistics of Education School Leavers CSE & GCE*, 1985, Table 32

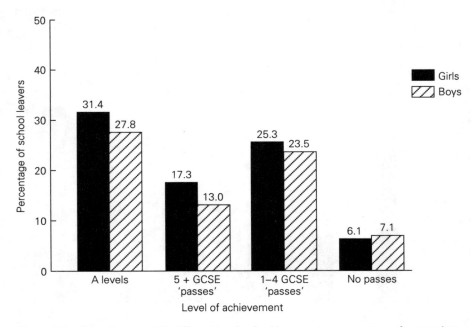

Figure 6.6:   School leavers with different levels of achievement as percentage of appropriate age group of each sex, UK 1991/2
Source: Derived from Mackinnon *et al.* 1995, Figure 11.5, p. 174. Based on GSS, 1994, *Educational Statistics for the United Kingdom*, 1993, Table 32, London, HMSO.

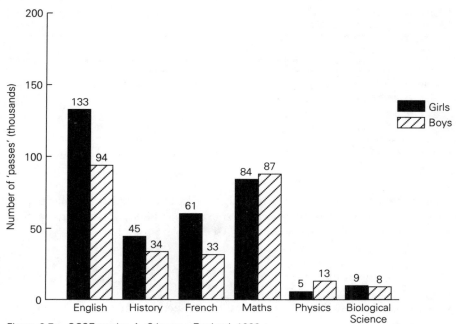

Figure 6.7: GCSE grades A–C by sex, England, 1992
Source: Derived from Mackinnon *et al.* 1995, Figure 11.6, p. 175 Based on DFE, 1993,
Statistics of Education Public Examinations: GCSE and GCE, 1992, Table 8, London, HMSO.

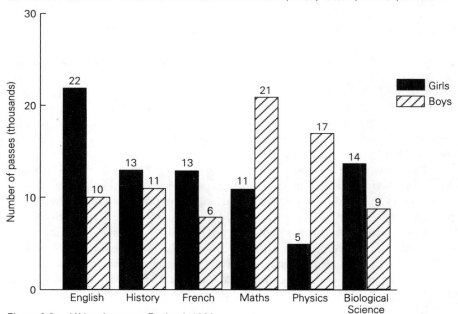

Figure 6.8: 'A' level passes, England, 1992
Source: Derived from Mackinnon, *et al.* 1995, Figure 11.7, p. 175. Based on DFE, 1993, Table 14
Note: 'AS' levels are included, with each 'AS' level pass counted as half an 'A' level pass

Table 6.3: Percentage of estimated population aged 18 on first degree courses in Higher Education Institutions, England.

	1983/4		1992/3	
	Females	**Males**	**Females**	**Males**
UFC universities	3.6	4.7	7.0	7.8
Former polytechnics	1.8	2.2	4.9	4.5
Other FHE institutions	1.2	0.5	2.4	1.1
Total	6.6	7.4	14.3	13.4

Source: Derived from DFE, Statistical Bulletin Issue 10/94 1994, Tables 7 & 8

of all higher-education institutions, at age 18 women now have a higher participation rate than men, though they still have a slightly lower participation rate in relation to the 'old universities' (see Table 6.3).

'Racial'/Ethnic Differences

As with social class, data about educational outcomes in relation to 'racial'/ethnic differences are not available in official statistics. However, since the 1970s, especially, there has been a considerable amount of research in this area. In a comprehensive review of the literature from 1960–82, Tomlinson notes a variety of local studies which tended to show the average levels of qualifications achieved by Afro-Caribbean students as lower than those of their white peers; though she also reports some conflicting findings (see Driver, 1980a and b; Taylor, 1981, pp. 113–22). As regards Asian students, the results of local studies from the 1970s were much more mixed, with some claiming that Asians do as well or even better than whites at 16+ (Taylor, 1973 and 1976), but others reporting that they underachieve compared to whites (Allen and Smith, 1975). Some studies found that while Asians were less likely to take 'O' levels they obtained slightly more passes than other students when they did so (Brooks and Singh, 1978).

The most comprehensive data relating to the 1970s and early 1980s are those reported by the Rampton/Swann Committee, collected in 1979 and 1982 in five LEAs that had high proportions of ethnic minority students. Figure 6.9 compares the performance of Afro-Caribbean and Asian students with that of others, at various levels. This shows the performance of Asian students to be quite close to the average, but that of Afro-Caribbean students to be lower at all levels; though the proportion of Afro-Caribbeans gaining five or more higher-grade passes at 16+ and one or more 'A' levels at 18+ increased between the two surveys (1978/9–1981/2) (Mackinnon and Statham, 1995, pp. 180–1).

Drew and Gray (1991) have provided the most recent and detailed review of studies concerned with inequalities in educational outcome as regards 'race'. They focus on the white–black gap in achievement in 16+ examination results.

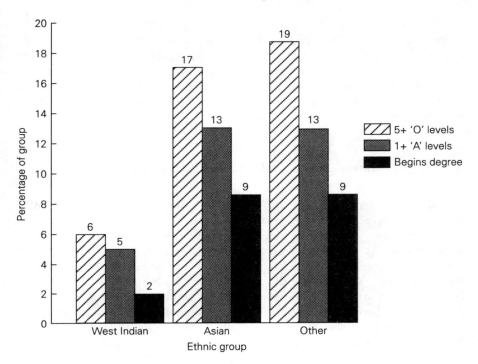

Figure 6.9: Educational attainment of ethnic groups 1981–2
Source: Derived from Mackinnon, et al 1995, Figure 11.3, p. 179. Based on DES, 1985, Education for All: Report of the Committee of Inquiry into the Education of Children from Ethnic Minority Groups (The Swann Report) Chapter 3, London, HMSO.

The studies they review cover the period from 1972 to the mid-1980s. They note that the ten studies present 'a relatively stable picture of the association between ethnic group and educational achievement' (Drew and Gray, 1991, p. 163). Once again, this portrays Afro-Caribbean students as performing less well than others. Drawing on the Youth Cohort Study, which relied on national data relating to the mid-1980s, they report that 20 per cent of all students and 19 per cent of Asian students achieved five or more 'higher-grade' passes, compared with 7 per cent of Afro-Caribbean students. And a similar, but smaller, disparity was also to be found at lower levels of achievement: 51 per cent of all students obtained one or more higher-grade passes, compared with 38 per cent of Afro-Caribbean students.

Until recently there was very little solid information about the participation of ethnic-minority students in higher education, though it was generally assumed that they were underrepresented. Ethnic monitoring data has begun to provide a clearer picture; though it is a complex one. It seems that, for the 1990 and 1991 cohorts of entrants, students of Bangladeshi origin are the only substantial minority group underrepresented in higher education, by comparison with numbers in the relevant age group. In these terms, white students are under-represented, in comparison with most other 'racial'/ethnic groups. However, as with gender, the situation is slightly different if one distinguishes between the 'old universities' and other higher education institutions. In the former, students of Pakistani and Afro-Caribbean descent join Bangladeshi students in being under-represented; though here again whites are also under-represented (Modood, 1993).

Interpreting Data on Educational Outcomes

The data presented in the previous section reveal a range of comparative inequalities and equalities, and also some changes over time. It is worth noting that, taking these data at face value, what stands in need of explanation varies somewhat across the three dimensions of social differentiation. In the case of social class, the persistence of inequalities seems to be the main issue, though the paucity of data available about recent trends makes precise assessment difficult. The situation is more complex with gender and ethnic differences. Even in 1970 there seems to have been little overall disparity in performance between girls and boys at 16+, in terms of 'higher-grade passes' achieved. There was, however, a gender imbalance in mathematics and scientific subjects. And while this has been reduced over time, a substantial imbalance still persists at 18+. There was also a gender imbalance in the humanities, in the opposite direction, and this has increased over time. These trends obviously call out for explanation; as does the closing of the difference between males and females in the proportions attending university, and the lag in this within higher-status institutions. As regards ethnic inequalities, whatever differences in performance at 16+ and 18+ there may have been in the past between whites and Asians, these seem to have largely disappeared. However, there appears to be continuing underachievement by Afro-Caribbean students. Both these features of the situation invite investigation.[2] So, too, does the relative success of students from some ethnic minorities compared to those from others in gaining access to higher education.

Three observations seem appropriate at this point. First, in terms of a concern with explaining inequality in educational outcomes, and changes in them over time, the research on schools we examined in the previous two chapters has been very selective in its focus. It has been concerned almost exclusively with explaining the persistence of inequalities rather than their reduction. Furthermore, the emphasis has been almost entirely on inequalities

---

[2] We are using 'underachievement' here in a purely descriptive way to refer to a factual inequality. In some usages it carries explanatory connotations, and this has led to criticism of the term: see, for example, Troyna, 1984 and Plewis, 1991. The same caveat applies to 'over-achievement', and also to 'over-representation'/'under-representation'.

which are taken to disadvantage working-class, female, and ethnic-minority students. Very little attention has been given to the improvement which has taken place in the performance of girls at 16+ and 18+, an improvement which has occurred even in the areas of mathematics and science. And there has been virtually no research on schools concerned with the worsening achievement of boys compared to girls at 16+.[3] In the same way, very little attention has been given to the apparent reduction in outcome inequalities between Asian and white students, or to the over-representation of many ethnic minorities in higher education.

The second point to be made is that there has been an almost exclusive focus on the *existence* of inequalities between social categories of student, rather than on the *extent* of inequality. Thus, whole categories of student have been treated as existing in a state of inequality with others. What the outcome data indicate, however, is that in terms of educational outcomes most of the comparisons show the majority of students within each category to be in an equal situation compared with most of those in other categories; for example in gaining or not gaining a particular level of qualification. Inequalities generally occur only at the margin: their probabilistic character of inequalities must not be forgotten. And it certainly must not be assumed that marginal differences necessarily indicate the operation of some factor, or set of factors, which discriminates against all members of a particular category.

A third observation is that some studies of school processes have been in search of an explanation for outcome inequalities which were diminishing or had already disappeared. This is particularly obvious in the case of sex differences in overall performance; but much the same point can be made about research on Asian students. Here too claims about the effects of unequal treatment have continued when, in terms of the available data, there is apparently little or no outcome inequality of the relevant kind to be explained.

However, we should not accept these data about educational outcomes at face value. They only deal with some sorts of outcome. And, like all data, they are constructions which are reliant on both factual and value assumptions (Troyna, 1984; Tanna, 1990). We will discuss three sets of problems involved in the construction of such data, relating to operationalization and measurement, sampling, and interpreting the significance of outcome inequalities.

Operationalization and Measurement Issues

We discussed the problems associated with operationalizing different social categories of student in Chapter 3. How these are resolved can have significant

---

[3] It is of some significance that in a discussion of sex differences in educational outcomes which *does* note the increasing success of girls, Skeggs (1989, p. 110) treats this as an indication of 'a trend towards diminishing differentials between girls and boys'. In fact, as we have seen, some of the differentials are now greater than they were in the past.

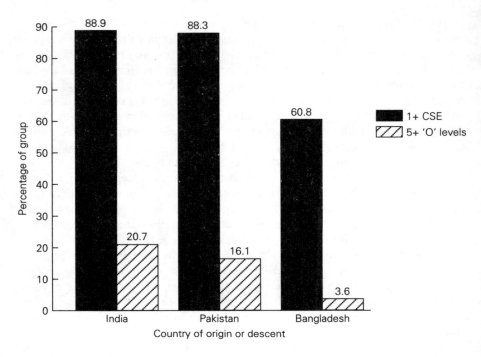

Figure 6.10: Examination results of fifth-year Asian pupils in the ILEA, by country of origin or descent, 1986
Source: Mackinnon, et al 1995, Figure 11.14. Based on ILEA Research and Statistics, 1987, Table 6
Note: '1+ CSE' means at least one CSE grade 5 or higher; '5+ 'O' levels' means at least five O levels grade C or higher.

consequences for conclusions about inequalities in outcomes. To take just one example, there are substantial differences between ethnic groups which are obscured by the general category 'Asian' (see Figure 6.10). Similar effects may be found if one varies social-class categorizations.

There are also problems of operationalization and measurement in relation to educational outcomes themselves. There are different ways of assessing level of educational performance. For example, at 16+ this can be presented in terms of overall numbers of higher-grade passes, according to some metric which measures level of performance across all subjects (see, for example, Jesson *et al.*, 1992), or on the basis of performance in particular key subjects, and in other ways. Furthermore, estimates of the proportions of students from different categories gaining any level of qualification will vary depending on what base figure is used. There are several possibilities here: for instance, proportion of that category in the population, in the relevant age group, among school leavers at the relevant age, or among those who took the examination.

The different base figures can produce very different results, since they measure different mixes of contributory factors. Thus, comparing the numbers of students from different social classes or ethnic groups achieving at a particular level at 18+ as a proportion of the numbers from that category in the age group measures survival in the education system to 18 and entry to the examination, as well as performance in it. Similarly, comparing the numbers of girls and boys obtaining a pass in the humanities and the sciences in terms of any base figure other than the proportion entering the relevant examinations conflates the effect of differential examination performance, differential entry, *and* differential choice of subject.

Another issue relating to the operationalization and measurement of outcomes is raised by Tanna (1990). She points to the significance of differences between ethnic groups in whether they achieve qualifications at a single point in time, or over several years. One implication of this is that any measure of the examination performance of school leavers in a particular year will under-represent the achievement level of any category of student whose members tend more than others to obtain qualifications through subsequent further study; which seems to be true of both Asian and Afro-Caribbean students (Smith and Tomlinson, 1989, p. 14). The same point applies in relation to university attendance. Women are over-represented amongst mature students, so that any measure of participation rates at age 18, of the kind we used earlier (see Table 6.3), is likely to underestimate their level of participation.

Equally important, the proportion of students from a category obtaining a particular educational qualification will be affected by other relevant characteristics of the population which makes up that category. This is a point which Troyna (1984, pp. 162–3) and others have made about the significance of differences in the social-class composition of different ethnic groups for the relative underachievement of Afro-Caribbean students.[4] In comparing Afro-Caribbean achievements with those of whites, populations with different balances between working- and middle-class groups are being compared. As a result, whatever differences are found may be as much the result of social class as of ethnicity. Conversely, gender differences in performance within ethnic groups can obscure underachievement on the part of males or females belonging to those groups. For example, it seems that Afro-Caribbean males may be under-represented in higher education, despite the fact that overall their ethnic group is over-represented (Modood, 1993, p. 171).

There are also some factors which may vary between different social categories of student whose relevance depends directly upon the particular definition of inequality adopted: notably, differences in average ability and aspiration.

Ability has sometimes been taken into account in relation to research on social-class inequalities, but there is little data available on the period with

---

[4] For some evidence, see Craft and Craft, 1983.

which we are concerned. Halsey, Heath and Ridge do offer a model of differential staying-on rates which allows for the distribution of measurable ability across social classes.[5] However, as they note, their estimates contain a considerable margin for error, not least because they did not have ability data for their sample and relied instead on assumptions about the distribution of ability between social classes based on data from elsewhere (Halsey, Heath and Ridge, 1980, pp. 136–40; see also Sauders, 1995, pp. 31–3).

There has been even less research on social-class inequalities in educational outcomes which has taken account of differences in levels of aspiration and motivation. As Murphy (1990) has pointed out, most research on educational inequality assumes equal levels of aspiration between the classes, or treats any differences in aspiration which might exist as themselves the product of inequality.[6] This will be reasonable on the basis of some definitions of opportunity, but it is by no means implied by all of them. Moreover, the measurement of differences in aspiration and motivation is even more problematic than the measurement of ability.

In the case of sex and ethnic differences, control for ability has been virtually non-existent. It seems to have been assumed by many researchers, often as a matter of principle, that there are no significant differences in ability between the sexes and across ethnic groups. However, some evidence is provided by studies which have sought to examine the progress of children from different ethnic backgrounds. For example, Blatchford *et al.* (1985) tested samples of Afro-Caribbean and white 5-year-olds in terms of early reading, early mathematical, and early writing skills, and they found no significant ethnic differences.[7] However, as the authors note, there are some methodological problems that need to be borne in mind when interpreting these findings, including the danger of possibly unrepresentative samples (Blatchford *et al.*, 1985, p. 59).

In their study of eighteen secondary schools, Smith and Tomlinson compared ethnic groups in terms of attainment in reading, writing, mathematics, non-verbal and verbal reasoning early in their secondary school careers. They found that mean scores for ethnic-minority children were below average, though in the case of Afro-Caribbean children only marginally so (Smith and Tomlinson, 1989, p. 136). Using these data as a base-line, they investigated progress over the course of secondary schooling by comparing them with 16+ examination results. They found ethnic-minority students, including Afro-Caribbean stu-

[5] They emphasize that they see the distribution of ability as 'the end-product of a set of social processes involving culturally generated abilities to secure O and A levels' (Halsey, Heath and Ridge, 1980, p. 117).
[6] For a sophisticated version of this, see Boodon 1973. See Saunders 1995 for criticism of social mobility studies for failing to take account of differences in ability and aspiration.
[7] This study did find ethnic inequalities emerging over the course of primary schooling. Smith and Tomlinson, 1989, Ch. 2, provide a useful review of this and other studies.

dents, making the same progress as, or greater progress than, white students. However, as Drew and Gray have noted, there are particular methodological problems involved in interpreting these findings, to do with sampling and the setting of the original benchmark level of ability or achievement on the basis of which progress was assessed (Drew and Gray, 1990, pp. 166–7).

Differences in aspiration levels have been almost entirely neglected in research on sex and ethnic differences. Yet, were we in a position to control for aspiration and motivation, as Tanna (1990) suggests, it might be revealed that the apparent equality between Asians and whites masks deeper inequalities. And much the same is true in relation to the performance of girls and boys. Thus, change in aspiration level may explain the improvement which has taken place in the performance of girls; and if this factor was investigated and it were found that, on average, girls had greater motivation than boys, then a claim could be made that measures of outcome inequalities which ignore this factor underestimate female disadvantage.

Sampling

A second set of methodological issues concerning the construction of outcome inequalities relates to sampling. In the case of social class and ethnic inequalities reliance is usually placed on samples rather than on total numbers; and these may not always be representative of the relevant populations. Thus, Troyna has pointed out that outcome data in relation to ethnic differences are often based on relatively small samples from which generalization is hazardous (Troyna, 1984, p. 161). And Tanna (1990, p. 352) has made the important point that in the case of the Rampton/Swann data, the performance of ethnic-minority students is being compared with that of 'some of the most disadvantaged white British groups', whereas if a comparison is made with all leavers from maintained schools in England, Asian students are still underachieving. By contrast, Smith and Tomlinson (1989, p. 8) argue that these data probably underestimate the achievement of Asians and Afro-Caribbean school leavers because 'it is well established that Asians and West Indians living in areas of high ethnic [minority] concentration are much more likely to have lower job levels and educational qualifications than those living in mainly white areas'. Moreover, the clustering of different Asian groups in different geographical areas means that research on Asian educational outcomes in one part of the country may well not be representative of Asians elsewhere, given that as we noted earlier there seem to be significant differences in educational performance among these groups.[8]

There is also the issue of sampling over time. Troyna (1984, p. 161) points

[8]   However, it should be noted that the data on which this finding is based come from a local study, Kysel, 1988.

out that some studies have relied on outdated data. And this problem is compounded by the fact that the impact on educational outcomes of school processes studied in particular schools at particular times will only occur several years later, when the students concerned reach 16+ or 18+: they will not be represented in outcome data contemporaneous with the school study, though the effects of similar processes at an earlier date may be.

The Significance of Outcome Inequalities

A third issue concerns the meaning given to outcome data. These are not usually taken to be of significance in themselves, but rather for what they imply about occupational prospects and future life chances. In other words, they are used as an indicator of the latter. And, as we made clear in Chapter 3, in assessing indicators we must consider not only the validity of the data themselves but also the strength of the link between them and what they are taken to indicate.

It is widely assumed in the literature that there is a strong relationship between educational qualifications and occupational destinations, as regards both levels of achievement and inequalities in achievement across subjects. Thus, it is expected that those leaving school with a higher level of qualification will obtain higher-status jobs, or will enter higher level FE or HE courses, than those with lower qualifications. It is also expected that achievement in some subjects will give access to higher-status courses and occupations than others.

Indeed, it is a general assumption of much research on educational inequality that during the twentieth century the education system has become increasingly important in determining occupational recruitment, through the allocation of educational qualifications (see, for instance, Measor and Sikes, 1992, p. 88). This is quite a complex issue, however, as Payne (1987, Ch. 6) makes clear (see also Tyler, 1977, Ch. 2). Certainly, the upward mobility experienced over the course of this century by a substantial proportion of those with working-class origins seems to have owed little to increased levels of education and much more to the proliferation of higher-status jobs. At the same time, it is true that educational credentials are frequently used today as a screening device, so that only those with a particular level of qualification may be considered for a given level of post (Dore, 1976). Nonetheless, it is necessary to remember that an increase in the role of paper qualifications does not mean that these are now all-important in occupational recruitment; or even that they are always more important than other factors. Their significance is likely to vary somewhat according to context. For example, they will be more important in recruitment to first job than to subsequent appointments, where relevant experience and references from previous employers will usually be significant. The implication of this is that the degree to which people's educational performance determines their occupational position may start from a relatively high point but will decline somewhat subsequently. Furthermore, there is now some scope for people to improve their level of qualifications later in life, through part-time and full-time courses which are open to mature entrants. As a result, schools no longer control access to qualifications-bearing courses to the extent that they once did.

The degree to which educational qualifications determine occupational destinations also varies somewhat across occupational sectors and over time. Educational credentials probably play their strongest role within the education system itself, both in recruitment to further- and higher-education courses and in appointments to posts. In other employment sectors the importance of qualifications varies according to custom and practice and level of post, and over time with changes in the supply and demand for labour of the relevant kinds. Furthermore, there are factors operating within the labour market which work against members of particular social categories, irrespective of their possession of qualifications. For instance, working-class, female, and black people may find that their educational credentials do not always carry the same weight as similar ones held by middle-class, white males. This is true even though those within each category who have a particular level of qualification may be better placed than those without it (Smith, 1977; Heath and Ridge, 1982; Roberts *et al.*, 1983; Jenkins, 1987).

In the area of gender the focus has, of course, been not so much on the exchange value of different levels of educational qualification as on that of qualifications in different subjects. It has been generally assumed that qualifications in mathematics and the sciences provide access to higher status and more highly paid occupations than those in the humanities (Deem, 1978, p. 69; Stanworth, 1983, p. 11; Skeggs, 1989; Measor and Sikes, 1992, p. 76). Thus, Skeggs argues that, despite improvements, girls' success 'still remains in subject areas traditionally associated with females, areas such as English and languages which arguably have less value in terms of specific employment outcomes or higher education demands'. She claims that 'mathematical skills are a "critical filter" regulating entry into high-status occupations' (Skeggs, 1989, p. 112). Evidence is not provided in support of this argument, however. And while it is true that a qualification in mathematics at 16+ probably acts as a filter, so too does one in English language. Nor is it clear that mathematics qualifications at higher levels facilitate access to high-status occupations more than those in all other subjects. While mathematical and scientific qualifications are required for access to some occupations, the latter by no means exhaust all high-status ones; and specialization in these subjects may represent a barrier in relation to some occupations, such as the law.

In addition to questions about the factual assumptions built into the use of educational outcomes as a measure of occupational prospects or life chances, it is important to remember that there are also value assumptions involved. It is easy to forget this, reliance being placed on the outcome data which are routinely produced by the operation of the education system, such as examination results. Yet, as the literature on official statistics has warned, we must recognize the organizational priorities and assumptions which go into the production of such statistics (Douglas, 1967; Hindess, 1973; Cicourel, 1976). Thus, the treatment of inequalities in educational qualifications as an indicator of differential occupational futures and life chances relies on the assumption that an important aspect of education, if not the most important one, is the extent to which it contributes to obtaining high status and highly paid jobs. Implicit here is a particular, and rather materialistic, conception of the good life; and it is one that is by no means a matter of consensus. Rejection of bourgeois values was a major element of the new sociology of education; though much subsequent research seems to have lapsed into a reliance on those values to document outcome inequalities. Moreover, rejection of this materialistic view of life is by no means restricted to the radical Left, it is shared by many interpretations of Christianity, by the religious values of some ethnic minorities, by the commitments of environmentalists and of New Age travellers etc. We do not wish to argue for, or against, this conception of the good life here. What is important is that the value assumptions involved in the selection of outcomes for attention should be made explicit; and that the focus of research must not be restricted, wittingly or unwittingly, to outcomes which are defined as significant only from a particular value perspective.[9]

There has been some recognition of other kinds of outcome in the literature. Thus, Measor and Sikes suggest that schools 'are or should be about more than just qualifications'. They note that:

> some writers have seen education as important for maintaining a democratic nation. Humanist thinkers have seen education as having a unique function in liberating the individual and enabling us to achieve our full potential. (Measor and Sikes, 1992, p. 2)

In addition, these authors and others have emphasized the socialization effects of schooling, for example in reproducing attitudes which motivate and legitimate social-class, sex/gender, and racist hierarchies. It is necessary to note, however, that, whatever the gaps in information and methodological problems surrounding the interpretation of the sorts of educational outcome we have discussed here, the situation is very much worse as regards these more elusive outcomes. In fact, we have very little evidence about, for example, the effects of schooling on attitudes to social inequality, even though substantial claims have been made about this (Althusser, 1971; Bowles and Gintis, 1976).[10]

Summarizing our argument in this section, then, the picture of inequalities in educational outcomes available from official statistics and research is a good

---

[9] It is also worth emphasizing that, to the extent that commitment to this materialistic view of life is unevenly distributed across social categories, part of any inequality between the latter measured in terms of outcomes like examination results will stem from this, see Murphy, 1990.

[10] As Hickox, 1982 points out, what evidence there is suggests that if producing positive attitudes towards various forms of inequality is the function of schools under capitalism, they may not have been very successful.

deal more complex and uncertain than seems to be assumed by many studies of school processes. Moreover, these studies have tended to treat inequalities in educational outcomes as simple matters of fact, when they are actually constructions based on factual and value assumptions. Indeed, very often they seem to have been primarily concerned with highlighting inequalities believed to disadvantage particular categories of students, with a view to influencing policy priorities. This is even true of the articles by Troyna (1984) and Tanna (1990), which we cited earlier for their recognition of the constructed character of outcome inequalities. Both these authors are preoccupied with countering interpretations of outcome data which they see as working against the interests of black students. Their discussions of methodological problems are subordinated to this practical task, and are therefore highly selective — rather than being concerned with presenting a balanced picture of the range of equalities and inequalities to be found in educational outcomes.

Estimating the School Effect

The second step in assessing the explanatory validity of research on school processes is to examine how effectively these processes have been shown to contribute to inequalities in educational outcomes. Some studies in this area have appealed to quantitative research on 'school effects' in support of their arguments (see Troyna, 1991a, p. 363; Wright, 1992a, p. 23). School-effects research, like qualitative analysis of school processes, arose in large part as a reaction against the earlier emphasis in educational research on the extent to which differences in home background affect children's educational performance (see Reynolds, 1985). However, it represented not so much a rejection of the conclusions of earlier studies as of the way in which these had frequently been interpreted. As Smith and Tomlinson (1989, p. 19) comment, referring to American studies which had suggested that schooling has little effect on social inequality: 'whereas Coleman and then Jencks had concluded that schooling was not effective as a means of reducing individual inequality, their conclusions were taken to mean that schooling has little influence on whether or not children can read, write and do arithmetic.'

The research on school effects provides some evidence for differences among schools in their impact on students' educational achievement. However, several points need to be made about the contribution it can make to conclusions about the role of school processes in generating outcome inequalities. First, there is a variety of methodological problems surrounding the measurement of school effects, relating for example to the sampling of schools and the measurement of relevant features of school intakes.[11] Also, it is important to recognize that school effects are often estimated by calculating

---

[11] See Gray *et al.* 1990 for a useful discussion of these in relation to their own and other studies.

the residual variance, once allowance has been made for variation in relevant characteristics of school intakes; rather than by measuring any correlation between particular features of schools and variations in outcome data. This means that any failure fully to measure relevant differences in the student intakes of schools may inflate estimates of 'the school effect'. It also has the consequence that this research can tell us little about which features of schools are responsible for any such effect. The studies of Rutter *et al.* (1979) and Mortimore *et al.* (1988) are unusual in seeking to identify features which are significant for 'effectiveness'; but this is the least convincing aspect of their work (Heath and Clifford, 1981; Smith and Tomlinson, 1989, pp. 24–7).

A second point is that the contribution of schools, as measured by this research, is a great deal less than that of social-class differences in children's home background and of differences in their attainment levels before they enter the schools. Thus, Gray *et al.* (1990) report that differences among secondary schools explain up to 5 per cent of the variance in 16+ examination performance, if differences between schools in the attainment levels of students entering them are controlled, the latter accounting for between 40 per cent and 60 per cent of the variance (Gray *et al.*, 1990, pp. 153–4).[12]

Finally, it must be emphasized that differences in the effectiveness of schools do not necessarily contribute to inequalities in educational performance between different social categories of student. For this to happen there must be differential recruitment from the social categories to more and less effective schools, and/or schools must treat members of different social categories systematically in more and less effective ways. We will look at each of these issues in turn.

Differential Recruitment

The concern with the differential recruitment of students from different social categories to more and less effective schools parallels an argument which was of central importance in relation to social-class inequalities in the 1950s and early 1960s. Then, the focus was on the recruitment of working-class children to grammar schools. As we saw in Chapter 1, the free-place system was criticized as inadequate because it did not give all working-class children who had the requisite level of ability the opportunity to attend a grammar school. Moreover, even after the 1944 reforms, this criticism continued to be pressed. Not only was there some evidence that, even on the basis of measurable intelligence, 11+ selection was discriminating against working-class children at the margin (Douglas, 1964), but there were also doubts about the accuracy of intelligence tests and (in particular) about the degree to which they were

---

[12] Where only social background of students is controlled, the school effect ranges between 3.5 per cent and 25 per cent, though most of the results are less than 8 per cent. Social background accounts for between 10.8 per cent and 20.4 per cent, but with all but one of the results between 10 per cent and 15 per cent.

neutral between the social classes. Ability was increasingly regarded as a product of environment, and was often assumed therefore to be open to change
by schools, rather than being fixed by genetic endowment. Given this, even
if equality relative to measured ability was achieved, it could still be argued
that working-class students who could have benefitted from a grammar-school
education were being denied access to one.

What is of particular significance for us here is that, to a considerable
extent, failure to obtain access to a grammar school ruled out the possibility
of gaining 16+ and 18+ qualifications, and virtually eliminated the chance of
going to university.[13] By contrast, the difference in opportunity between those
students assigned to a less and those assigned to a more effective school today
is much less substantial. It has been estimated as amounting, on average, to a
difference of, say, two grades in two subjects or of one grade in four at GCSE
(Gray *et al.*, 1990, pp. 145–7). We are not wanting to suggest that this is of
no consequence. Our point is rather that inequalities of treatment must be
assessed for their degree of consequentiality: for the sort of impact they are
likely to have on outcome inequalities. A sense of proportion is required.

Another important element of the argument that outcome inequalities
between particular social categories have been produced by differential recruitment to more and less effective schools is, of course, to show that
working-class and/or black and ethnic-minority students are in fact disproportionately assigned to less effective schools. There is little reliable evidence
about this; though it is perhaps not unlikely given the uneven geographical
distribution of social classes and ethnic groups.[14] Once again, however, it is
important to recognize that what would be involved here is a matter of degree.
It is not that all working-class or all black students are likely to be assigned to
poor schools, while all middle-class white students are sent to effective ones.
For this reason, too, any overall effect is likely to be small.

Differential Treatment within Schools

Showing that differential treatment within schools has produced inequalities in
educational outcomes is of course precisely what much of the research we
have discussed in the previous two chapters has been concerned to do; even

[13] It did not deny these opportunities completely, for several reasons: there was some
transfer from secondary modern to grammar schools at 13+; there were some comprehensive schools in existence from the early 1950s and these grew in number over time;
and from the mid-1950s onwards an increasing number of secondary modern schools
entered students for 16+ examinations, including the GCE, and this enabled some of
them to transfer to comprehensive or grammar schools to pursue 'A' level courses.
Nonetheless, for much of the period, the vast majority of students who were assigned
a secondary-modern place (and they were the vast majority of students) had little
chance of sitting GCE examinations.
[14] There is some evidence about this from local studies. See Mortimore *et al.*, 1988,
p. 213.

though their focus was not on 'effectiveness'. However, establishing the effects of differential treatment is even more difficult than determining the effects of differential recruitment. Here the question arises of what constitute consequential differences in treatment. Many of the studies we discussed in earlier chapters rely on plausible theories about, for instance, the effects of allocation to different levels and types of course, or of differential distribution of teachers' attention in the classroom, for educational outcomes such as examination results. However, they rarely provide credible evidence to show that these effects actually occurred in the schools studied. Indeed, given the range of other factors likely to be operating, the size of the samples of students generally involved would probably be too small to detect such effects, even apart from the problems of identifying and measuring differential treatment.

In fact, few of these studies even provide evidence about the educational achievement of students, or (in the case of studies of secondary schools) of the educational outcomes they obtained. An exception is Troyna's (1991a) work on Jayleigh school, and some of what he reports is surprising given his analysis of intra-school processes, which we discussed earlier. He notes that 'of those Asian students who passed GCSE, 32 per cent obtained higher grades (A–C) compared to 24 per cent of whites'. However, he comments that '[. . .] these data are of limited value. They tell us simply that there is no *prima facie* case for assuming that Asian pupils were discriminated against in the marking of GCSE examinations' (Troyna, 1991a, p. 367). While he is right not to accept such outcome data at face value, as we have seen, this is a curious interpretation of his data. Had the proportions been reversed, this would surely have been *prima facie* evidence that the treatment of Asian students in the school had depressed their educational achievement (rather than that GCSE markers had discriminated against them). The superior performance of Asian students in this respect, therefore, might be taken to suggest that (other things being equal) whatever differential treatment there had been in the school had not been consequential for examination performance, or that it had actually aided the Asian students.

There were, though, other respects in which Asian students achieved less than white students at Jayleigh, notably in terms of the number of passes obtained (5.5 compared to 6.0); and this reflected differences in the average number of examinations for which these two categories of students were entered. Troyna argues that this variation in entry rates resulted from the operation of the set system. However, the difference in overall performance is reported to be not statistically significant (CRE, 1992, p. 19); and, as we saw in Chapter 4, Troyna fails to establish that the set system affected the relative examination entry rates of Asians and whites.

Overall, then, there is little evidence that differences among schools in their effectiveness produce outcome inequalities between different social categories of student; either in terms of differential recruitment or differential treatment. This does not mean that such differences are of no significance, simply that at present the evidence is insufficient to draw reasonable conclusions about their relationship to outcome inequalities; though it seems likely that the contribution of school factors is considerably less than that of prior attainment and social-class background.

The Role of Schooling in Constructing Educational Inequalities

It is important to notice that estimates of the size of the school effect are concerned with the *differential* effects of schools, rather than with the contribution of schooling *per se*. And much of the literature on school processes which we have examined in earlier chapters has not been interested in identifying differences between schools. Quite the reverse, it has claimed to document general features of schooling and their consequences. Two conditions must be met here: generalizability and causal efficacy.

Generalizability

A first requirement is to show that the unequal treatment which studies have claimed in the schools investigated occur on a sufficiently general scale to have an effect in national terms. This is not a requirement which studies of single schools or of very small samples of schools can easily meet. Moreover, as we noted in Chapter 5, studies of school process have generally not been very successful even in establishing that the events they document were common *within* the schools investigated. Very often, the data presented relate to relatively small proportions of the teachers and students, and to small samples of their behaviour.

Moreover, most of these studies give very little consideration to the problem of generalizability across schools. Instead, they often seem to assume that the school investigated is a microcosm of the whole education system. However, this is to presuppose a degree of homogeneity in school processes which is implausible given that schools vary considerably in the characteristics of their student intakes and in the educational outcomes they produce. It is also worth emphasizing that outcome inequalities in aggregate terms are not simply produced by some identifiable set of students who are not doing as well as they should be, in some sense. These inequalities are determined by the relationship between the scores of *all* the students in one category with those of *all* the students in another. It is significant, for example, that while the examination performance of Asian students at Troyna's Jayleigh was quite close to that of white students, the level of performance in the school as a whole was below the national average: this school seems to lie within the group of schools where less than 60 per cent of students achieve five or more GCSEs. In other words, the performance of both Asian and white students in this school was effectively pulling down the respective national averages of each category of student. What this highlights is that interpreting the relationship between outcomes in particular schools and inequalities in terms of national aggregates is by no means straightforward.

Of course, it might be argued that if we put all the different studies which have been carried out together they will provide us with grounds for generalization. Yet, while this may improve the basis for generalization, it will not necessarily make that basis adequate. At least two conditions are required for this to be achieved. First, studies must provide the necessary comparative information, both about school processes and about the social composition of student intakes and the achievement levels of different categories of student. As we have noted, this is by no means always done.[15] The second condition is, of course, that the sample of schools must be reasonably representative, in relevant respects, of the larger population to which generalization is being made. For reasons already indicated, this is not easy to judge. However, on the basis of the information provided, it seems that many of the schools studied have been at the lower end of the range of examination performance. We have already seen that this is true of Jayleigh, and much the same applies to the schools studied by Wright (1986) and Foster (1989). Even if these studies had been carefully coordinated to provide us with relevant comparative data, this would have constituted a rather unrepresentative sample of English schools in terms of examination performance, and this is *prima facie* evidence of unrepresentativeness in other relevant respects.

As we saw in Chapter 3, generalizability can be claimed in terms of theoretical inference as well as empirical generalization. However, with the exception of research on differentiation–polarization theory, these studies do not begin to meet the requirements of theoretical inference (Hammersley, 1985). And, even if they did, this in itself would not provide a basis for generalization to the relevant population of schools in England, or to any other finite population. This is because theoretical inference is condition-dependent. The same processes and effects would only be found in other schools if the conditions built into the theory were met in those schools. To establish generality on this basis we would once again need empirical evidence about the larger population of schools to which generalization is being made. Moreover, it is quite possible that whatever contribution is made by schools to outcome inequalities in national terms is the result of diverse internal processes, rather than of the same process having the same effects in each school.

All of this is not to imply that case studies of schools are of no value. Rather, it is to suggest that, if they are to illuminate the way in which outcome inequalities are produced, the position of each school needs to be plotted in relation to the patterns of relevant heterogeneity in the education system as a

---

[15] For example, despite providing a detailed discussion of 'achievement and opportunity' at national level, Gillborn 1990a offers no information about the achievement levels of different ethnic groups within the school he studied.

whole. And, at present, we have insufficient information for this to be done very effectively.

Causal Efficacy

The other issue which needs to be addressed in assessing the contribution of schooling to outcome inequalities is one which we considered earlier: the causal effect of school processes must be established. And the task of showing that there are general features of schools which produce outcome inequalities is even more difficult than that of establishing that there are differences *between* schools in this respect. This is because the comparison which is implied is between the school system as it currently exists and what would happen if it did not exist (Smith and Tomlinson, 1989, p. 20) or if it were quite different in character. Yet, of course, it is impossible to obtain data about either of these hypothetical possibilities.

Again, this problem is rarely addressed by school studies. Instead, it seems to be assumed that any inequalities discovered in schools must play a key role in the reproduction of inequalities in educational outcomes. This is the complement to the assumption that inequality in outcomes implies inequalities in opportunity (Halsey, 1981, p. 111). Inequality of treatment in schools is effectively treated as both a necessary and a sufficient condition of outcome inequalities. This is reminiscent of a feature of much early criminological research, where the 'evil' of crime could only be explained in terms of some other evil, such as poverty, 'broken homes' etc. (Matza, 1969, p. 21).

What underlies this, very often, is a reliance on reproduction theory. Thus, Ball (1986, p. 88) claims that 'systems of streaming in the comprehensive school contribute to the [. . .] reproduction of class relations [. . .]' by channelling and differentiating students and thereby exercising 'considerable constraint' on their life chances. Similarly, Gillborn declares his focus to be the role of teachers as 'agents in the reproduction of inequalities of educational opportunity' (Gillborn, 1990a, p. 162), while Mac an Ghaill argues that:

> schools can be seen as latently recreating the social relations of the wider society, including such structural divisions as those of class, 'race', and gender. This is achieved through a number of pedagogical practices which serve selectively to reproduce the dominant culture by differentially skilling, both technically and socially, different social groups for their future place within the socio-economic division of labour. (Mac an Ghaill, 1988, p. 150)

Riddell (1992, p. 21) also explicitly draws on social reproduction theory in examining 'the way in which option choice is used by the school to bring about traditional gender divisions in the curriculum'.

Deem spells out the macro context of this argument in relation to gender more fully. She claims that since 'in most capitalist societies there remains a strongly entrenched sexual division of labour, separating what women do from what men do', '[. . .] it is both possible and feasible to argue that the sexual division of labour must be essential to the maintenance of capitalist society [. . .]'. And, following an appeal to the work of Althusser to establish the central significance of schooling in modern capitalist societies, she concludes: 'It is claimed, then, that there are strong connections between the subordinate position of women in capitalist society and the maintenance of that form of society, and that the maintenance of the sexual division of labour has, since the nineteenth century, been carried out increasingly by the school as well as by the family' (Deem, 1978, pp. 2–4).

This sort of reproduction theory forms the background to much research on inequalities in schools. And its effect is to turn the data reported in these studies into little more than illustrations of what is taken as already known to be happening in schools, on theoretical grounds. This might be reasonable if reproduction theory had been independently tested and its validity established. But this is not the case. Indeed, reproduction theory is rarely formulated in a way that would allow empirical testing.

To make it open to test would require, at the very least, some clarification of what it means to claim that schools reproduce inequality. There is considerable ambiguity here. We can identify several possible relationships between the inputs into and outputs from schools, which might or might not come under the heading of 'reproduction'. If we think of these inputs and outputs, first of all, in terms of the abilities of students on entry, and their educational achievements on exit, schools might simply produce a range of achievements which is isomorphic in terms of its extent and ordering with students' initial levels of academic ability. This is reproduction in a quite literal sense: in these terms schools make no independent contribution of their own, they simply translate inequalities of input into inequalities of output. Alternatively, schools could amplify the original differences in ability, producing a wider range of inequalities in achievement than the range of inequalities among students on entry, but still retaining the ordering of students within those ranges; an ordering that may reflect membership of social-class, gender, or ethnic categories. Again, though, schools might conceivably reduce the original differences among students, but yet still retain their ordering; so that social-class, gender, or 'racial'/ethnic differences are nevertheless reproduced in this sense. Another possibility is that, whatever happens to the *extent* of differences among students, instead of the original ordering among them, there is some level of 'mobility'; and, of course, on this model different levels of mobility on the part of members of relevant social categories might be taken as distinguishing non-reproduction from reproduction. Finally, reproduction of inequality could conceivably be defined as any situation in which there is not equality of educational achievement across all students. Here, a non-reproductive school would aim for, and produce, some base-line of achievement; and presumably not educate any student beyond that.

This exploration of the scope for different definitions of what constitutes reproduction of educational inequalities by schools deals with only one element of the notion of social reproduction. That concept is also used to refer to socialization into attitudes that accept inequality as normal and natural. And, here again, we could reasonably ask whether reproduction entails schools leaving the distribution of students' attitudes much the same as they were, or increasing acceptance of the 'status quo'. And, if schools were actually to reduce such acceptance, how much reduction would need to be achieved before they were no longer seen as engaged in social reproduction?

Even this does not exhaust the meaning of 'reproduction'. Part of the appeal of reproduction theory is that it combines the 'liberal' focus on social-class, gender, or ethnic inequalities in educational achievement with the more radical approach developed by the new sociologists of education. It does not take educational abilities and achievements as given but treats them as social constructions which serve the needs of a capitalist, patriarchal and/or racist society. In this way, reproduction theory incorporates social constructionism; and this is not surprising given the origins of that approach in the sociology of knowledge, and the influence of Marx on that subdiscipline. However, where Marx's account of the way in which capitalism reproduces itself was located within a philosophy of history which identified, albeit very sketchily, what would follow the overthrow of capitalism and why, reproduction theory has become relatively autonomous, if not completely detached, from any philosophy of history. This has made it usable by feminists and anti-racists as well as Marxists; but it has rendered obscure what would count as non-reproduction in these more radical terms.[16]

However, even if this lack of clarity about what constitutes social reproduction could be resolved, it remains to be seen whether reproduction theory would be testable, even in principle. The functionalist character of what have come to be referred to as direct reproduction theories has long been recognized (see Cohen and Rosenberg, 1977; Erben and Gleeson, 1977; Hirst 1979; Edwards, 1980; Hickox, 1982).[17] And one of the central criticisms of structural functionalism was that it was not an empirical theory at all (see, for example,

---

[16] There is an ambivalence within reproduction theory between a lingering commitment to a political philosophy of history and the adoption of a theoretical position which is indifferent in its attitude towards different social systems, being concerned solely with academic study of how they manage to reproduce themselves and how they are changed. This parallels the contradiction within social constructionism which we identified in Chapter 1: between critique based on ontological gerrymandering and a thoroughgoing constructionism which provides no basis for critique, because it implies that all social phenomena are constituted in and through accounts of them. It is these ambivalences, in large part, which have led to reprimands for 'academicism' within both Marxism and feminism (Shaw, 1975; Mies, 1991).

[17] Cohen, 1978 has argued convincingly that Marx's theory of capitalism is functionalist, though he does not regard this as a weakness, but see also Cohen, 1988. For criticisms of functionalism, see Demerath and Peterson, 1967; and for an assessment of Cohen's defence of Marxist functionalism, see Halfpenny, 1983.

Homans, 1964). Moreover, as Hargreaves (1982) has shown, the more sophisticated Marxist analyses of education which developed after the initial influence of Althusser and Bowles and Gintis, and which have framed the thinking of many feminists and anti-racists, suffer from much the same lack of theoretical openness and neglect of empirical rigour. They still assume that there is a *telos* in the system which serves to bring about social reproduction, in terms of which all empirical data must be interpreted. The only difference is that this *telos* is now treated as much less overt and direct than it was previously assumed to be: the process of reproduction is regarded as more complex and mediated, and as subject to at least potential resistance. This lack of change in the basic character of reproduction theory, despite increased recognition of complexity, is underlined by the fact that, as Hargreaves points out, direct reproduction theories were rejected not so much because of theoretical and empirical inadequacies but because they failed to allow any scope for resistance, and therefore had unacceptable political implications for those committed to 'radical change' (Hargreaves, 1982, p. 111).

Like the cruder forms of normative functionalism, then, reproduction theory (direct and indirect) has a tendency to be logically circular and thereby self-confirming. And it could be argued that this is no accident. These features are attuned to the function which it serves in sociological texts: it provides a social scientific vehicle for critique, one which keeps the values on which the criticism is based under cover and therefore protected from scrutiny. In this context it is a boon that reproduction theory leaves obscure what would and would not count as reproduction. It maximizes the scope for critique, since anything short of the realization of some unspecified ideal society can be criticized as furthering social reproduction.

There is an interesting parallel here, but also an instructive contrast, with recent developments in criminology; an area of sociology where social constructionism and reproduction theory have also been very influential. It was a feature of some versions of the 'labelling theory' of the 1960s that the existence of deviance was treated as simply the product of the creation and enforcement of moral rules and laws. Where previous work in criminology had been preoccupied with the abnormal or pathological factors which led some people to become deviant, behaviour labelled as criminal now came to be treated as rational, and as intrinsically no different from any other sort of behaviour. Its sole distinction lay in the fact that it had been criminalized; and the focus of investigation became the labelling process itself. This constructionist perspective was later inherited by the 'new criminology', and was combined with a form of reproduction theory (Taylor *et al.*, 1973). Crime was now seen as produced by the courts and the police, these institutions functioning to serve the needs of capitalist society.

As some critics pointed out, though, labelling theory rarely applied constructionism in a fully consistent manner (Pollner, 1974; Rains, 1975). Here too there was ontological, and also moral, gerrymandering. Labelling theory was originally developed in relation to 'victimless crimes', such as alcohol and marihuana use, homosexual activity, etc. While it was occasionally turned into a criminological policy of 'radical non-interventionism' (see Schur, 1973), its later extension to other sorts of crime was often more qualified, and met with opposition. One important source of resistance was feminism, since feminists insisted that rape and sexual harassment were not mere social constructions, and were not restricted to capitalist societies. Rather, these crimes were to be seen as the products of pathological, patriarchal attitudes on the part of men; attitudes which have been universal in history. Also significant was the growing realization that a very substantial proportion of the victims of crime were working-class. As a result of this, it became difficult to see crime as no more than an ideological construct functioning to reproduce capitalism.[18]

As Cohen (1979) has pointed out, by moving between constructionist and realist positions in an opportunistic way, sociologists of deviance had initially avoided dealing with the difficult issue of the proper function of law, and of what it should and should not proscribe. He spells out the problem, highlighting the awkward contradictions produced and the *ad hoc* strategies used to deal with them:

If — so one of the public's questions ran — deviants were not pathological beings driven by forces beyond their control, then surely as rational, responsible beings they should be punished *more* severely? Ah no, that's not *quite* what we meant. And when we talked about being on the side of the deviant, did this mean that we were actually in favour of what he did? Here, our answers were really tortuous. Faced with behaviour like vandalism or football hooliganism which we couldn't openly approve of (in the sense of advocating tolerance or non-punishment), then our main message was that actually there was much *less* of this than the public thought (because of moral panics, selective perception, stereotyping, scapegoating, etc.). Simultaneously, of course, to other audiences, we welcomed such behaviour and pointed to the evidence which showed that if society didn't Radically Change, then indeed the public's fears would materialise and more of the behaviour would occur. With other forms of deviance easier to support openly within the liberal consensus — abortion, the gay movement, dope smoking — we happily advocated tolerance, even in public. And this time we would say that there was not less, but far, far *more* of such behaviour than anyone could imagine through their stereotypes. [. . .] Already apparent in these stances was the vacillation between the image of the deviant as mismanaged victim and the deviant as cultural hero [. . .] (Cohen, 1979, pp. 18–19)

While labelling theory and the new criminology originally operated on the basis of a vague and contradictory set of oppositional values which was

---

[18] See Young, 1975 and Downes, 1979, pp. 12–13. This is one of the factors which led to the development of so-called left realism in criminology: Young and Matthews, 1992.

disguised by their use of constructionism and reproduction theory, in more recent years criminologists have been forced to face questions about what sort of law and legal system are justified. Crime can no longer be seen simply as a social construction which functions to meet the needs of capitalism, and it cannot be assumed that it will disappear with the abolition of that system.

No parallel development has taken place within the sociology of education. Here, constructionism and reproduction theory have continued to be used as a basis for critique.[19] Relying on these 'theories', the contribution of school processes to the production of inequalities in educational outcomes has simply been assumed. Siraj-Blatchford and Troyna are perhaps representative here in being unable to imagine the situation otherwise: 'Given the proclaimed role of state education as the foremost official agency of socialisation in society, we find it inconceivable that it does not function to some degree in reproducing inequality' (Siraj-Blatchford and Troyna, 1993, p. 224). This probably explains why there has been so little attempt to investigate the explanatory power of school factors in relation to outcome inequalities.

The Pragmatics of Explaining Educational Inequalities

What our analysis suggests is that the switch in the sociology of education, over the past twenty years or so, from explanations of educational inequalities which emphasize factors outside the education system to a focus on school processes, was not motivated by empirical (or even by purely theoretical) arguments, but rather by the shift in political values we described in Chapters 1 and 2. Explanations appealing to the nature of working-class homes were rejected largely because they came to be seen as politically unacceptable. However, this was not how the change was usually presented. Instead, it was portrayed as the emergence of a new theoretical paradigm within the sociology of education; by analogy with the 'scientific revolutions' documented by Kuhn (1970), though with a much stronger sense of the superiority of the new paradigm to what had gone before than the Kuhnian analogy strictly allowed.[20]

As we argued in Chapter 2, explanation always relies on value judgments. Thus, ethical, and political considerations are unavoidable in selecting explanations. We argued, though, that these should not be adopted as practical commitments; and that they must be made explicit, at least to the extent that they are not a matter of general consensus. Not to do so is to obscure the

---

[19] And the more recent influences of post-structuralism and post-modernism have often been used in much the same way.

[20] Even those criticisms of earlier explanations of educational failure which had value connotations — such as that they 'blamed the victim' (Ryan, 1971) — were also open to interpretation in factual or scientific terms. Thus, in part at least, victims should not be blamed because they are by definition powerless, a factual matter not a value judgment.

nature of the arguments being presented: it implies that they are purely factual when they are necessarily value-dependent; and it also has the effect of treating the value assumptions on which the explanations being promoted rely as if they were the only legitimate ones, thereby apparently validating them on the basis of research.

As we have seen, much of the research on educational inequality has failed to make explicit the values on which it is based. This has allowed those values to remain obscure, for the most part being expressed solely in negative, oppositional terms. Indeed, it has enabled analysis to shift between different value positions, to select the one which offers the most effective point of criticism.[21] Here what is involved is negative critique, a critical sociology that is concerned simply to 'interrupt' existing social relationships and which cannot offer any justification for its own role (Hammersley, 1995a, Ch. 2). Of course, values are sometimes mentioned in this literature, but their content, implications, and justification are not explicated. For instance, very often critique is carried out in the name of eradicating inequality. But, for the reasons we outlined in Chapter 3, such a goal is meaningless. Inequality cannot be eliminated, even in principle. There will always be inequalities because what is an equality from one point of view is an inequality from others. Moreover, while not all inequalities are inequitable, what is and is not equitable depends on the moral perspective one adopts; and there are conflicting perspectives. What we have in the literature concerned with explaining educational inequalities, then, is a shift in explanatory preference which was motivated by political considerations, disguised as a scientific finding validated by evidence.

Conclusion

In this chapter, we have examined the explanatory validity of research on inequalities in schools. We began by outlining some of the information which is currently available about outcome inequalities. These proved to be a good deal more diverse and complex than most school studies seem to assume. We also emphasized that outcome inequalities are constructions which rely on factual and value assumptions. Different assumptions produce different patterns of equality and inequality. In general, though, research on schools has treated outcome inequalities as if they were simple matters of fact.

In the second half of the chapter we examined the extent to which a causal relationship had been established between unequal treatment in schools and outcome inequalities. We concluded that the studies examined in this book have hardly begun to meet the conditions necessary to establish this

---

[21] Thus, Ball (1986, p. 84), in claiming that there is a 'strong and enduring relationship between streaming and social class differentiation' moves, without giving notice, between a conception of inequality as relative to ability and one which is defined in terms of proportional representation of the social classes in streams.

relationship. Generally, they fail to show both the generalizability of their findings about school processes and the consequentiality of these processes for educational outcomes. Instead, they simply assume that schools must play a role in producing outcome inequalities, basing this conviction on reproduction theory and social constructionism. Yet, neither of these is a well-established empirical theory; rather, they seem to be interpretative schemes which are used to engage in political critique masquerading as social-science research.

We concluded that the shift in the study of educational inequality from an emphasis on external factors to a stress on school processes arose from a change in political values. There is nothing illegitimate about this, since explanations are always value-dependent. However, this is not how the change in explanatory strategy was presented, or how it has subsequently been defended. Rather it was portrayed as a shift in theoretical paradigm, and the role of values in the selection of explanatory factors was thereby disguised. The result of this has been the illegitimate promotion of the value judgments implicit in research on school processes as if they were the product of social science, and a failure to subject them to adequate scrutiny. This is perhaps the most fundamental sense in which recent research on educational inequality has failed to be reflexive.

Chapter 7

Conclusion

Educational inequality has been an important focus for British sociological research over the past forty years. And, in general, what has been reported is persisting inequalities in the education system, despite reforms of various kinds. Moreover, increasingly over time, the source of this inequality has been located in the structure and functioning of schools, these being taken to reflect the character of British society as capitalist, patriarchal, and/or racist. Teachers are frequently portrayed by this literature as implicated in a system which, despite the best efforts of many, discriminates against working-class, female, and/or ethnic-minority students (Ball, 1986; Troyna and Carrington 1990; Riddell, 1992; Wright, 1992b).

We regard educational inequalities of the kinds identified in this literature as an important topic for inquiry and as a significant public issue; and we believe that research has made, and continues to make, a significant contribution to our understanding of it. However, a central purpose of our book has been to suggest that research findings in this area need more careful scrutiny than they typically receive. Indeed, we suggest that many of them are subject to very considerable doubt.

In the first three chapters we outlined the recent history of this field of research, located our own position in relation to the main approaches to be found within it, and spelled out the kind of methodological reflexivity which we believe is required. We argued that inquiry into inequalities cannot but be value-based, but that this does not mean that it is necessarily committed to, or that it should be directed towards promoting, certain definitions of educational inequality, and to engaging in the practical evaluation of schooling. Rather, in our view the task of educational research is limited to producing factual information which is relevant to public debates about inequalities and other issues. One of the reasons for this is that the equity, and other, principles involved in such debates are multiple and may conflict; and research cannot resolve such conflicts. Thus, researchers must use value principles to identify inequalities for study, and must make these principles explicit. However, their task is solely to produce factual information about value relevant inequalities, and their primary duty is to try to ensure that the conclusions they draw are sound. This involves a process of collective assessment within the research community, taking due note of the various threats to validity which can affect empirical findings. Thus, in Chapter 3 we laid out the methodological framework in terms of which we believe research in this field should be assessed.

Subsequent chapters reviewed a large amount of the literature on inequality in schools. Our conclusion was that many of the claims made in that literature cannot be sustained on the evidence currently available. In Chapter 4 we argued that research on school processes often lacks clarity about what is to count as discrimination. Moreover, almost whatever definition is adopted, it generally fails to establish that systematic discrimination has taken place in the allocation of students to levels and types of course. And, while some research on schools has identified processes which have the potential to amplify social class and other differences in educational performance, the evidence is weak that this effect has occurred. In Chapter 5, we showed that much the same lack of clarity about definitions prevails in research on classrooms, analysis of observed incidents and/or of informants' accounts is often speculative, failing to take account of significant threats to its validity. Furthermore, the interpretations presented, relating to a relatively small number of incidents, are frequently used as grounds for generalizations which cannot be sustained. In both areas, then, claims are often made about discrimination based on insufficient relevant data, and on questionable interpretations of these. And there is widespread failure to distinguish clearly between evaluative and factual considerations, and to make explicit the values on which the identification and explanation of inequalities is based.

In Chapter 6 we looked at the inequalities in educational outcomes which differential treatment in schools is often held to cause. We noted that our knowledge about outcome inequalities is by no means complete or entirely reliable. Indeed, for some outcomes, notably those concerned with the effects of school experience on attitude and behaviour later in life, there is little or no relevant evidence. But, even on the basis of the information that is available, the picture is much more complex and diverse than is assumed by most studies of inequality in schools. While there is almost certainly some persisting underachievement, particularly in relation to working-class and Afro-Caribbean students, there have also been substantial reductions in the underperformance of girls and of some ethnic-minority groups, sometimes to the point of reversing previous disparities. At the same time, there is underachievement of boys at both 16+ and 18+ on some important outcome measures. Furthermore, the task of establishing the causal link which is assumed between differential treatment in schools and inequality in educational outcomes is far more demanding than most studies in this area recognize; and what evidence there is suggests that school factors play only a slight role, compared to differences among students in ability. In short, there is no convincing evidence currently available for any substantial role on the part of schools in generating inequalities in educational outcomes between social classes, genders, or ethnic groups. Studies simply assume that schools play such a role, often on the basis of appeals to reproduction theory and social constructionism; neither of which can provide the necessary support.

What we find in this literature, then, is a general tendency to overinterpret the data available, and this results in part from neglect of some important and difficult methodological problems. We are not criticizing researchers for having failed to resolve these problems; nor are we suggesting that they are easy to resolve, quite the reverse. But we *are* critical of the fact that the problems have not been given the attention they deserve; and, more important still, that their implications for the likely validity of the conclusions drawn in this field have often been underplayed or even ignored. A considerable amount of further research would be required before we could come to any sound conclusion about the role that school factors play in determining educational outcomes, one way or the other. Moreover, the deficiencies in the literature seem to have become considerably worse in the past decade or so. Much of the more recent work on educational inequality is less explicit about the methodological problems involved, less systematic in its orientation, and less restrained in its conclusions.

Of course, there is a temptation in all areas of inquiry for researchers to overclaim, for them to declare significant findings which the evidence will not bear. No-one finds inconclusive results satisfying and, increasingly, the pressure is on researchers to produce definitive and newsworthy conclusions, and to do this earlier rather than later. Such conditions do not provide a context in which methodological probity and theoretical modesty are encouraged. However, it is not just that the discovery of inequality has been privileged in this literature, but also that some kinds of inequality have been preferred as findings to others. As we have noted, there has been an almost exclusive focus on the discovery of inequalities which are believed to disadvantage working-class, female, and 'black' students, and on the persistence of these. What seems to be involved, then, is a form of systematic bias towards the discovery of particular sorts of inequality in schools, and their treatment as consequential for the persistence of inequalities in educational outcomes. Moreover, there is some evidence to suggest that this bias is not a contingent matter, but is actually built into the analytic orientation of many researchers.

One aspect of this is the use of shifting definitions. Thus, the meaning of 'educational equality' has been redefined over time, in ways which expand the scope for discovering inequalities. On the earliest interpretation, in terms of sheer access to secondary education, equality was achieved for almost all children via the 1944 Act: access to state-funded secondary schools was now determined on the basis of judgments of academic merit not by the financial resources of parents. Indeed, some evidence suggests that equality of opportunity was also achieved at that time in the slightly more stringent sense that access to grammar schools matched the distribution of measured ability between the social classes (see Floud, Halsey, and Martin, 1956, pp. 57–8 and 65; but see also Douglas, 1964).[1] However, at this point the concept of educational

[1] There was one clear sense in which allocation to grammar schools was not based on measured ability. The numbers of girls and boys allocated a grammar school place were equalized and, given that the performance of girls in the 11+ was generally better than that of boys, some girls went to secondary-modern schools who had a higher 11+ score than some boys who went to grammar school.

opportunity was redefined so that it no longer meant mere access to secondary education according to ability, but required provision for working-class students of the material and cultural resources necessary for them to achieve outcomes equivalent to those of members of the middle-class (Halsey, 1972). And when, subsequently, this formulation came to be rejected as itself presupposing the superiority of bourgeois culture, the 'reality' of a high level of educational inequality was preserved by portraying the nature of the education on offer in British schools as biased against the aspirations and capacities of members of the working-class. As a result of such redefinitions, it has been possible to dismiss every reform designed to reduce social-class inequalities as having had little impact on them. Indeed, reforms have sometimes been treated not just as failing to contribute to the solution of the problem but as playing an active role in maintaining the status quo by giving the appearance of change and so legitimating persisting inequalities (Young and Whitty, 1977, p. 16; see Silver, 1981).

Similar revisions of the meaning of 'equal educational opportunity' have also shaped research on sexual and 'racial' inequalities. These have reflected the shifts from liberal to more radical forms of feminism, and from multi-culturalism to anti-racism (Weiner, 1985; Troyna, 1987). 'Indirect' as well as 'direct' forms of discrimination have been emphasized, the former coming to be defined in such a way as to include any policy or practice which has differential consequences in relation to sex or ethnicity that can be held to disadvantage female or ethnic minority students (see Gillborn and Drew 1993, p. 356). Here again each earlier conceptualization of the problem, and interventions based on it, has often been dismissed as ineffective or even as representing a subtle strategy to preserve inequality. Revisions to the definition of educational equality have not been treated as alternatives. Rather, each new definition has been presented as capturing the *true* level of educational inequality; as superseding the previous ones, indeed as revealing them to have been ideological.

These changes in the definition of educational equality are often formulated as involving a movement from the concept of equality of opportunity to that of equality of outcome. Thus, in the later period, any inequality in educational outcomes has tended to be regarded as a sign of unequal treatment within schools. This has served as an invitation for researchers to investigate school processes with a view to documenting the inequalities already 'known' to be operating there. The result is that almost any apparent difference in treatment by schools and teachers can be treated as discrimination, through exploitation of the uncertainty which surrounds our understanding of the effects of treatments on outcomes.

Symptomatic of this is that apparently contradictory claims are advanced. Thus, on the one hand, we have Sharp and Green (1975) arguing that 'less able', working-class children are disadvantaged because they are given *less* attention than children judged by teachers to be 'more able'; whereas Tickle

(1983) claims that less able children are disadvantaged by being given *more* teacher attention. Similarly, a number of authors have criticized option-selection schemes for implying that students have a free choice when in fact they do not; especially not working-class, female and ethnic-minority students. Yet the same authors also criticize option-choice arrangements for discriminating against these categories of student by not providing them with a 'balanced curriculum' (Tomlinson, 1987), or for not ensuring that they are distributed across types of course in the same proportions as white or male students (Grafton *et al.*, 1983; Riddell, 1992). In this research it seems as if, almost whatever occurs, working-class, female, or ethnic-minority students are treated as subject to discrimination. And, indeed, this follows logically from the reproduction theory on which much of this research relies. That theory *presupposes* that the cunning of the system involves institutional bias against these categories of student. From this point of view, schools are inevitably engaged in social reproduction, whether this is achieved directly through successful indoctrination and regimentation (Althusser, 1971; Bowles and Gintis, 1976) or indirectly by their failing in these tasks, triggering off a subculture which is oppositional to school values, but one which nevertheless prepares students for 'appropriate' occupational destinations (Willis, 1977). *Whether* schools produce educational inequalities is never an issue, it is assumed that they must; the focus for research is simply *how* they do this.

The 'discovery' of discrimination has also been greatly facilitated by the overinterpretation of data which we mentioned earlier. Frequently one or two 'atrocity stories' (Dingwall, 1977) have been reported and treated as evidence of routine discrimination on the part of the teachers concerned, and of others. And this has been supported by the selective interpretation of informants' accounts. For instance, there has been considerable reliance on student reports about teacher racism (Wright, 1986; Mac an Ghaill, 1988; Gillborn, 1990a), with little attention being given to the well-known problems entailed in reliance on informants' accounts. Yet these problems are exacerbated in this case by the indeterminacies surrounding the meaning of 'racism'. It is also noticeable that while students' accounts have been reported (at least as far as they conform to the assumptions of the researcher about 'what must be occurring'), there has been much less attempt to document the perspectives of allegedly racist teachers; and where this *has* been done it has fallen far short of being convincing, taking the form of speculative 'ideology critique' (see, for example, Mac an Ghaill, 1988, Ch. 2 and Connolly, 1995, pp. 78–9).[2]

What we see in operation here, then, is a very powerful analytic machinery for generating inequality claims. It allows the construction of inequalities of the relevant kinds from almost whatever empirical material is available. Of

---

[2] For an attempt to handle informants' accounts about racist teachers in a more methodologically adequate manner, see Foster, 1989 and 1990a. For a study which aims to understand and explain the racist views of one group of teachers, see Hammersley, 1980, Ch. 2.

course, from one point of view this bias is perhaps not very surprising. As we saw in Chapters 1 and 2, research in this area has been closely related to a political campaign designed to promote the problem of educational inequality on the agendas of public policy and professional education. And the occurrence of bias has been facilitated by the substantial shift from the use of quantitative to qualitative methods; since there is much less agreement about what methodological rules apply to the latter.

Both the old and the new sociologists of education saw their work as political. For the old sociologists this meant that topics for research were selected on political grounds and that the findings were interpreted from a particular political point of view; though for them the actual process of research was treated as properly subject to scientific canons.[3] With the shift from the old to the new sociology this demarcation between politics and science was abandoned by many. The whole process of research now came to be seen as political, and as quite properly directed towards the achievement of political goals, often formulated as the eradication of inequality of one kind or another, or even of all inequality. Thus, we have Sharp (1981, p. 149) arguing that it is '[. . .] the responsibility of the social scientist [. . .] to work toward achieving that kind of society [which is] characterized by both formal and substantive equality [. . .]'. As a result, many researchers seem to have become more concerned with engaging in radical critique in order to bring about 'change' than with making a balanced assessment of educational inequalities, their causes and consequences.

Of course, those who regard social research as necessarily political, in some global sense, may reject the very idea that research should be neutral as between different kinds of potential finding. To the extent that research is regarded as properly partisan, bias of the right kind can become a desirable feature, not a negative one. This is made explicit in one article advocating politically committed research in education, where the authors declare that: 'the question is not whether the data are biased; the question is whose interests are served by the bias' (Gitlin *et al.*, 1989, p. 245). In much the same way, Lather (1986) has called for research to be 'openly ideological', and Troyna has declared that he is 'committed to the integration of antiracist and related egalitarian convictions into the design, execution and interpretation' of his research. (Troyna, 1993, p. 168). On the basis of the arguments presented in Chapter 2 (and developed elsewhere: Hammersley, 1995a), we believe that this represents an abandonment of research in favour of the production of propaganda. Its only virtue is that it makes explicit what some researchers have been, and probably still are, engaged in under the cover of 'research'.

That there is political pressure within academia to produce the 'right' conclusions, and to avoid the 'wrong' ones, has been illustrated on a number

---

[3] See Halsey's 1972, pp. 3–4 discussion of the importance of distinguishing scientific from value problems. This distinction was also adopted by some feminists. See, for example, Kelly, 1978.

of occasions in recent years. One of these was the response to Smith and Tomlinson's (1989) report that in the schools they studied the achievement levels of both south Asians and Afro-Caribbeans are 'distinctly *better*' than whites, when allowance is made for social class and attainment in reading at the end of the second year of secondary schooling. This was challenged on the grounds that '[it leaves the way] clear for the New Right to state that the report shows ethnic-minority pupils "doing as well in our schools as white children — in some cases better"' (Gillborn and Drew, 1993, p. 556; see also Gillborn, 1990a, pp. 131–8; Troyna and Hatcher, 1992). This reprimand was accompanied by selective methodological criticism designed to discredit this aspect of Smith and Tomlinson's findings (see Hammersley and Gomm, 1993). In much the same way, Troyna (1991b) has criticized quantitative research on racism in schools generally, suggesting that it underestimates the incidence of racism, the evidence for this being the findings of qualitative work. He accepts the latter on the basis of little or no explicit methodological assessment, with the sole exception of a study which did *not* discover much evidence of teacher racism, this being subjected to dismissive critique (Hammersley, 1993).[4]

In short, there has been a systematic distortion of the research process for political ends by some of the new sociologists of education and by many of their successors.[5] However, there is an even more fundamental problem with the literature on educational inequality than this problem of bias. And it is one which affects the old as much as the new sociology. This is that inequality has been treated as if it were an objective and unitary feature of social arrangements. As we have emphasized, while claims about descriptive inequalities are factual not valuational, they cannot but be selected on the basis of value assumptions adopted for methodological purposes. Descriptions of inequalities depend on assumptions about what constitutes equity, opportunity, and education. And there are diverse views about these matters. Similarly, explanations for inequalities rely on assumptions about what it is feasible to change, what changes are justifiable in terms of their value in relation to associated and opportunity costs, who is responsible for what and within what limits etc. However, not only has it been rare for researchers to make these value assumptions explicit, but also the inequalities focused on have been treated as if they were necessarily inequities, and as demanding policy intervention. Their inequitable character has been taken for granted, as has the assumption that they can and should be remedied. Yet, establishing claims about equity and about what is desirable requires ethical and political

---

[4] The study which was treated as an exception was that by Foster, 1990a. On the debates surrounding this study and Foster's criticisms of other work in this field, see Hammersley, 1995a, Ch. 4. The kind of self-censorship to which this climate can lead is illustrated by Finch's discussion of the problems of reporting her research findings about play groups, Finch, 1985, pp. 117–21.

[5] It is perhaps worth emphasizing that this is by no means the only source or direction of distortion currently operating on social and educational research. See Hammersley and Scarth, 1994, and Pettigrew, 1994.

judgments which cannot be validated by research. A value consensus has effectively been assumed, but there is little evidence that such a consensus exists, even amongst educational researchers.

To leave implicit the value and factual assumptions on which claims about inequalities are made is to misrepresent the nature of educational inequalities: it is to reify them. Descriptive equalities and inequalities abound in the education system, and elsewhere, but they are not all of a piece. There are all manner of respects in which students from different categories can be judged to be equal or unequal. Students who all sat an examination are equal in that respect, even though their results were different. Moreover, whether their results were different, how different, and in what direction, depends in part on how the researcher treats those results: whether their scores are grouped (and if so how broad the groups are), whether the concern is solely with whether they reached a particular threshold mark or whether a norm-referenced approach is adopted, whether or not their performance is judged relative to some measure of their ability or previous achievement; and, if so, what measure of that is adopted etc. Nor are the categories of student which are employed in this research simply 'given' features of contemporary societies. As we saw in Chapter 3, there are various social-class schemas and different (and highly contested) bases for identifying 'racial'/ethnic groups; even 'gender' is by no means an entirely unproblematic category. And there are, of course, many other ways than these of distinguishing among students, each of which would reveal various equalities and inequalities. These include, for instance, differences in motivational level, specific aptitude, personality type, position in the family etc.

Above all, of course, to treat inequality as a unitary, objective feature of the world is to obscure the role of the researcher in constructing it. It is ironic that the new sociologists and their successors, who have criticized others for lack of reflexivity, should have so signally failed to be reflexive about their own role in the construction of educational inequalities. This lack of reflexivity is made considerably worse, however, by the fact that, as we have seen, much of this literature draws conclusions about inequality which, despite being presented as factual claims, have the character of practical evaluations and prescriptions. In this way, value conclusions are presented as though they have been validated by sociological research. This is not only a transgression of the proper limits of social science but it leads to a distortion of rational discussion about educational inequalities. One aspect of this is that academic evaluations of situations, in terms of a single value complex, are treated as if they were equivalent to the sort of practical evaluation necessary in teaching or policymaking, which must be sensitive to the context in which action is to take place and must therefore encompass a much wider range of factual and value considerations. In other words, the contribution which research can make to policymaking and practice has been grossly exaggerated (Hammersley, 1995a, Ch. 7).

Of course, the attempted derivation of value conclusions from factual investigations is by no means unusual in sociology. Indeed, there are two influential paradigms for this within the discipline: positivism, of a Comtean or Durkheimian kind, and Marxism. Both assume that such conclusions can be drawn from analysis of the nature of contemporary society, viewed in the context of a process of necessary development. Thus, for Durkheim, the sociologist was a diagnostician, identifying the pathological in nineteenth-century and early twentieth-century society: that which was transitional in the emergence of a truly modern society characterized by organic solidarity. And this was thought to provide the basis for the recommendation of remedies designed to facilitate the process of social change (Lukes, 1973; Bryant, 1976). Similarly, in the work of Marx analysis of capitalist society against the background of its development is used as a basis for understanding the potential built into it for change to a higher form of society. He insists that there is no ethical component in his scientific socialism; but this is simply an assertion of an extreme form of ethical naturalism, whereby evaluative and prescriptive conclusions can be scientifically validated.[6] Like Hegel, Marx sought to derive evaluative conclusions about what is, and prescriptive conclusions about what should be, from socio-historical analysis (Lukes, 1985; Wood, 1991).

These two paradigms shaped the old and the new sociologies to varying degrees, and so too did the work of Max Weber. However, Weber's position on this issue contrasts sharply with those of Durkheim and Marx. He insisted on the difference between facts and values, and that the one cannot be derived from the other. He also believed that there was a considerable danger in modern society that science would be used to legitimate political decisions. His insistence that scholarship must be value-neutral was designed to counter this.[7]

Our position is closest to that of Weber. We believe that sociological research must be pursued as a non-political activity, in the specific sense that it should not be directed towards the achievement of any particular political goal, not even the elimination of educational inequities (Hammersley, 1995a, Ch. 6). In our view neither science, nor any other kind of academic inquiry, can offer answers to evaluative and prescriptive questions; though it can provide important resources for answering those questions. In other words, what

---

[6] The whole realm of morality is supposedly discarded, as it was with Hegel. This is done on the grounds that it is either ineffective, because detached from social reality, or ideological, because it functions as part of that reality in ways which are not understood by the morally committed.

[7] Until recently, Weber has tended to be interpreted through the distorting lens of Parsons' synthesis (Parsons, 1937). For a critical commentary on the reception of Weber's work, see Tribe's introduction to Hennis, 1988, and Hennis's book itself. This distortion of Weber's position probably affected the old sociology in significant respects. However, Weber's argument that science can assess the rationality of value judgments, given commitment to certain ultimate values, and that it can recommend the most efficient means for the achievement of specified goals, provides a potential bridge between his position and that of Durkheim and Marx; even though it is one which leaves a chasm to be leapt at one end.

social science produces can never be sufficient for the guidance of practical action. Essential to such guidance, but not available from research, are commitments to particular values, and judgments based on experience and local knowledge.

From this point of view, the task of research on educational inequalities is to present factual information relevant to debates among professionals, policymakers, and relevant publics. Researchers must select from the vast range of descriptive equalities and inequalities that are to be found in the education system those which they or others take to be relevant, in one way or another, to the value of equity. But it is important to recognize that no evaluative or prescriptive conclusions follow from this process of selection. This is because there is always scope for different views about the value significance of any inequality: given the potential for different interpretations of equity, and for disagreements about the relative importance of equity as against other values. Moreover, prescriptive conclusions do not follow automatically from evaluations, because the former necessarily involve judgments about what is feasible for particular agents in the circumstances they face, the relative opportunity costs of interventions of various kinds etc. The relationship between values and research which provides for the relevance of the phenomena studied by sociologists is an academic one, then: it implies no practical commitment to those values on the part of the researcher (though he or she may as a matter of fact be so committed); and it does not provide a sufficient basis for recommending policies.

Our argument is not that researchers must never have strong political commitments. Indeed, we are inclined to agree with Weber that as citizens we should all have these. But these commitments must not control our research. They can motivate us to investigate particular topics, and can provide theoretical insights; but the research process should be governed, above all else (though not to the *exclusion* of all else), by commitment to the task of producing knowledge. Nor should we pretend that our convictions can be justified by research. To reiterate, the goal of substantive academic research is to provide the information relevant to debates about public issues, rather than to produce evidence designed to support one side in those debates. In other words, research on educational inequality must be guided by a commitment to its description and explanation, not to its eradication; not least because, in literal terms, such a political project is quixotic.

The most basic of our complaints in this book, then, is that sociologists have engaged in political debates about educational equality under the guise of scientific research. And in doing so they have served *both* research and politics badly. They have treated inequality as if it were an objective and unitary feature of the world, and have shown a bias towards finding inequalities of particular kinds. On the basis of a detailed analysis of particular studies, we have argued that the conclusions drawn have often lacked sufficient clarity, have relied on over-interpretation of evidence, and have failed to consider equally plausible and credible alternative interpretations. Under the pressure of a political campaign concerned with promoting educational inequality as a social problem, researchers seem often to have fixed on particular findings which suited their purposes, presenting these as 'the facts' about educational inequality. Furthermore, these conclusions have frequently been evaluative and/or prescriptive in nature, and have been presented as if they were justified by sociological analysis. Thus, research in this field has operated under a systematic deception: it is purportedly about educational inequality, which appears to be a purely factual matter, something about which science can in principle provide evidence; yet, inequalities have been treated as obvious inequities. So the effect has been to promote political views about the education system on the basis of a spurious appeal to science. In these various ways, the proper work of research has been seriously distorted, and the authority of social science has been abused.

Of course, political and practical action in relation to the problem of educational inequalities cannot wait for progress in research. But in our view it would benefit from not being hampered by bogus scientific claims made by researchers; and it could gain a great deal from genuine progress in documenting and explaining the range of value-relevant equalities and inequalities which prevail in the British education system.

References

ABERNETHY, G.L. (1959) *The Idea of Equality: An Anthology*, Richmond, Virginia, John Knox Press.

ABRAHAM, J. (1989a) 'Testing Hargreaves' and Lacey's differentiation-polarisation theory in a setted comprehensive', *British Journal of Sociology*, **40**, 1, pp. 46–81.

ABRAHAM, J. (1989b) 'Teacher ideology and sex roles in curriculum texts', *British Journal of Sociology of Education*, **10**, 1, pp. 33–51.

ALCOFF, L. (1988) 'Cultural feminism vs post-structuralism: The identity crisis in feminism', *Signs*, **13**, 3, pp. 405–36.

ALLEN, S. and SMITH, C. (1975) 'Minority group experience of the transition from education to work', in BRANNEN, P. (Ed) *Entering the World of Work*, London, HMSO.

ALTHUSSER, L. (1971) 'Ideology and ideological state apparatuses', in ALTHUSSER, L. *Lenin and Philosophy and Other Essays*, London, New Left Books.

APPIAH, K.A. (1990) 'Racisms', in GOLDBERG, T. (Ed) *Anatomy of Racism*, Minneapolis, University of Minnesota Press.

ARISTOTLE (1925) *The Nicomachean Ethics*, Oxford, Oxford University Press (Ross translation).

ARNOT, M. and WEINER, G. (Eds) (1987) *Gender and the Politics of Schooling*, London, Hutchinson.

ARNOT, M. and WHITTY, G. (1982) 'From reproduction to transformation: Recent radical perspectives on the curriculum from the USA', *British Journal of Sociology of Education*, **3**, pp. 93–103.

ASHBY, W.R. (1956) *An Introduction to Cybernetics*, London, Chapman and Hall.

ASHMORE, M. (1989) *The Reflexive Thesis*, Chicago, University of Chicago Press.

ATKINSON, P.A. (1985) *Language, Structure and Reproduction: An Introduction to the Sociology of Basil Bernstein*, London, Methuen.

ATKINSON, P.A. (1992) *Understanding Ethnographic Texts*, Newbury Park, Sage.

ATKINSON, P.A., DELAMONT, S. and HAMMERSLEY, M. (1993) 'Qualitative research traditions', in HAMMERSLEY, M. (Ed) *Educational Research: Current Issues*, London, Paul Chapman.

BACHMAN, J. and O'MALLEY, P. (1986) 'Self-concepts, self-esteem, and educational experiences: The frog pond revisited (again)', *Journal of Educational Psychology*, **50**, 1, pp. 35–46.

BALL, S.J. (1981) *Beachside Comprehensive*, Cambridge, Cambridge University Press.

BALL, S.J. (1983) 'Case study research in education', in HAMMERSLEY, M. (Ed) *The Ethnography of Schooling*, Driffield, Nafferton Books.

BALL, S.J. (1986) 'The sociology of the school: Streaming and mixed ability and social class', in ROGERS, R. (Ed) *Education and Social Class*, London, Falmer Press.

BALL, S.J. (1990) 'Self-doubt and soft data: Social and technical trajectories in ethnographic fieldwork', *Qualitative Studies in Education*, **3**, 2, pp. 157–71.

BANKS, O. (1955) *Parity and Prestige in English Secondary Education*, London, Routledge and Kegan Paul.

BANKS, O. (1971) *The Sociology of Education*, (second edition), London, Batsford.

BANKS, O. (1982) 'The sociology of education 1952–1982', *British Journal of Educational Studies*, **30**, 1, pp. 18–31.

BARKER LUNN, J. (1970) *Streaming in the Primary School*, Slough, NFER.

BARRETT, M. (1980) *Women's Oppression Today: Problems in Marxist Feminism*, London, Verso.

BARTH, F. (1969) *Ethnic Groups and Boundaries*, London, Allen and Unwin.

BARTON, L. and WALKER, S. (Eds) (1983) *Race, Class and Education*, London, Croom Helm.

DE BEAUVOIR, S. (1973) *The Second Sex*, New York, Vintage Press.

BECKER, H.S. (1967) 'Whose side are we on?', *Social Problems*, **14**, pp. 239–47.

BEETHAM, D. (1985) *Max Weber and the Theory of Modern Politics*, (2nd ed.), Cambridge, Polity Press.

BENN, S.I. (1967) 'Equality, moral and social', in EDWARDS, P. (Ed) *The Encyclopaedia of Philosophy*, New York, Macmillan.

BENTLEY, D. and WATTS, M. (1987) 'Courting the positive virtues: A case for feminist science', in KELLY, A. (Ed) *Science for Girls?*, Milton Keynes, Open University Press.

BERGER, P. and LUCKMANN, T. (1967) *The Social Construction of Reality*, Harmondsworth, Penguin.

BERLAK, A., BERLAK, H., BAGENSTOS N.T. and MIKEL, E.R. (1975) 'Teaching and learning in English primary schools', *School Review*, **83**, 2, pp. 215–43.

BERNBAUM, G. (1977) *Knowledge and Ideology in the Sociology of Education*, London, Macmillan.

BERNSTEIN, B. (1970) 'Education cannot compensate for society', *New Society*, 26 February, pp. 344–7.

BERNSTEIN, B. (1974) 'Sociology and the sociology of education: A brief account', in REX, J. (Ed) *Approaches to Sociology*, London, Routledge and Kegan Paul.

BLAIR, M. (1993) 'Review of Peter Foster: Policy and practice in multicultural and antiracist education', *European Journal of Intercultural Studies*, **2**, 3, pp. 63–4.

BLATCHFORD, P., BURKE, J., FARQUAR, C., PLEWIS, I. and TIZARD, B. (1985) 'Educational achievement in the infant school: The influence of ethnic origin, gender and home on entry skills', *Educational Research*, **27**, pp. 52–60.

BLAUG, M. (1987) *The Economics of Education and the Education of an Economist*, Aldershot, Elgar.

BLUMER, H. (1969) *Symbolic Interactionism*, Englewood Cliffs NJ, Prentice-Hall.

BOUDON, R. (1973) *Education, Opportunity and Social Inequality* (English translation 1974), New York, Wiley.

BOWLES, G. and DUELLI KLEIN, R. (Eds) (1983) *Theories of Women's Studies*, London, Routledge and Kegan Paul.

BOWLES, S. and GINTIS, H. (1976) *Schooling in Capitalist America*, London, Routledge and Kegan Paul.

BROOKS, D. and SINGH, K. (1978) *Aspirations versus Opportunities: Asian and White School-leavers in the Midlands*, Walsall and Leicester Community Relations Councils.

BRUUN, H.H. (1972) *Science, Values, and Politics in Max Weber's Methodology*, Copenhagen, Munksgaard.

BRYANT, C.G.A. (1976) *Sociology in Action: A Critique of Selected Conceptions of the Social Role of the Sociologist*, London, Allen and Unwin.

BULMER, M. (Ed) (1975) *Working Class Images of Society*, London, Routledge and Kegan Paul.

BULMER, M. (1986) 'Race and ethnicity', in BURGESS, R.G. (Ed) *Key Variables in Social Investigation*, London, Routledge and Kegan Paul.

BURGESS, R.G. (Ed) (1984) *The Research Process in Educational Settings*, Lewes, Falmer Press.

BURGESS, R.G. (Ed) (1985a) *Issues in Educational Research: Qualitative Methods*, Lewes, Falmer Press.

BURGESS, R.G. (Ed) (1985b) *Strategies of Educational Research: Qualitative Methods*, Lewes, Falmer Press.

BURGESS, R.G. (Ed) (1985c) *Field Methods in the Study of Education*, Lewes, Falmer Press.

BURGESS, R.G. (Ed) (1986) *Key Variables in Social Investigation*, London, Routledge and Kegan Paul.

BURGESS, R.G. (Ed) (1989) *The Ethics of Educational Research*, Lewes, Falmer Press.

BUSWELL, C. (1981) 'Sexism in school routines and classroom practices', *Durham and Newcastle Research Review*, **9**, 46, pp. 195–200.

BUTLER, J. (1987) 'Variations on sex and gender: Beauvoir, Wittig and Foucault', in BENHABIB, S. and CORNELL, D. (Eds) *Feminism as Critique: Essays on the Politics of Gender in Late-capitalist Societies*, Cambridge, Polity Press.

BUTTON, G. and SHARROCK, W.W. (1993) 'A disagreement over agreement and consensus in constructionist sociology', *Journal for the Theory of Social Behaviour*, **23**, 1, pp. 1–25.

BYRNE, E. (1978) *Women and Education*, London, Tavistock.

CARBY, H. (1982) 'White woman listen! Black feminism and the boundaries of sisterhood', in Centre for Contemporary Cultural Studies, *The Empire Strikes Back: Race and Racism in 70s Britain*, London, Hutchinson.

CARRINGTON, B. (1983) 'Sport as a side-track: An analysis of West Indian involvement in extra-curricular sport', in BARTON, L. AND WALKER, S. (Eds) *Race, Class and Education*, London, Croom Helm.

CENTRE FOR CONTEMPORARY CULTURAL STUDIES (1981) *Unpopular Education: Schooling and Social Democracy in England since 1944*, London, Hutchinson.

CHADWICK, H. (1967) *The Early Church*, Harmondsworth, Penguin.

CICOUREL, A.V. (1976) *The Social Organisation of Juvenile Justice*, London, Heinemann.

CLARRICOATES, K. (1980) 'The importance of being Ernest . . . Emma . . . Tom . . . Jane: The perception and categorisation of gender conformity and gender deviation in primary schools', in DEEM, R. (Ed) *Schooling for Women's Work*, London, Routledge.

COHEN, D.K. and ROSENBURG, B.H. (1977) 'Functions and fantasies: Understanding schools in capitalist America', *History of Education Quarterly*, **17**, pp. 113–68.

COHEN, G.A. (1978) *Karl Marx's Theory of History: A Defence*, Oxford, Oxford University Press.

COHEN, G.A. (1988) *History, Labour and Freedom: Themes from Marx*, Oxford, Oxford University Press.

COHEN, S. (1979) 'Guilt, justice and tolerance: Some old concepts for a new criminology', in DOWNES, D. and ROCK, P. (Eds) *Deviant Interpretations*, Oxford, Martin Robertson.

COLEMAN, J. (1968) 'The concept of equality of educational opportunity', *Harvard Educational Review*, **38**, 1, pp. 7–22.

COLLINS, R. (1977) 'Some comparative principles of educational stratification', *Harvard Educational Review*, **47**, 1, pp. 1–27.

COMMISSION FOR RACIAL EQUALITY (1992) *Set to Fail? Setting and Banding in Secondary Schools*, London, Commission for Racial Equality.

COMMITTEE OF THE SECONDARY SCHOOL EXAMINATIONS COUNCIL (1943) *Curriculum and Examinations in Secondary Schools*, London, HMSO (Norwood Report).

CONNOLLY, P. (1992) 'Playing it by the rules: The politics of research in "race" and education', *British Educational Research Journal*, **18**, 2, pp. 133–48.

CONNOLLY, P. (1995) 'Racism, masculine peer-group relations and the schooling of African/Caribbean infant boys', *British Journal of Sociology of Education*, **16**, 1, pp. 75–92.

CONSULTATIVE COMMITTEE OF THE BOARD OF EDUCATION (1926) *The Education of the Adolescent*, London, HMSO (The Hadow Report).

COSER, R. (1959) 'Some social functions of laughter', *Human Relations*, **12**, pp. 171–82.

CRAFT, M. (Ed) (1970) *Family, Class and Education*, London, Longman.

References

CRAFT, M. and CRAFT, A. (1983) 'The participation of ethnic minority pupils in further and higher education', *Educational Research*, **25**, 1, pp. 10–19.

CRAFT, M., RAYNOR, J. and COHEN, J. (1972) *Linking Home and School*, 2nd ed., London, Longman.

CRAIB, I. (1993) 'Social constructionism as social psychosis', Paper given at the British Sociological Association annual conference, University of Essex.

CROLL, P. (1985) 'Teacher interaction with individual male and female pupils in junior-age classrooms', *Educational Research*, **27**, 3, pp. 220–3.

CROSSMAN, M. (1987) 'Teachers' interactions with girls and boys in science lessons', in KELLY, A. (Ed) *Science for Girls?*, Milton Keynes, Open University Press.

DEEM, R. (1978) *Women and Schooling*, London, Routledge and Kegan Paul.

DEEM, R. (Ed) (1980) *Schooling for Women's Work*, London, Routledge.

DEEM, R. (1986) 'Gender and social class', in ROGERS, R. (Ed) *Education and Social Class*, London, Falmer Press.

DEMERATH, N.J. and PETERSON, R.A. (Eds) (1967) *System, Change and Conflict*, New York, Free Press.

DENNIS, N. and HALSEY, A.H. (1988) *English Ethical Socialism*, Oxford, Oxford University Press.

DEPARTMENT FOR EDUCATION (1994) *Statistical Bulletin, Issue No 10/94: Participation in Education by 16–18 year olds in England, 1983/4 to 1993/94*, London, Government Statistical Service.

DEPARTMENT OF EDUCATION AND SCIENCE (1975) *Education Survey 21: Curricular Differences for Boys and Girls*, London, HMSO.

DINGWALL, R. (1977) 'Atrocity stories' and professional relations', *Sociology of Work and Occupations*, **4**, 4, pp. 371–96.

DORE, R. (1976) *The Diploma Disease*, London, George Allen and Unwin.

DOUGLAS, J.D. (1967) *The Social Meanings of Suicide*, Princeton, Princeton University Press.

DOUGLAS, J.W.B. (1964) *The Home and the School*, London, MacGibbon and Kee.

DOWNES, D. (1979) 'Praxis makes perfect: A critique of critical criminology', in DOWNES, D. and ROCK, P. (Eds) *Deviant Interpretations*, Oxford, Martin Robertson.

DOWNES, D. and ROCK, P. (Eds) (1979) *Deviant Interpretations*, Oxford, Martin Robertson.

DOYLE, W. (1977) 'Learning the classroom environment', *Journal of Teacher Education*, **28**, pp. 51–5.

DRAPER, J. (1993) 'We're back with Gobbo: The re-establishment of gender relations following a school merger', in WOODS, P. and HAMMERSLEY, M. (Eds) *Gender and Ethnicity in Schools*, London, Routledge.

DREW, D. and GRAY, J. (1990) 'The fifth-year examination achievements of black young people in England and Wales', *Educational Research*, **32**, 2, pp. 107–17.

DREW, D. and GRAY, J. (1991) 'The black–white gap in examination results: A statistical critique of a decade's research', *New Community*, **17**, 2, pp. 159–72.

DRIVER G. (1980a) 'How West Indians do better at school (especially the girls)', *New Society*, January 17th.

DRIVER, G. (1980b) *Beyond Underachievement*, London, Commission for Racial Equality.

DUBBERLEY, W. (1988a) 'Social class and the process of schooling: A case study of a comprehensive school in a mining community', in GREEN, A.G. and BALL, S.J. (Eds) *Progress and Inequality in Comprehensive Education*, London, Routledge.

DUBBERLEY, W. (1988b) 'Humor as resistance', *Qualitative Studies in Education*, **1**, 2, pp. 104–23.

DRUDY, S. (1991) 'The classification of social class in sociological research', *British Journal of Sociology*, **42**, 1, pp. 21–45.

EDWARDS, P. (Ed) (1967) *The Encyclopedia of Philosophy*, New York, Macmillan.

EDWARDS, T. (1980) 'Schooling for change: Function correspondence and cause', in BARTON, L., MEIGHAN, R. and WALKER, S. (Eds) *Schooling Ideology and Curriculum*, London, Falmer Press.

ENNIS, R. (1978) 'Equality of educational opportunity', in STRIKE, K.A. and EGAN, K. (Eds) *Ethics and Educational Policy*, London, Routledge and Kegan Paul.

EPSTEIN, D. (Ed) (1995) *Challenging Gay and Lesbian Inequalities in Education*, Buckingham, Open University Press.

ERBEN, M. and GLEESON, D. (1977) 'Education as production: A critical examination of some aspects of the work of Louis Althusser' in YOUNG, M. and WHITTY, G. (Eds) *Society, State and Schooling*, London, Falmer Press.

ESHEL, Y. and KURMAN, J. (1991) 'Academic self-concept, accuracy of perceived ability and academic attainment' *British Journal of Educational Psychology*, **61**, 2, pp. 187–96.

FINCH, J. (1985) 'Social policy and education: Problems and possibilities of using qualitative methods', in BURGESS, R.G. (Ed) *Issues in Educational Research*, Lewes, Falmer Press.

FLAX, J. (1986) 'Gender as a problem: In and for feminist theory', *American Studies*, **31**, 2, pp. 193–213.

FLAX, J. (1987) 'Postmodernism and gender relations in feminist theory', *Signs*, **12**, 4, pp. 621–43.

FLOUD, J.E. and HALSEY, A.H. (1956) 'Education and occupation: English secondary schools and the supply of labour', in KING HALL, R. and LAUWERYS, J.A. (Eds) *The Year Book of Education 1956*, London, Evans.

FLOUD, J. and HALSEY, A.H. (1958) 'The sociology of education: A trend report and bibliography, *Current Sociology*, **VII**, 3, pp. 165–235.

FLOUD, J.E., HALSEY, A.H. and MARTIN, F.M. (1956) *Social Class and Educational Opportunity*, London, Heinemann.

FLUDE, M. (1974) 'Sociological accounts of differential educational attainment', in FLUDE, M. and AHIER, J. (Eds) *Educability, Schools and Ideology*, New York, Wiley.

FOSTER, P. (1989) 'Policy and practice in multicultural and anti-racist education', PhD thesis, Open University.

FOSTER, P. (1990a) *Policy and Practice in Multicultural and Anti-racist Education*, London, Routledge.

FOSTER, P. (1990b) 'Cases not proven: An evaluation of two studies of teacher racism', *British Educational Research Journal*, **16**, 4, pp. 335–48.

FOSTER, P. (1991) 'Case still not proven: A reply to Cecile Wright', *British Educational Research Journal*, **17**, 2, pp. 165–70.

FOSTER, P. (1992) 'What are Connolly's rules?: A reply to Paul Connolly', *British Educational Research Journal*, **18**, 2, pp. 149–54.

FOSTER, P. (1993a) 'Teacher attitudes and Afro-Caribbean achievement', *Oxford Review of Education*, **18**, 3, pp. 269–82.

FOSTER, P. (1993b) 'Some problems in identifying racial/ethnic equality or inequality in schools', *British Journal of Sociology*, **44**, 3, pp. 519–35.

FOSTER, P. (1993c) 'Equal treatment and cultural difference in multi-ethnic schools: A critique of teacher ethnocentrism theory', *International Studies in the Sociology of Education*, **2**, 1, pp. 89–103.

FRENCH, J. and FRENCH, P. (1984) 'Gender imbalances in the primary classroom', *Educational Research*, **26**, 2, pp. 127–36.

FULLER, M. (1980) 'Black girls in a London comprehensive school', in DEEM, R. (Ed) *Schooling for Women's Work*, London, Routledge.

FULLER, M. (1982) 'Young, female and black', in CASHMORE, E. and TROYNA, B. (Eds) *Black Youth in Crisis*, London, Allen and Unwin.

FULLER, M. (1983) 'Qualified criticism, critical qualifications', in BARTON, L. and WALKER, S. (Eds) *Race, Class and Education*, London, Croom Helm.

GALLAGHER, A.M., CORMACK, R.J. and OSBORNE, R.D. (1994) 'Religion, equity and education in Northern Ireland', *British Educational Research Journal*, **20**, 5, pp. 507–18.

GARFINKEL, H. (1960) 'The rational properties of scientific and commonsense activities', *Behavioral Science*, **5**, 1, pp. 72–83.

GARFINKEL, H. (1967) *Studies in Ethnomethodology*, Englewood Cliffs NJ, Prentice-Hall.

GERGEN, K.J. (1985) 'The social constructionist movement in modern psychology', *American Psychologist*, **40**, 3, pp. 266–75.

GEUSS, R. (1981) *The Idea of Critical Theory*, Cambridge, Cambridge University Press.

GIBSON, J.J. (1979) *The Ecological Approach to Visual Perception*, Boston, Houghton-Miflin.

GILLBORN, D. (1990a) *'Race', Ethnicity and Education*, London, Unwin Hyman.

GILLBORN, D. (1990b) 'Sexism and curricular "choice"', *Cambridge Journal of Education*, **20**, 2, pp. 161–74.

GILLBORN, D. (1995) *Racism and Antiracism in Real Schools*, Buckingham, Open University Press.

GILLBORN, D. and DREW, D. (1993) 'The politics of research: Some observations on "methodological purity"', *New Community*, **19**, 2, pp. 354–60.

GILLIGAN, C. (1982) *In a Different Voice: Psychological Theory and Women's Development*, Cambridge, MA, Harvard University Press.

GITLIN, A.D., SIEGEL, M. and BORU, K. (1989) 'The politics of method: From Leftist ethnography to educative research', *Qualitative Studies in Education*, **2**, 3, pp. 237–53.

GLASS, D.V. (1950) 'The application of social research', *British Journal of Sociology*, **1**, pp. 17–30.

GLASS, D.V. (Ed) (1956) *Social Mobility in Britain*, London, Routledge and Kegan Paul.

GOLDTHORPE, J.H. (1980) *Social Mobility and Class Structure in Britain*, Oxford, Oxford University Press.

GOMM, R. (1991) 'An assessment of C. Wright: School processes', Unpublished paper.

GOMM, R. (1993) 'Figuring out ethnic equity', *British Educational Research Journal*, **19**, 2, pp. 149–65.

GOMM, R. (1994) 'Quantitative research', in *Educational Research Methods*, E824, Milton Keynes, Open University.

GOMM, R. (1995) 'Strong claims, weak evidence: A response to Troyna's "Ethnicity and the organisation of learning"', *Educational Research*, **37**, 1, pp. 79–86.

GOODACRE, E. (1968) *Teachers and the Pupils' Home Backgrounds*, Slough, NFER.

GOODACRE, E. (1971) 'Teachers and the pupils' home backgrounds', in COSIN, B., DALE, I.R., ESLAND, G. and SWIFT, D. (Eds) *School and Society*, London, Routledge and Kegan Paul.

GORBUTT, D. (1972) 'The "new" sociology of education', *Education for Teaching*, Autumn.

GORDON, P. (1980) *Selection for Secondary Education*, London, Woburn Press.

GORDON, P. (1992) 'The racialization of statistics', in SKELLINGTON, R. and MORRIS, P. *'Race' in Britain Today*, London, Sage.

GOULDNER, A.W. (1970) *The Coming Crisis of Western Sociology*, New York, Basic Books.

GRAFTON, T., MILLER, H., SMITH, L., VEGODA, M. and WHITFIELD, R. (1983) 'Gender and curriculum choice: A case study', in HAMMERSLEY, M. and HARGREAVES, A. (Eds) *Curriculum Practice: Some Sociological Case Studies*, Lewes, Falmer Press.

GRAY, J., JESSON, D. and SIME, N. (1990) 'Estimating differences in the examination performances of secondary schools in six LEAs: A multilevel approach to school effectiveness', *Oxford Review of Education*, **16**, 2, pp. 137–58.

GRAY, J.L. and MOSHINSKY, P. (1938) 'Ability and opportunity in English education' and 'Ability and educational opportunity in relation to parental occupation', in HOGBEN, L. (Ed) *Political Arithmetic*, London, Allen and Unwin.

GREEN, P.A. (1983) 'Teachers' influence on the self-concept of pupils of different ethnic origins', Unpublished PhD Thesis, University of Durham.

References

GUBA, E. (Ed) (1990) *The Paradigm Dialog*, Newbury Park, Sage.

HABERMAS, J. (1971) *Theory and Practice* (English translation), Cambridge, Polity Press, 1988.

HADOW REPORT (see Consultative Committee of the Board of Education (1926)).

HALFPENNY, P. (1983) 'A reflection of historical materialism?' *Social Science Information*, **22**, 1, pp. 61–87.

HALPIN, D. and TROYNA, B. (Eds) (1994) *Researching Education Policy: Ethical and Methodological Issues*, London, Falmer Press.

HALSEY, A.H. (Ed) (1961) *Ability and Educational Opportunity*, Paris, OECD.

HALSEY, A.H. (Ed) (1972) *Educational Priority*, London, HMSO.

HALSEY, A.H. (1981) *Change in British Society*, (2nd ed), Oxford, Oxford University Press.

HALSEY, A.H. (1982) 'Provincials and professionals: The British post–war sociologists', *Archives Européennes de Sociologie*, **23**, 1, pp. 150–75.

HALSEY, A.H. (1994) 'Sociology as political arithmetic', *British Journal of Sociology*, **45**, 3, pp. 427–44.

HALSEY, A.H. and GARDNER, L. (1953) 'Selection for secondary education and achievement in four grammar schools', *British Journal of Sociology*, **4**, 1, pp. 60–75.

HALSEY, A.H., HEATH, A. and RIDGE, J. (1980) *Origins and Destinations*, Oxford, Oxford University Press.

HAMMERSLEY, M. (1980) 'A peculiar world?: Teaching and learning in an inner-city school', Unpublished PhD thesis, University of Manchester.

HAMMERSLEY, M. (1981) 'Ideology in the staffroom?: A critique of false consciousness', in BARTON, L. and WALKER, S. (Eds) *Schools, Teachers and Teaching*, Lewes, Falmer Press.

HAMMERSLEY, M. (Ed) (1983) *The Ethnography of Schooling*, Driffield, Nafferton Books.

HAMMERSLEY, M. (1985) 'From ethnography to theory', *Sociology*, **19**, pp. 244–59.

HAMMERSLEY, M. (1990a) 'An assessment of two studies of gender imbalance in the classroom', *British Educational Research Journal*, **16**, 2, pp. 125–43.

HAMMERSLEY, M. (1990b) *Reading Ethnographic Research*, London, Longman.

HAMMERSLEY, M. (1991) 'A myth of a myth?: An assessment of two studies of option choice in secondary schools', *British Journal of Sociology*, **42**, 1, pp. 61–94.

HAMMERSLEY, M. (1992) *What's Wrong with Ethnography?*, London, Routledge.

HAMMERSLEY, M. (1993) 'On methodological purism: A response to Barry Troyna', *British Educational Research Journal*, **19**, 4, pp. 339–41.

HAMMERSLEY, M. (1995a) *The Politics of Social Research*, London, Sage.

HAMMERSLEY, M. (1995b) 'Theory and evidence in qualitative research', *Quality and Quantity*, **29**, pp. 55–66.

HAMMERSLEY, M. (1995c) 'The methodology of ethnomethodology', Unpublished paper.

HAMMERSLEY, M. and ATKINSON, P.A. (1983) *Ethnography: Principles in Practice*, London, Tavistock. (2nd ed., Routledge, 1995).

HAMMERSLEY, M. and GOMM, R. (1993) 'A response to Gillborn and Drew on "race", class and school effects', *New Community*, **19**, 2, pp. 348–53.

HAMMERSLEY, M. and SCARTH, J. (1993) 'Beware of wise men bearing gifts: A case study of educational research', *British Educational Research Journal*, **19**, 5, pp. 489–98.

HAMMERSLEY, M. and WOODS, P. (Eds) (1976) *The Process of Schooling*, London, Routledge and Kegan Paul.

HAMMERSLEY, M. and WOODS, P. (Eds) (1984) *Life in Schools*, Milton Keynes, Open University Press.

HAMMOND, M., HOWARTH, R. and KEAT, R. (1991) *Understanding Phenomenology*, Oxford, Basil Blackwell.

HARDING, S. (1986) *The Science Question in Feminism*, Milton Keynes, Open University Press.

HARGREAVES, A. (1982) 'Resistance and relative autonomy theories: Problems of distortion and incoherence in recent Marxist theories of education', *British Journal of Sociology of Education*, **3**, 2, pp. 107–26.

HARGREAVES, A. and HAMMERSLEY, M. (1982) 'CCCS gas: Politics and science in the work of the Centre for Contemporary Cultural Studies', *Oxford Review of Education*, **8**, 2, pp. 139–44.

HARGREAVES, A. and WOODS, P. (Eds) (1984) *Classrooms and Staffrooms*, Milton Keynes, Open University Press.

HARGREAVES, D.H. (1967) *Social Relations in a Secondary School*, London, Routledge and Kegan Paul.

HARGREAVES, D.H. (1974) 'Deschooling and the new romantics' in FLUDE, M. and AHIER, J. (Eds) *Educability Schools and Ideology*, London, Croom Helm.

HARGREAVES, D.H., HESTER, S. and MELLOR, F. (1975) *Deviance in Classrooms*, London, Routledge and Kegan Paul.

HARRIS, D. (1992) *From Class Struggle to the Politics of Pleasure: The Effects of Gramscianism on Cultural Studies*, London, Routledge.

HARTSOCK, N. (1983) 'The feminist standpoint: Developing the ground for a specifically feminist historical materialism', in HARDING, S. and HINTIKKA, M.B. (Eds) *Discovering Reality*, Dordrecht, Reidel.

HEARNSHAW, L.S. (1979) *Cyril Burt, Psychologist*, London, Hodder and Stoughton.

HEATH, A. (1984) Unit 14, Open University Course E205, *Conflict and Change in Education*, Milton Keynes, Open University Press.

HEATH, A. and CLIFFORD, P. (1981) 'The measurement and explanation of school differences', *Oxford Review of Education*, **7**, 1, pp. 3–40.

HEATH, A. and RIDGE, J. (1982) 'Schools, examinations and occupational attainment', in CAPELLO, F.S., DEI, M. and ROSSI, M. (Eds) *L'immobilità Sociale*, Bologna, Il Mulino, reprinted in PURVIS, J. and HALES, M. (Eds) *Achievement and Inequality in Education*, London, (1983), Routledge and Kegan Paul.

HEGEL, G.W.F. (1821) *The Philosophy of Right*, (English translation, 1952), London, Oxford University Press.

HENNIS, W. (1988) *Max Weber: Essays in Reconstruction*, London, Allen and Unwin.

References

HICKOX, M.S.H. (1982) 'The Marxist sociology of education: A Critique', *British Journal of Sociology*, **33**, 4, pp. 563–78.

HICKS, D. (1980) 'Bias in geography textbooks: Images of the Third World and multi-ethnic Britain', Centre for Multicultural Education, University of London Institute of Education, Working Paper No. 1.

HINDESS, B. (1973) *The Use of Official Statistics in Sociology*, London, Macmillan.

HINDESS, B. (1987) *Freedom, Equality and the Market: Arguments on Social Policy*, London, Tavistock.

HIRST, P. (1979) *On Law and Ideology*, London, Macmillan.

History of the Human Sciences (1994) **7**, 1, special section on 'Constructing the Social', pp. 81–123.

HOBSBAWM, E. (1962) *The Age of Revolution 1789–1848*, London, Weidenfeld and Nicolson.

HOLSTEIN, J.A. and MILLER, G. (Eds) (1993) *Reconsidering Social Constructionism: Debates in Social Problems Theory*, New York, Aldine de Gruyter.

HOMANS, G.C. (1964) 'Structural, functional and psychological theories', in FARIS, R.E.L. (Ed) *Handbook of Modern Sociology*, Chicago, Rand McNally.

HOOD, R. (1992) *Race and Sentencing*, Oxford, Oxford University Press.

HUDSON, L. (Ed) (1970) *The Ecology of Human Intelligence*, Harmondsworth, Penguin.

HURMAN, A. (1978) *A Charter for Choice: A Study of Option Schemes*, Windsor, NFER.

IBARRA, P.R. and KITSUSE, J.I. (1993) 'Vernacular constituents of moral discourse: An interactionist proposal for the study of social problems', in HOLSTEIN, J.A. and MILLER, G. (Eds) *Reconsidering Social Constructionism: Debates in Social Problems Theory*, New York, Aldine de Gruyter.

IRIGARAY, L. (1985) *The Sex Which Is not One*, Ithaca, NY, Cornell University Press.

JACKSON, B. (1964) *Streaming: An Education System in Miniature*, London, Routledge and Kegan Paul.

JENKINS, R. (Ed) (1987) *Racism and Equal Opportunities Policies in the 1980s*, Cambridge, Cambridge University Press.

JENKS, C. (Ed) (1977) *Rationality, Education and the Organization of Knowledge*, Papers for a reflexive sociology of education, London, Routledge and Kegan Paul.

JESSON, D., GRAY, J. and TRANMER, M. (1992) *GCSE Performance in Nottinghamshire 1991: Pupil and School Factors*, Nottingham, Nottinghamshire County Council, Education, Advisory and Inspection Service.

JEWSON, N. and MASON. D. (1987) 'Monitoring equal opportunities policies: Principles and practice', in JENKINS, R. (Ed) *Racism and Equal Opportunity Policies in the 1980s*, Cambridge, Cambridge University Press.

JONES, C. (1985) 'Sexual tyranny: Male violence in a mixed secondary school', in WEINER, G. (Ed) *Just a Bunch of Girls*, Milton Keynes, Open University Press.

KELLY, A. (1978) 'Feminism and research', *Women's Studies International Quarterly*, **1**, pp. 225–32.

KELLY, A. (1981) 'Choosing or channelling?', in KELLY, A. (Ed) *The Missing Half: Girls and Science Education*, Manchester, Manchester University Press.

KELLY, A. (1987) 'The construction of masculine science', in KELLY, A. (Ed) *Science for Girls?*, Milton Keynes, Open University Press.

KOGAN, M. (1971) *The Politics of Education: Edward Boyle and Anthony Crosland in Conversation with Maurice Kogan*, Harmondsworth, Penguin.

KRESS, G. (1993) 'Against arbitrariness: The social production of the sign as a foundational issue in critical discourse analysis', *Discourse and Society*, **4**, 2, pp. 169–92.

KUHN, A. and WOLPE, A. (Ed) (1978) *Feminism and Materialism: Women and Modes of Production*, London, Routledge and Kegan Paul.

KUHN, T.S. (1970) *The Structure of Scientific Revolutions*, (2nd edn), Chicago, University of Chicago Press.

KYSEL, F. (1988) 'Ethnic background and examination results', *Educational Research*, **30**, 2, pp. 83–9.

LACEY, C. (1966) 'Some sociological concomitants of academic streaming in a grammar school', *British Journal of Sociology*, **17**, pp. 245–62.

LACEY, C. (1970) *Hightown Grammar*, Manchester, Manchester University Press.

LACEY, C. (1975) 'Destreaming in a "pressured" academic environment', in EGGLESTON, S.J. (Ed) *Contemporary Research in the Sociology of Education*, London, Methuen.

LACEY, C. (1976) 'Problems of sociological fieldwork: A review of the methodology of Hightown Grammer', in SHIPMAN, M. (Ed) *The Organisation and Impact of Social Research*, London, Routledge and Kegan Paul.

LAKOFF, S.A. (1964) *Equality in Political Philosophy*, Cambridge MS, Harvard University Press.

LAMBART, A. (1976) 'The sisterhood', in HAMMERSLEY, M. and WOODS, P. (Eds) *The Process of Schooling*, London, Routledge and Kegan Paul.

LAMBART, A. (1982) 'Expulsion in context: A school as a system in action', in FRANKENBERG, R. (Ed) *Custom and Conflict in British Society*, Manchester, Manchester University Press.

LA RUE, L. (1970) 'The black movement and women's liberation', *The Black Scholar*, May, pp. 36–42.

LASSMAN, P. and VELODY, I. (Ed) (1989) *Max Weber's 'Science as a Vocation'*, London, Unwin Hyman.

LATHER, P. (1986) 'Issues of validity in openly ideological research', *Interchange*, **17**, 4, pp. 63–84.

LAZARSFELD, P. (1949) 'The American soldier: An expository review', *Public Opinion Quarterly*, **13**, pp. 377–404.

LICHT, B.G. and DWECK, C.S. (1987) 'Sex differences in achievement orientations', in ARNOT, M. and WEINER, G. (Eds) *Gender and the Politics of Schooling*, London, Hutchinson.

LINDSAY, K. (1926) *Social Progress and Educational Waste*, London, Routledge and Kegan Paul.

LITTLE, A. and WESTERGAARD, J.H. (1964) 'The trend of class differentials in educational opportunity in England and Wales', *British Journal of Sociology*, **15**, pp. 301–16.

LOBBAN, G. (1975) 'Sex-roles in reading schemes', *Educational Review*, **27**, 3, pp. 202–10.

LÖWITH, K. (1949) *Meaning in History*, Chicago, University of Chicago Press.

LUGONES, M.C. and SPELMAN, E.V. (1983) 'Have we got a theory for you!: Feminist theory, cultural imperialism and the demand for "the woman's voice"', *Women's Studies International Forum*, **6**, 6, pp. 573–81.

LUKES, S. (1973) *Emile Durkheim: His Life and Work*, London, Allen Lane.

LUKES, S. (1985) *Marxism and Morality*, Oxford, Oxford University Press.

MAC AN GHAILL, M. (1988) *Young, Gifted and Black*, Milton Keynes, Open University Press.

MAC AN GHAILL, M. (1995) *The Making of Men: Masculinities, Sexualities and Schooling*, Buckingham, Open University Press.

MACKINNON, D. (1986) 'Equality of opportunity as fair and open competition', *Journal of Philosophy of Education* **20**, 1, pp. 69–71.

MACKINNON, D., STATHAM, J. and HALES, M. (1995) *Education in the UK: Facts and Figures*, London, Hodder and Stoughton.

MACLEOD, J. (1987) *Ain't no Makin' It*, Boulder, CO, Westview Press.

McCALL, G. (1984) 'Systematic field observation', *Annual Review of Sociology*, **10**, pp. 263–82.

McCARTHY, T. (1978) *The Critical Theory of Jurgen Habermas*, London, Hutchinson.

McDOWELL, L. and PRINGLE, R. (Eds) (1992) *Defining Women: Social Institutions and Gender Divisions*, Cambridge, Polity Press.

MAHONEY, P. (1985) *Schools for the Boys? Co-education Reassessed*, London, Hutchinson.

MARSH, C. (1986) 'Social class and occupation', in BURGESS, R.G. (Ed) *Key Variables in Social Investigation*, London, Routledge and Kegan Paul.

MARSH, H. (1990) 'Influences of internal and external frames of reference on the formation of maths and English self-concepts', *Journal of Educational Psychology*, **82**, 1, pp. 107–16.

MARSHALL, G., NEWBY, H., ROSE, D. and VOGLER, C. (1988) *Social Class in Modern Britain*, London, Hutchinson.

MARX, K. and ENGELS, F. (1845–6) *The German Ideology Part One*, ARTHUR, C.J. (Ed) (1970) London, Lawrence and Wishart.

MASON, D. (1990) 'A rose by any other name . . . ?: Categorisation, identity and social science', *New Community*, **17**, 1, pp. 123–33.

MATZA, D. (1969) *Becoming Deviant*, Englewood Cliffs, NJ, Prentice-Hall.

MEASOR, L. and SIKES, P.J. (1992) *Gender and Schools*, London, Cassell.

MERRETT, F. and WHELDALL, K. (1992) 'Teachers' use of praise and reprimands to boys and girls', *Educational Review*, **44**, 1, pp. 73–9.

MERTON, R.K. (1936) 'The unanticipated consequences of purposive social action', *American Sociological Review*, **1**, pp. 894–904.

MERTON, R.K. (1972) 'Insiders and outsiders', *American Journal of Sociology*, **78**, pp. 9–47.

MERTON, R.K. (1973) *The Sociology of Science: Theoretical and Empirical Investigations*, Chicago, University of Chicago Press.

MIES, M. (1983) 'Towards a methodology for feminist research', in BOWLES, G. and DUELLI KLEIN, R. (Eds) *Theories of Women's Studies*, London, Routledge and Kegan Paul.

MIES, M. (1991) 'Women's research or feminist research?: The debate surrounding feminist science and methodology', in FONOW, M.M. and COOK, J.A. (Eds) (1991) *Beyond Methodology: Feminist Scholarship as Lived Research*, Bloomington IND, Indiana University Press.

MIRZA, H.S. (1992) *Young, Female and Black*, London, Routledge.

MODOOD, T. (1988) *Not Easy Being British*, Runnymede Trust and Trentham Books.

MODOOD, T. (1993) 'The number of ethnic minority students in British higher education: Some grounds for optimism', *Oxford Review of Education*, **19**, 2, pp. 167–82.

MOERMAN, M. (1974) 'Accomplishing ethnicity', in TURNER, R. (Ed) *Ethnomethodology*, Harmondsworth, Penguin.

MOORE, A. (1993) 'Genre, ethnocentricity and bilingualism in the English classroom', in WOODS, P. and HAMMERSLEY, M. (Eds) *Gender and Ethnicity in Schools*, London, Routledge.

MORELAND, R., MILLER, J. and LAUCKA, F. (1981) 'Academic achievement and self-evaluations of academic performance', *Journal of Educational Psychology*, **73**, 3, pp. 335–44.

MORGAN, D.H. (1986) 'Gender' in BURGESS, R.G. (Ed) *Key Variables in Social Investigation*, London, Routledge and Kegan Paul.

MORGAN, V. and DUNN, S. (1988) 'Chameleons in the classroom: Visible and invisible children in nursery and infant classrooms', *Educational Review*, **40**, 1, pp. 3–12.

MORLEY, D. (1992) *Television, Audiences and Cultural Studies*, London, Routledge.

MORTIMORE, P., SAMMONS, P., STOLL, L., LEWIS, D. and ECOB, R. (1988) *School Matters: The Junior Years*, Wells, Open Books.

MURPHY, J. (1990) 'A most respectable prejudice: Inequality in educational research and policy', *British Journal of Sociology*, **41**, 1, pp. 29–54.

NAGEL, E. (1961) *The Structure of Science*, London, Routledge and Kegan Paul.

NASH, R. (1973) *Classrooms Observed*, London, Routledge and Kegan Paul.

NEI, M. and ROYCHOUDHURY, A.K. (1983) 'Genetic relationship and evolution of human races', *Evolutionary Biology*, **14**, New York, Plenum Press.

NORTHAM, J. (1982) 'Girls and boys in primary maths books', *Education*, **10**, 1, pp. 11–14.

NORWOOD REPORT, see Committee of the Secondary School Examinations Council (1943).

OAKES, G. (1988) *Weber and Rickert: Concept Formation in the Cultural Sciences*, Cambridge, MA, Massachusetts Institute of Technology Press.

OCHS, E. (1979) 'Transcription as theory', in OCHS, E. (Ed) *Developmental Pragmatics*, New York, Academic Press.

OPEN UNIVERSITY (1972) *E282 School and Society*, Open University Press.

OSSOWSKI, S. (1963) *Class Structure in the Social Consciousness*, London, Routledge and Kegan Paul.

PARSONS, T. (1937) *The Structure of Social Action*, New York, McGraw Hill.

PAYNE, C. (1987) *Employment and Opportunity*, London, Macmillan.

PAYNE, G.C.F. and CUFF, E.C. (Eds) (1982) *Doing Teaching: The Practical Management of Classrooms*, London, Batsford.

PETTIGREW, M. (1994) 'Coming to terms with research: The contract business', in HALPIN, D. and TROYNA, B. (Eds) *Researching Education Policy*, London, Falmer.

PHILLIPS, D.C. (1990a) 'Subjectivity and objectivity: An objective inquiry', in EISNER, E. and PESHKIN, A. (Eds) *Qualitative Inquiry: The Continuing Debate*, New York, Teachers College Press.

PHILLIPS, D.C. (1990b) 'Postpositivistic science: Myths and realities', in GUBA, E. (Ed) *The Paradigm Dialog*, Newbury Park, Sage.

PLEWIS, I. (1991) 'Understanding: A case of conceptual confusion', *British Educational Research Journal*, **17**, 4, pp. 377–85.

POLLNER, M. (1974) 'Sociological and commonsense models of the labelling process', in TURNER, R. (Ed) *Ethnomethodology*, Harmondsworth, Penguin.

POLSKY, N. (1971) 'Research method, morality and criminology', in *Hustlers, Beats, and Others*, Harmondsworth, Penguin.

PRATT, J. (1985) 'The Attitudes of Teachers', in WHYTE, J., DEEM, R., KANT, L. and CRUICKSHANK, M. (Eds) *Girl Friendly Schooling*, London Methuen.

PRATT, J., BROOMFIELD, J. and SEALE, C. (1984) *Option Choice: A Question of Equal Opportunity*, Windsor, NFER-Nelson.

PRIESWERK, R. (Ed) (1980) *The Slant of the Pen: Racism in Children's Books*, Geneva, World Council of Churches.

PRING, R. (1972) 'Knowledge out of Control', *Education for Teaching*, **89**, pp. 19–28.

PROKOPCZYK, C. (1980) *Truth and Reality in Marx and Hegel: A Reassessment*, Amherst Mass., University of Massachusetts Press.

PURVIS, J. (1991) *A History of Women's Education in England*, Milton Keynes, Open University Press.

RAINS, P. (1975) 'Imputations of deviance: A retrospective essay on the labelling perspective', *Social Problems*, **23**, pp. 1–11.

RATTANSI, A. (1992) 'Changing the subject?: Racism, culture and education', in DONALD, J. and RATTANSI, A. (Eds) *'Race', Culture and Difference*, London, Sage.

REID, M.I., BARNETT, B.R. and ROSENBERG, H.A. (1974) *A Matter of Choice: A Study of Guidance and Subject Options*, Windsor, NFER.

REYNOLDS, D. (1985) 'Ten years on: A decade of school effectiveness research reviewed', in Reynolds, D. (Ed) *Studying School Effectiveness*, London, Falmer Press.

Reynolds, D., Sullivan, M. and Murgatroyd, S. (1987) *The Comprehensive Experiment*, Lewes, Falmer.

Riddell, S.I. (1992) *Gender and the Politics of the Curriculum*, London, Routledge.

Roberts, K., Cook, F.G., Clark, S.C. and Semeonoff, E. (1977) *The Fragmentary Class Structure*, London, Heinemann.

Roberts, K., Duggan, J. and Noble, M. (1983) 'Racial disadvantage in youth labour markets', in Barton, L. and Walker, S. (Eds) *Race, Class and Education*, London, Croom Helm.

Rock, P. (1979a) *The Making of Symbolic Interactionism*, London, Macmillan.

Rock, P. (1979b) 'The sociology of crime, symbolic interactionism and some problematic qualities of radical criminology', in Downes, D. and Rock, P. (Eds) *Deviant Interpretations*, Oxford, Martin Robertson.

Rogers, C. (1982) *The Social Psychology of Schooling*, London, Routledge and Kegan Paul.

Rogers, R. (Ed) (1986) *Education and Social Class*, London, Falmer Press.

Rose, V.M. (1977) 'Rape as a social problem: A byproduct of the feminist movement', *Social Problems*, **26**, 1, pp. 75–89.

Rosenthal, R. and Jacobson, L. (1968) *Pygmalion in the Classroom*, New York, Holt, Rinehart and Winston.

Rubinstein, D. (1993) 'Opportunity and structural sociology', *Journal for the Theory of Social Behaviour*, **23**, 3, pp. 266–83.

Rubinstein, D. and Simon, B. (1969) *The Evolution of the Comprehensive School, 1926–66*, London, Routledge and Kegan Paul.

Rutter, M., Yule, B. and Berger, M. (1975) 'Attainment and adjustment in two geographical areas' *British Journal of Psychiatry*, **126**, pp. 520–33.

Rutter, M., Maughan, B., Mortimore, P. and Ouston, J. (1979) *Fifteen Thousand Hours: Secondary Schools and their Effects on Children*, London, Open Books.

Ryan, W. (1971) *Blaming the Victim*, London, Orbach and Chambers.

Sadler, D.R. (1981) 'Intuitive data processing as a potential source of bias in naturalistic evaluations', *Educational Evaluation and Policy Analysis* , 3, 4 July–August, pp. 25–31, Reprinted in House, E. (Ed) *Evaluation Studies Review Annual*, **7**, 1982, Beverley Hills, Sage.

Saunders, P. (1990) *Social Class and Stratification*, London, Routledge.

Saunders, P. (1995) 'Might Britain be a meritocracy?', *Sociology*, **29**, 1, pp. 23–41.

Scarth, J. and Hammersley, M. (1986) 'Some problems in assessing the closedness of classroom tasks', in Hammersley, M. (Ed) *Case Studies in Classroom Research*, Milton Keynes, Open University Press.

Schneider, J.W. and Kitsuse, J.I. (Eds) (1984) *Studies in the Sociology of Social Problems*, Norwood, Ablex.

Schools Council (1970) *Cross'd with Adversity: The Education of Socially*

Disadvantaged Children in Secondary Schools, London, Evans/Methuen Educational.

SCHUR, E.M. (1973) *Radical Nonintervention: Rethinking the Delinquency Problem*, Englewood Cliffs, NJ, Prentice Hall.

SCHUTZ, A. (1943) 'The problem of rationality in the social world', *Economica*, **10**, pp. 130–49.

SECADA, W.G. (Ed) (1989) *Equity in Education*, New York, Falmer Press.

SHARP, R. (1980) *Knowledge, Ideology, and the Politics of Schooling*, London, Routledge and Kegan Paul.

SHARP, R. (1981) 'Marxism, the concept of ideology, and its implications for fieldwork', in POPKEWITZ, T.S. and TABACHNICK, B.R. (Eds) *The Study of Schooling: Field-based Methodologies in Educational Research and Evaluation*, New York, Praeger.

SHARP, R. and GREEN, A. (1975) *Education and Social Control*, London, Routledge and Kegan Paul.

SHARP, S.A. (1980) 'Godfrey Thomson and the concept of intelligence' in SMITH, J.V. and HAMILTON, D. (Eds) *The Meritocratic Intellect: Studies in The History of Educational Research*, Aberdeen, Aberdeen University Press.

SHARROCK, W.W. (1974) 'On owning knowledge', in TURNER, R. (Ed) *Ethnomethodology*, Harmondsworth, Penguin.

SHAW, M. (1975) *Marxism and Social Science*, London, Pluto Press.

SHIPMAN, M. (1973) 'Bias in the sociology of education', *Educational Review*, **25**, 3, pp. 190–200.

SHORT, G. (1985) 'Teacher expectation and West Indian underachievement' *Educational Research*, **27**, 2, pp. 95–101.

SILVER, H. (Ed) (1973) *Equal Opportunity in Education: A Reader in Social Class and Educational Opportunity*, London, Methuen.

SILVER, H. (1981) 'Policy as history and as theory', *British Journal of Sociology of Education*, **2**, 3, pp. 293–9.

SIMON, B. (1953) *Intelligence, Psychology and Education: A Marxist Critique*, London, Lawrence and Wishart.

SIMON, B. (1974) *The Politics of Educational Reform 1920–40*, London, Lawrence and Wishart.

SIRAJ-BLATCHFORD, I. and TROYNA, B. (1993) 'Equal opportunities, research and educational reform: Some introductory notes', *British Educational Research Journal*, **19**, 3, pp. 223–6.

SISMONDO, S. (1993) 'Some social constructions', *Social Studies of Science*, **23**, pp. 515–53.

SKAALVIK, E. and HAGTVET, K. (1990) 'Academic achievement and self-concept: An analysis of causal predominance in a developmental perspective', *Journal of Personality and Social Psychology*, **58**, 2, pp. 292–307.

SKEGGS, B. (1989) 'Gender differences in education', in REID, I. and STRATTA, E. (Eds) *Sex Differences in Britain*, (2nd ed), Aldershot, Gower.

SMITH, D.E. (1987) *The Everyday World as Problematic: A Feminist Sociology*, Milton Keynes, Open University Press.

Sмiтн, D.J. (1977) *Racial Disadvantage in Britain*, Harmondsworth, Penguin.

Sмiтн, D.J. and Tomlinson, S. (1989) *The School Effect: A Study of Multi-racial Comprehensives*, London, Policy Studies Institute.

Southern, R.W. (1970) *Western Society and the Church in the Middle Ages*, Harmondsworth, Penguin.

Spear, M.G. (1985) 'Teachers' attitudes towards girls and technology', in Whyte, J., Deem, R., Kant, L. and Cruickshank, M. (Eds) *Girl Friendly Schooling*, London, Methuen.

Spear, M.G. (1987) 'Teachers' views about the importance of science to boys and girls', in Kelly, A. (Ed) *Science for Girls?*, Milton Keynes, Open University Press.

Spector, M. and Kitsuse, J.I. (1977) *Constructing Social Problems*, Menlo Park, CA, Cummings.

Spelman, E.V. (1988) *Inessential Woman: Problems of Exclusion in Feminist Thought*, London, Women's Press Ltd.

Spender, D. (1982) *Invisible Women: The Schooling Scandal*, London, Writers and Readers Publishing Cooperative.

Squibb, P. (1973) 'The concept of intelligence: a sociological perspective', *Sociological Review*, **21**, 1, pp. 57–75.

Stanworth, M. (1983) *Gender and Schooling: A Study of Sexual Divisions in the Classroom*, London, Hutchinson. (originally published London, Women's Research and Resources Centre, 1981).

St John-Brooks, C. (1980) 'The transmission of values in English teaching', Unpublished PhD thesis, University of Bristol.

St John-Brooks, C. (1983) 'English: A curriculum for personal development?', in Hammersley, M. and Hargreaves, A. (Eds) *Curriculum Practice*, Lewes, Falmer Press.

Storing, H. (Ed) (1962) *Essays on the Scientific Study of Politics*, New York, Holt Rinehart and Winston.

Strauss, L. (1953) *Natural Right and History*, Chicago, University of Chicago Press.

Strong, P. (1979) Sociological imperialism and the profession of medicine: A critical examination of the thesis of medical imperialism', *Social Science and Medicine*, **13A**, 2, pp. 199–215.

Swann, J. and Graddol, D. (1988) 'Gender inequalities in classroom talk', *English in Education*, **22**, 1, pp. 48–65.

Tanna, K. (1990) 'Excellence, equality and educational reform: the myth of South Asian achievement levels', *New Community*, **16**, 3, pp. 349–68.

Taylor J.H. (1973) 'Newcastle-upon-Tyne Asians do better than whites', *British Journal of Sociology*, **24**, pp. 431–47.

Taylor, J.H. (1976) *The Half-way Generation*, Slough, National Foundation for Educational Research.

Taylor, I., Walton, P. and Young, J. (1973) *The New Criminology*, London, Routledge and Kegan Paul.

Taylor, I., Walton, P. and Young, J. (Eds) (1975) *Critical Criminology*, London, Routledge and Kegan Paul.

TAYLOR, M. (1981) *Caught Between: A Review of Research into the Education of Pupils of West Indian Origin*, Windsor, National Foundation for Educational Research-Nelson.

TICKLE, L. (1983) 'One spell of ten minutes or five spells of two . . . ?: Teacher–pupil encounters in art and design education', in HAMMERSLEY, M. and HARGREAVES, A. (Eds) *Curriculum Practice*, Lewes, Falmer Press.

THOMPSON, D. (1973) *Discrimination and Popular Culture*, (2nd ed), London, Heinemann.

TOMLINSON, S. (1979) 'Decision-making in special education ESN(M): With some reference to children of immigrant parentage', Unpublished PhD thesis, University of Warwick.

TOMLINSON, S. (1981) *Educational Subnormality: A Study in Decision-making*, London, Routledge and Kegan Paul.

TOMLINSON, S. (1983) *Ethnic Minorities in British Schools: A Review of the Literature 1960–82*, London, Heinemann.

TOMLINSON, S. (1987) 'Curriculum option choices in multi-ethnic schools', in TROYNA, B. (Ed) *Racial Inequality in Education*, London, Routledge.

TRIBE, K. (1988) 'Translator's introduction', in HENNIS, W. *Max Weber: Essays in Reconstruction*, London, Allen and Unwin.

TROYNA, B. (1984) 'Fact or artefact: The "educational underachievement" of black pupils', *British Journal of Sociology of Education*, **5**, 2, pp. 153–66.

TROYNA, B. (1987) 'A conceptual overview of strategies to combat racial inequality in education: Introductory essay', in TROYNA, B. (Ed) *Racial Inequality in Education*, London, Routledge.

TROYNA, B. (1991a) 'Underachievers or underrated?: The experiences of pupils of South Asian origin in a secondary school', *British Educational Research Journal*, **17**, 4, pp. 361–76.

TROYNA, B. (1991b) 'Children, "race" and racism: The limitations of research and policy', *British Journal of Educational Studies*, **39**, 4, pp. 425–36.

TROYNA, B. (1992) 'Ethnicity and the organisation of learning groups: A case study', *Educational Research*, **34**, 1, pp. 45–55.

TROYNA, B. (1993) 'Underachiever or Misunderstood?: A reply to Roger Gomm' *British Educational Research Journal*, **19**, 2, pp. 167–74.

TROYNA, B. (1994) 'Reforms, research and being reflexive about being reflective', in HALPIN, D. and TROYNA, B. (Eds) *Researching Education Policy: Ethical and Methodological Issues*, London, Falmer Press.

TROYNA, B. and CARRINGTON, B. (1989) 'Whose side are we on?: Ethical dilemmas in research on "race and education"', in BURGESS, R.G. (Ed) *The Ethics of Educational Research*, Lewes, Falmer Press.

TROYNA, B. and CARRINGTON, B. (1990) *Education, Racism and Reform*, London, Routledge.

TROYNA, B. and HATCHER, R. (1992) *Racism in Children's Lives*, London, Routledge.

TYLER, W. (1977) *The Sociology of Educational Inequality*, London, Methuen.

UNESCO (1969) *Four Statements on the Race Question*, Paris, UNESCO.

VERMA, G.K. and BAGLEY, C. (Eds) (1982) *Self-concept, Achievement and Multicultural Education*, London, Macmillan.

VERNON, P. (1969) *Intelligence and Cultural Environment*, London, Methuen.

VERNON, P. (1979) 'Intelligence testing and the nature/nurture debate 1928–78: What next?', *British Journal of Educational Psychology*, **49**, pp. 1–14.

WALFORD, G. (1980) 'Sex bias in physics textbooks', *School Science Review*, **62**, pp. 220–27.

WALFORD, G. (Ed) (1987) *Doing Sociology of Education*, London, Falmer Press.

WALFORD, G. (Ed) (1991) *Doing Educational Research*, London, Routledge.

WALFORD, G. (Ed) (1994) *Researching the Powerful in Education*, London, UCL Press.

WALKER, J.C. (1986) 'Romanticising resistance, romanticising culture: Problems in Willis's theory of cultural production', *British Journal of Sociology of Education*, **7**, 1, pp. 59–80.

WALKER, R. and ADELMAN, C. (1975) 'Interaction analysis in informal classrooms' *British Journal of Educational Psychology*, **45**, pp. 73–6.

WALLMAN, S. (1979) 'The application of anthropological theory to boundary processes', in MASON, D. and REX, J. (Eds) *Theories of Ethnic and Race Relations*, Cambridge, Cambridge University Press.

WEBER, M. (1948) *From Max Weber*, GERTH, H. and MILLS, C.W. (Eds), London, Routledge.

WEINER, G. (1985) 'Equal opportunities, feminism and girls' education: Introduction', in WEINER, G. (Ed) *Just a Bunch of Girls: Feminist Approaches to Schooling*, Milton Keynes, Open University Press.

WEINER, G. and ARNOT, M. (Eds) (1987) *Gender Under Scrutiny*, London, Hutchinson.

WERTHMAN, C. (1963) 'Delinquents in schools', *Berkeley Journal of Sociology*, **8**, 1, pp. 39–60.

WESTEN, P. (1990) *Speaking of Equality: An Analysis of the Rhetorical Force of 'Equality' in Moral and Legal Discourse*, Princeton, NJ, Princeton University Press.

WHITE, J. and YOUNG, M.F.D. (1975) 'The sociology of knowledge', *Education for Teaching*, **98**, pp. 4–13.

WHITTY, G. (1977) 'Sociology and the problem of radical educational change: Notes towards a reconceptualisation of the "new" sociology of education', in YOUNG, M.F.D. and WHITTY, G. (Eds) *Society, State and Schooling*, Ringmer, Falmer Press.

WHITTY, G. (1985) *Sociology and School Knowledge: Curriculum Theory, Research and Politics*, London, Methuen.

WHITTY, G. and YOUNG, M.F.D. (Eds) (1976) *Explorations in the Politics of School Knowledge*, Driffield, Nafferton Books.

WHYTE, J. (1986) *Girls into Science and Technology*, London, Routledge and Kegan Paul.

WILLIAMS, B. (1962) 'The idea of equality', in LASLETT, P. and RUNCIMAN, W.G. (Eds) *Philosophy, Politics and Society*, 2nd Series, Oxford, Basil Blackwell.

References

WILLIAMS, M. (1991) *Unnatural Doubts: Epistemological Realism and the Philosophical Basis of Scepticism*, Oxford, Basil Blackwell.

WILLIAMSON, B. (1974) 'Continuities and discontinuities in the sociology of education', in FLUDE, M. and AHIER, J. (Eds) *Educability, Schools and Ideology*, New York, Wiley.

WILLIS, P. (1977) *Learning to Labour*, Farnborough, Saxon House.

WOOD, A. (1991) 'Marx against morality', in SINGER, P. (Ed) *Handbook on Ethics*, Oxford, Blackwell.

WOODS, P.E. (1979) *The Divided School*, London, Routledge and Kegan Paul.

WOOLGAR, S. (Ed) (1988) *Knowledge and Reflexivity: New Frontiers in the Sociology of Knowledge*, London, Sage.

WOOLGAR, S. and PAWLUCH, D. (1985) 'Ontological gerrymandering: The anatomy of social problems explanations', *Social Problems*, **32**, 3, pp. 314–27.

WRIGHT, C. (1986) 'School processes: An ethnographic study', in EGGLESTON, J., DUNN, D. and ANJALI, M. (Eds) *Education for Some: The Educational and Vocational Experiences of 15–18 Year Old Members of Minority Ethnic Groups*, Stoke-on-Trent, Trentham Books.

WRIGHT, C. (1992a) 'Early education: Multiracial primary school classrooms', in GILL, D., MAYOR, B. and BLAIR, M. (Eds) *Racism and Education: Structures and Strategies*, London, Sage.

WRIGHT, C. (1992b) *Race Relations in the Primary School*, London, David Fulton.

WRIGHT, E.O. (1985) *Classes*, London, Verso.

WRIGHT, P. and TREACHER, A. (Eds) (1982) *The Problem of Medical Knowledge: Examining the Social Construction of Medicine*, Edinburgh, University of Edinburgh Press.

YOUNG, J. (1975) 'Working class criminology', in TAYLOR, I., WALTON, P. and YOUNG, J. (Eds) *Critical Criminology*, London, Routledge and Kegan Paul.

YOUNG, J. and MATTHEWS, R. (Eds) (1992) *Rethinking Criminology: The Realist Debate*, London, Sage.

YOUNG, M.F.D. (Ed) (1971) *Knowledge and Control*, London, Collier-Macmillan.

YOUNG, M.F.D. (1973) 'Taking sides against the probable: Problems of relativity and commitment in teaching and the sociology of knowledge', *Educational Review*, **25**, pp. 210–22.

YOUNG, M.F.D. and WHITTY, G. (Eds) (1977) *Society, State and Schooling*, Ringmer, Falmer Press.

Author Index

Subject Index

'acceptability' as an occupational selection criterion 78
analytic approach (as contrasted with possibilitarianism) 25–6, 31–2, 34
antiracism 15, 28, 35
argument, types of 43–4

bias in the analysis of educational inequalities 175–9
black box, concept of 68
black power movement 16

causal efficacy, establishing 161–3, 165–70
clarity as a methodological requirement 41–55
constructionism (see social constructionism)
credibility as a methodological criterion 55–66

data, types of 56
decisionism 26, 27, 28, 30, 35
descriptive adequacy as a methodological requirement 55–66
differential educational provision, effects of 99–103
differentiation-polarisation theory 65, 66, 96–9
discrimination, conceptualisation of 49–50
  direct 49–50
  indirect 50, 86–7
  in allocation to different levels of course 69, 71–81
  in allocation to courses in different subjects 69–70, 81–93

discriminatory consequences of allocation to low status courses 70, 93–104
discriminatory consequences of differential allocation to subjects 104–5

educational inequalities (see also equality, concept of)
as a social problem 5–13
ethnic and 'racial' 1, 16, 19, 20–1, 147–50
gender 11, 15–16, 19, 20–1, 143–7
social class 1, 5–15, 19, 20, 141–3
produced by the process of selection 68–70, 71–93
produced by the effects of selection 70–1, 93–105
in the distribution of classroom resources 107–8, 109–25
produced by differential classroom treatment 109, 134–7
in school knowledge and values 108–9, 125–31
produced by socialisation into inequality 109, 131–4
in outcomes 139–59
operationalisation and measurement issues 152–5
sampling issues 155–6
problems in interpretation of 156–9
explaining 159–71
empirical generalization 65–6
epistemological foundationalism 2, 34–5, 36, 40